D1189764

Populism in the Mountain West

Populism in the Mountain West

Robert W. Larson

University of New Mexico Press

To Helen and Matthew

Design by Barbara Werden

Library of Congress Cataloging-in-Publication Data

Larson, Robert W., 1927–
  Populism in the Mountain West.

  Bibliography: p.
  Includes index.
    1. Populism—Rocky Mountains Region—History—
19th century.   2. Rocky Mountains Region—Politics
and government.   I. Title.
F721.L27   1986   322.4′4′0978   86-16160
ISBN 0-8263-0900-3

Contents

Illustrations

Acknowledgments

When one has spent more than a decade in the preparation of a manuscript, compiling a complete and accurate list of people and institutions for acknowledgment is no minor feat. The number of individuals who were both helpful and considerate is large, and the fear of forgetting someone or some institution in such a compilation is one of the last frustrations faced by an author. The most efficient way to go about this task is to start from the beginning when I was given such excellent assistance during the summer of 1975 by the staff of the Montana Historical Society library during a research trip to Helena. For the New Mexico portion of my study, the people associated with the State Archives and Records Center, the Museum of New Mexico, the State Library, and the University of New Mexico library, already acknowledged in my earlier volume on New Mexico Populism, continue to enjoy my gratitude. Closer to home are the alert archivists of the Wyoming State Archives and Historical Department in Cheyenne and those down the Front Range at the Colorado State Archives in Denver. Also helpful for my research on Colorado Populism are the able librarians under the direction of Eleanor M. Gehres at the Western History Department of the Denver Public Library and those at the Colorado State Historical Society.

The staff of my own library at the University of Northern Colorado was unflagging in its efforts to assist me, particularly Claude J. Johns, Jr., who was dean of the James A. Michener Library at the time, and Suzanne Schulze, who was then in charge of government documents. Also important for the progress of the manuscript was Bill R. Brown, the school's graduate dean who provided me with a quiet library office.

The Newberry Library in Chicago was another facility that proved invaluable for the preparation of this study, the Edward E. Ayer Collection being especially helpful. During my research trips in 1977 and 1981, I found D'Ann Campbell and Richard Jensen of the Family and Community History Center to be excellent guides in locating sources in the Newberry's distinctive treasure house of books and manuscripts; Jensen's help on two graphs prepared for the study was particularly appreciated. Brief visits to the Arizona State Library, Archives, and Public Records in Phoenix in 1982 and the Utah State Historical Society in Salt Lake City in 1983 made the annual meetings of the Western History Association a delightful combination of work and pleasure.

I am also grateful for three generous grants I received. An award from the University of Northern Colorado Faculty Research and Publications Committee helped me bear the expenses of my 1975 research trip to Helena. Through that same committee, I was also given released time from my teaching duties. Absolutely invaluable was a 1981 grant from the National Endowment for the Humanities which provided me with a free school quarter to begin writing my manuscript. Along with a sabbatical leave from my institution, the released time made available by the National Endowment for the Humanities enabled me to have two consecutive quarters to work on my first draft. In connection with the NEH grant, I would like to thank Willard G. Jones, director of the Office of Grants and Contracts at the University of Northern Colorado, for urging me to apply and Howard R. Lamar of Yale University, Lewis L. Gould of the University of Texas, and James Edward Wright of Dartmouth University for their willingness to recommend me.

Several people involved in the final steps of the study deserve my utmost appreciation. My colleague in the Department of English, L. Ben Varner, and Forrest W. Frease, who is now retired, both gave my manuscript the kind of review that only exceptional practionaires of the language can give. Harriet Shirley did her usual flawless job of typing the manuscript; Helen Stansbury and Barbara Mogck, however, were essential in retyping a number of the revisions. Richard N. Ellis of the University of New Mexico assisted my efforts at a crucial time for which I am most grateful. David V. Holtby and Barbara Guth of the University of New Mexico Press could not have been more helpful in nursing my manuscript through its last stage; David's talents in this regard could not fail to impress any author.

Finally, I'm grateful to my institution for cooperating with me fully to chronicle the events of Populism in the Mountain West and to the members of the Department of History for their complete support for the project; Alfred E. Cornebise, the chairman, knew how to give me that all-important boost when it really counted. My parents and my sister gave me the usual moral support as did my daughter and son who finally got their father to dedicate a book to them.

University of Northern Colorado   Robert W. Larson

Populism in the Mountain West

One

Mountain Populism:

A Mainstream

Movement?

In 1892, the People's party, which had been formally launched in Cincinnati the previous year, presented the American electorate with a bold political alternative. No longer would voters be forced to choose between the entrenched Republican and Democratic parties. A daring new political organization with fresh ideas existed, and its members hoped to steal the leadership away from its two older rivals. With this ambitious object in mind, the infant party fielded candidates on all levels of government—from the grass roots upward to the nation's pinnacle of power, the presidency. The party offered candidates for local office, candidates for state government, and candidates for the Congress of the United States. For the executive branch of the federal government, the Populists created a ticket calculated to reconcile the still-lingering differences between voters from the North and the South. Twenty-seven years after Appomattox the voters could elect a former Union general from Iowa, James B. Weaver, as the Populist choice for president and an ex-Confederate general from Virginia, James G. Field, as his running mate.

The young party also adopted a provocative platform at the Omaha convention, where Weaver and Field were chosen. The controversial document addressed itself to the myriad of ignored problems which

3

had accumulated during the nation's unprecedented industrial growth following the Civil War. For farmers, harried small businessmen by the 1890s, the Populists made a strident call for government ownership of the railroads as a solution to the problem of high and often unfair freight rates. For the urban workingmen, they passed resolutions demanding a shorter work week and calling for the restriction of "pauper" immigrants, who were lowering the wage level. For all citizens, the Populists demanded that government, too long considered corrupt and venal, be more responsive to the electorate. The party advocated a secret ballot and the institution of such devices of direct legislation as the initiative and referendum. Moreover, the Populists demanded that the members of that august and privileged body, the United States Senate, be elected directly by the people rather than indirectly by state legislators.

A stirring, yet profoundly, cynical preamble introduced the platform: ". . . We meet in the midst of a nation brought to the verge of moral, political, and material ruin. Corruption dominates the ballot-box, the legislatures, the Congress, and touches even the ermine of the bench." When its author, the flamboyant ex-Republican from Minnesota Ignatius Donnelly, first read the preamble at a party gathering in Saint Louis, the response was exuberant. Papers and hats were tossed into the air as cheering delegates, feeling that their innermost grievances had at last been articulated, stood waving wraps and umbrellas in warm approval.[1] The response at the Omaha convention was equally enthusiastic. In an atmosphere of pageantry and patriotism, the delegates, who had been convened for that purpose on the Fourth of July, approved the tough planks of the Omaha platform and chose the Weaver-Field ticket.

The Populists held conventions throughout the nation on the state and local level. At all of these gatherings, identification with the new national party usually took the form of an eager endorsement of the controversial planks of the Omaha platform. Populists sometimes unilaterally, and at other times, in cooperation with like-minded Democrats and Republicans in so-called fusion movements, nominated candidates for state and local office. Members of the young third party were particularly active in those regions where their reform proposals received the widest acceptance: the wheat-raising Midwest, the cotton-producing South, and the silver-producing West. General Weaver campaigned extensively, especially in those areas where he perceived the greatest ardor for his cause; for example, he was the first major presidential candidate to campaign personally in the remote mining state of Montana.[2] Often more like a holy crusade than a political campaign, the Populist effort continued energetically through the early fall until the votes were cast in November.

Because of their strong convictions and irrational expectations, the Populists were immensely disappointed when the ballots were finally tallied. Weaver and Field had not won; the Populist standard-bearers had polled less than 9 percent of the vote. The candidates from the two established parties, Grover Cleveland and Benjamin Harrison, had divided the lion's share of the ballots cast—Cleveland was returned to the White House after a four-year absence. Areas of the country where Populists had based their strongest hopes had simply not come through as anticipated. The South had remained loyal to the Democratic party: although Weaver and Field were able to win fifteen percent of the votes cast in six of the cotton-producing states of that region, they could not claim a single electoral vote south of the Mason-Dixon line. In that part of the Midwest where wheat was the staple crop, the results were better. Kansans had given all their state's electoral votes to Weaver and Field, had elected the entire Populist state ticket (including the governor), and had sent Populists to occupy five of the state's eight seats in Congress.[3] It was a triumph made possibly only by Democratic support; it was a triumph marred, however, by the loss of the lower house of the state legislature to the Republicans.

In the other states of the Middle Border, the Populist show was not so impressive. A Populist-Democratic fusion ticket in North Dakota captured the governorship and all the state offices except one, but lost both houses of the state legislature to the G.O.P. Republicans also elected North Dakota's only representative to the lower house of Congress and won one of the state's three electoral votes—Cleveland and Weaver split the other two. In Nebraska and South Dakota, the outcome was even more disappointing to the People's party. Because the Democrats had abandoned the Cleveland ticket to support Weaver and Field, Harrison managed to win the electoral votes of the Cornhusker state by the narrowest of margins. But in the competition for state office, the Republicans, to use the words of Populist historian John D. Hicks, won "everything as usual."[4] In South Dakota, there was more of the same—another convincing Republican victory.

One area where Populists did especially well, however, was in the mineral-rich Mountain West. In Colorado, the foremost silver-producing state of the nation, Populists captured the governorship, added the state's two seats in the House of Representatives to their column, and almost gained control of the state senate—successes made possible only by Democratic cooperation. In Idaho and Nevada with both Democratic and Republican cooperation, Weaver-Field electors were chosen by impressive majorities, more than 54 percent in the former, and almost 67 percent in the latter.[5] In Wyoming, fusion with the Democrats failed to win the state's electoral votes for Weaver and Field, but it did result in a victory for the Democratic gubernatorial candidate. A Populist-Democratic coalition also gained control of the lower house of the Wyoming legislature. In Montana, the Populists made an independent bid for power and lost: the popular vote for the Weaver-Field ticket was only 16.5 percent of the total. Moreover, the Republican candidate for governor won a narrow victory over his Democratic and Populist opponents, a success that never would have been possible had the two parties collaborated.[6] Even in the Territory of New Mexico, where the Constitution forbade presidential electors to be chosen, Populists were active and successful. In the 1892 race, they retained political control of San Miguel, the most populous county in the territory.[7]

One would conclude from this brief analysis of Populist successes in 1892 that historians of the movement, called the most important third party effort in America by Howard R. Lamar, would devote much of their time and energy to studying the three regions where Populist appeal was most widespread (particularly in light of the movement's poor showing in the industrial Northeast and in the corn and dairy states of the Midwest).[8] While historians have given ample attention to the movement in the wheat-producing states of the nation's hinterland and the cotton states stretching from Texas to North Carolina, they have, by comparison, ignored Populism in the Mountain West until recently. There are probably two major reasons for the niggardly attention given to this vast region west of the nation's wheat belt, where Populism enjoyed its most tangible successes. One was the remoteness of the Mountain West. How could settlers from such a sparsely populated region have had any significant impact on national politics? The other was the strong conviction on the part of historians that Populism took hold in this region only because it had made an unequivocal commitment to support the free coinage of silver.

John D. Hicks, probably the man most responsible for the Mountain West's one-dimensional silver image, expressed this latter belief most forcefully. In his definitive *The Populist Revolt: A History of the Farmers' Alliance and the People's Party* (1931), Hicks admitted that the Weaver-Field ticket garnered half of its electoral votes from the silver states of the Mountain West, but concluded that there was a "fly in the ointment." The region's inhabitants supported the third party not because of any genuine interest in the overall Populist program, but because of their preoccupation with the silver issue.

> They were interested in *silver*, and they supported the Populist ticket solely because of this one item in the Populist creed. Had the Populist program not included free coinage it could hardly have appealed seriously to any of the mountain states.[9]

Richard Hofstadter, a quarter of a century later in his revisionist *The Age of Reform: From Bryan to F.D.R.*, supported Hicks's stress on the silver issue. Although at odds with Hicks in most of his interpretations of the movement, Hofstadter did agree with the dean of Populist historians on one point: the Mountain West was a one-issue region. "The free-silver Populism of the mountain states variety was not agrarian Populism at all but simply silverism."[10] Thus, two of the most preeminent of American historical scholars had, in effect, written mountain Populism out of the mainstream of the movement.

Despite the long shadows cast by Hicks and Hofstadter, historians have raised serious questions about the one-issue interpretation of mountain Populism in a number of articles, theses, and monographs that have appeared since the publication of Hofstadter's book in 1955. In 1968, for instance, David B. Griffiths wrote an article in the *Annals of Wyoming* on the Populist movement in the Cowboy state. He concluded that the famous range war, the Johnson County War, had contributed more to the growth of Wyoming Populism in 1892 than had the free coinage issue.[11] Two carefully researched master's theses, from which Griffiths drew part of his findings, had reached the same conclusion.[12]

Two years later in 1970, Thomas A. Clinch published his monograph *Urban Populism and Free Silver in Montana*.[13] Clinch, too, concluded that silver was not as all-encompassing an issue as students of Populism had been led to believe. Indeed, the movement in Montana was much more than simply a crusade to institute free coinage. In 1974, James Edward Wright published a monograph on Populism in Colorado, a particularly significant study because Colorado produced three-fifths of the national silver product in 1890.[14] In his study *The Politics of Populism: Dissent in Colorado,* much of which was based upon quantitative evidence, Wright also discovered a much more complex motivation for the Colorado movement than "simply silverism."[15] During the same year as Wright's publication, the writer of this study published his *New Mexico Populism: A Study of Radical Protest in a Western Territory.*[16] Again, the one-issue concept failed to stand up to the evidence uncovered during the preparation of the monograph.

Despite the questions raised and the patterns developed by these individual state studies, Lawrence Goodwyn, the first historian to write a general history of the Populist movement since Hicks, generally ignored these more recent findings. In his *Democratic Promise: The Populist Movement in America* (1976), Goodwyn perpetuated the one-issue stereotype of mountain Populism. He thereby continued to downplay the genuineness of high-country Populism and kept the movement in the Mountain West isolated from its southern and midwestern roots. Goodwyn's work disappointed those historians who had hoped that he would make a more serious effort than Hicks to integrate mountain Populism into the mainstream of the movement.

Although Goodwyn referred to some of the more recent state studies discussed above, their findings did not affect his major thesis. Recognizing that the Johnson County War in Wyoming had considerable relevance to Populism and that the movement in Montana had an intriguing urban quality about it, he, nonetheless, maintained that Populism in the Mountain West was limited to one issue:

> Through the 1880s the politics of the mountain states had become increasingly centered around the issue of free coinage of silver, particularly in the mining regions of Colorado, Nevada, and Idaho. A kind of one-issue Populism immediately flourished there as soon as the third party was formed.[17]

Goodwyn, in the few pages that he did devote to mountain Populism, used such terms as "single-mindedness" to characterize western Populists and employed such expressions as "emotional pull" to describe their support of free coinage.

Goodwyn's rather arbitrary definition of the movement's essence limited his assessment of the nature of Populism in this region. To Goodwyn, true Populism was the theory and program worked out in the late 1880s by the Southern Alliance (or to be more exact, the National Farmers' Alliance and Industrial Union). "Alliance radicalism *was* Populism," according to Goodwyn.[18] If a Populist organization in any state or territory failed to make the "greenback doctrines" of that essentially "cooperative movement," the Southern Alliance, central to its existence, it was not Populism at all. It was, to use Goodwyn's term, part of that "shadow movement" that emerged in the 1890s and distorted the Populist doctrines that had been patiently hammered out in the mass gatherings and conventions of the Southern Alliance and then disseminated by the alliance's ubiquitous lecturers.

By stressing such doctrines of the Southern Alliance as business cooperation among farmers and the subtreasury plan, both of which were products of Charles W. Macune, the brilliant social theorist of the organization, Goodwyn gave Populism an unmistakable southern slant, thus subordinating even the wheat-raising Midwest, the traditional heartland of Populism. He questioned the very authenticity of Populism in the Midwest, with the exception of Kansas, and refused to elevate Nebraska Populism, which Hicks emphasized, even to the level of a so-called shadow movement.[19] In fact, Goodwyn challenged John Hicks's thesis that Populism was largely the result of intense economic and political agitation on the part of Northern Alliancemen.

On the one hand, Goodwyn's absorbing and gracefully written work stimulated other historians working on this topic. His extensive research on the Southern Alliance provided an important new dimension in Populist interpretation. On the other hand, Goodwyn's book narrowed the scope of Populism even beyond that of Hicks, who, while dismissing the Mountain West as a one-issue region, at least gave appropriate attention to Populism in the Midwest and South. Goodwyn went a step beyond: not only did he ignore western Populism, but he also minimized the midwestern movement. In his monograph, Goodwyn focused on one region—the South, and one time period—the late 1880s. His emphasis excluded any mention of the important function the Omaha platform performed in unifying many disparate groups under the Populist umbrella in 1892.[20] In the final analysis, the restrictive nature of Goodwyn's definition prevented him from writing the broad, comprehensive study of Populism he probably intended.

In addition to the criticisms regarding the scope of his book, Goodwyn's conclusions also raised a number of important questions. Perhaps the controversy that *Democratic Promise* has generated is the surest sign of its significance as a major Populist study. In an article published in the *Journal of American History* in 1983, for example, Stanley B. Parsons, Karen Toombs Parsons, Walter Killilae, and Beverly Boyers acknowledged the book's undeniable contribution to this field of study, although they were unconvinced by Goodwyn's major thesis. His carefully developed conclusions, they admitted, are now the standard interpretation of the Populist movement used in several major textbooks. Respected historians such as Robert C. McMath, Jr. and Charles A. Cannon, moreover, have given Goodwyn's volume positive and favorable reviews.[21] More importantly, Goodwyn's book has stimulated historians to initiate new studies that analyze and test his controversial conclusions just as the publication of Hofstadter's *Age of Reform* did for another generation of historians some thirty years ago. Post-Goodwyn Populist scholars, however, can now use techniques of quantitative analysis to scrutinize Goodwyn's study in ways that differ significantly from those used in the 1950s. The results of this type of analysis have negated certain aspects of Goodwyn's thesis. Using quantitative analysis in their study mentioned above, Parsons and his colleagues, for example, have convincingly refuted the sequential relationship Goodwyn claimed was essential to the development of the "movement culture" that arose largely from the radicalism of the Southern Alliance during the late 1880s. Their statistical evidence also did not support Goodwyn's contention that farmers initially joined alliances to participate in cooperatives. Nor did their findings sustain his belief that the failure of these cooperatives to promote radical monetary policies prompted would-be Populists to enter politics as a final stage in the evolution of their "movement culture." The quantitative data mustered by Parsons and his associates on the cooperatives in Kansas, Texas, and other states where Populism achieved significance simply did not support the kind of sequential relationship that Goodwyn perceived.[22]

In another study critical of Goodwyn's thesis, James Turner has used statistical evidence from farm counties in Texas to challenge Goodwyn, and many other Populist historians, who have "implicitly assumed" that it was economic hardship that turned farmers into Populists. According to Turner, some discontented farmers became Populists because of their geographic isolation from towns and villages; while others, in the same region or state, remained loyal to one of the older parties. Turner also contended that other studies, including Peter H. Argersinger's *Populism and Politics: William Alfred Pef-*

fer and the People's Party, Stanley B. Parsons's *The Populist Context: Rural versus Urban Power in a Great Plains Frontier,* and Sheldon Hackney's *Populism to Progressivism in Alabama* bear out this conclusion. Geographic isolation was the single common factor shared by Populists in Kansas, Nebraska, and Alabama, the states which these authors examined.[23]

Although the debates between Goodwyn and his critics about the scope of his study and his conclusions suggest new types of studies for the Mountain West, this writer has limited his quarrel with Goodwyn to his characterization of western Populism as a single-issue movement. The first step necessary for the creation of any new interpretation or revision of Populism in the mountain states is the determination of the nature of the issues that generated Populist protest. Unlike past studies by such historians as Hicks, Hofstadter, and Goodwyn, this analysis does not focus solely on the silver issue. It also examines the Populist response to such issues as railroad regulation, credit policies, monopoly control, land-use litigation, labor conditions, and direct legislation. Indeed, an analysis of the Populist position toward these divisive public policy questions constitutes the essence of this study. The author has drawn relevant evidence from as many different sources as possible in order to fulfill this broad goal. For example, this study carefully scrutinizes the model for many local, state, or territorial Populist groups, the planks and resolutions adopted at the 1892 Populist convention in Omaha. In addition, this study, relying primarily on newspaper items, editorials, campaign broadsides and personal correspondence, as well as pertinent published sources, applies these campaign positions to the often distinctive conditions of the Mountain West. The analysis is done on an issue-by-issue basis.

A systematic investigation of the more disruptive issues of this region, however, is not enough. Also necessary is an understanding of the social, political, and economic conditions that created the turmoil in the first place. Consequently, an analysis of the circumstances that created protest during the 1880s and 1890s in each of the Mountain West states and territories must precede any examination of the direction that such protest took. It is necessary, moreover, to ascertain the nature as well as the number of issues generated by pre-Populist politics, so that their importance can be effectively evaluated against that of the widely known silver issue.

Naturally, the scope of this study does not include all the important areas of Populist development in this region. It leaves many of them to the ongoing reassessment and revision characteristic of Populist historiography in any region where the movement was strong. Analysis of the Populist voting strength in Congress has already begun in excellent studies by O. Gene Clanton and Karel D. Bicha; one suspects more will be done on this subject with perhaps a sharper focus on the admittedly small mountain-states delegation in Congress.[24] Additional analysis is also needed for pre-Populist groups. (Obviously in a diverse geographical area such as the Mountain West, a study of protest and pressure groups would include more than just the familiar Farmers' Alliance.) The activities of western labor unions associated with mining, for instance, could benefit from more investigation, particularly where these activities had an important bearing on third party politics. Yet another possible subject for future study would be the geographic isolation of so many high-country Populists; as previously mentioned, a study such as Turner's could be especially valuable to a region as remote as the West.

The centerpiece of this study, however, is the motivations of people who were attracted to the controversial third party movement. What were the issues that motivated them to break their traditional political ties? Which issues aroused the most dedication in them? Such questions are crucial: the People's party in 1890 was, after all, an untested political organization aspiring to power in a society with a remarkably strong two-party system.

One factor that strikes even the casual student of Populism in this region is the intense emotionalism and the pronounced alienation of many of the movement's adherents. Such strong feelings toward monopoly, workers' rights, and related concerns not only emphasize the issue-orientation of these mountain states Populists, but also provide compelling evidence of the strong influence that these issues had on reform-minded individuals. The emotions generated by some of the issues not only affected the sense of well-being of many Populists, but when frustrations were met, these setbacks tended to diminish their self-image. Carlos A. Schwantes, in a provocative article published in the *Western Historical Quarterly*, characterized this intensity and the rationale that developed from it as the "ideology of disinheritance." People came west to the "promised land" with certain expectations; when these expectations were not met, they developed a certain militancy to deal with the circumstances that denied them their God-given inheritance. Many tended to blame the special privileges of corporate

America for this painful denial. There was an "unmistakable fear that monopoly unfairly threatened the political egalitarianism and economic opportunity that they believed to be the birthright of settlers in America's undeveloped West." Although Schwantes's study centered on protest in the Pacific Northwest, he did deal with one of the major monopolies in the Mountain West, the Northern Pacific Railroad. This powerful corporate entity not only threatened the mineral rights of many in the states below the Canadian border, but also used its immense political power to jeopardize the sovereignty and independence of those states.[25]

The emphasis that Schwantes gave to monopoly in this study is important because monopoly might be the one thread that held the fabric of the movement in this region together. At least at first glance, the fear of bigness, particularly in its corporate form, appears common to practically all those in the Mountain West who identified with the People's party. But the specter of monopoly control and the anxiety it caused was not unique to the West. Suspicion and antagonism toward monopolies were prevalent in the cotton-growing South and wheat-producing Midwest. In a recent study of southern Populism, Bruce Palmer asserted that southern Populists viewed the "specific issues of the Omaha platform as more than a collection of separate reforms in land, transportation, and finance." Indeed, they "usually unified . . . [these] major demands under a single heading that was older than any one of them, antimonopoly."[26] Palmer, in his issue-oriented study, not only examined the strength of southern anti-monopolism during the turbulent 1880s and 1890s, but traced its important historical antecedents as well.

In the wheat belt, Populist Senator William Alfred Peffer of Kansas was one of the most persistent foes of monopoly and an unwavering supporter of railroad regulation. (The common carriers were the most familiar monopolies to the farmers of the Midwest.) He even justified his eventual return to the Republican party on the basis of its anti-monopoly policies of the twentieth century. According to Peter H. Argersinger in his 1974 biography of Peffer, the bearded Kansan, in praise of the "trust buster" Theodore Roosevelt, insisted that Roosevelt, during his flamboyant tenure in office, was merely "applying the principles of Populism."[27] Finding evidence in the Midwest and South regarding the fear of corporate bigness is not a difficult feat. This study examines the role anti-monopolism played in the thinking of mountain state Populists. If it was as important as in the other two regions, then free silver is but one of a number of issues regarded by them as compelling. And if free silver must share the limelight with these other issues, then Populism in the Mountain West can hardly be a one-issue movement. Of course, acceptance of such an interpretation should not reduce the Silver Question to one of minor importance. Silver was a significant commodity in the West, just as cotton was in the South and wheat was in the Midwest. For Western Populists to promote free coinage, along with their regional Democratic and Republican rivals, was no different from Southerners of all political stripes promoting a higher price for cotton and farmers from the Middle Border promoting more lucrative wheat sales. But to regard the silver issue as the only one of real significance to Populists of the Mountain West and to consider silver's value solely in terms of the metal as a commodity rather than as an instrument for inflation is to question, in a basic way, the sincerity of all of those who committed their time, resources, and energy to the burgeoning third party movement.

In order to examine the monopoly, free silver and other issues that so thoroughly consumed the energies of high-country Populists, the writer used the individual state studies previously mentioned as well as data compiled from new research and from that utilized in his previous studies. His goal, from the very beginning, has been to author a suggestive volume that will initiate a long-needed reinterpretation of Populism as a national movement by correcting the rather conspicuous misconceptions of that movement's debatable role in the Mountain West.

Because such an effort could involve as many as eight states or territories (excluding the three Pacific coastal states), four were selected for purposes of manageability: Colorado, Wyoming, Montana, and New Mexico. These are often called the Front Range states. They form a tier of commonwealths that extend from the Canadian border southward along the Rocky Mountains to the crooked boundary shaped by Mexico and west Texas. They are excellent examples of Frederick Jackson Turner's "rectangular Territories . . . carved into checkerboard States."[28] All four stretch many miles to the east and west of the Great Divide to connect the Great Plains with the arid Intermountain Plateau.

The other states and territories of the Mountain West are not ignored. The writer points out patterns in Idaho, Utah, Nevada, and Arizona that are similar to those in the Front Range states, as well as compares the important differences among these high, arid commonwealths. He does not engage, however, in the same kind of detailed analysis of issues and sources of discontent in these latter states that he proposes to do in the four western states along the east slope of the Rocky Mountain

The selection of Colorado, Wyoming, Montana, and New Mexico as case studies seems to meet all the important demands for typicality as far as the Mountain West of the 1880s and 1890s is concerned. All were mountainous and appeared to have mineral wealth. The people, therefore, could be expected to respond to the issue of free silver. (Although Wyoming had very little of the precious metal, its citizens during the 1890s were unaware of the fact; moreover, as already noted, Colorado led the nation in silver production.) Each of them had some agriculture, although Wyoming's agricultural production was smaller than the other three. In the Great Plains region of each of the four, dryland farming was employed; the land in the Intermountain Plateau states and territories of Idaho, Utah, Nevada, and Arizona was too arid for this kind of cultivation. Yet there were also irrigation systems in the river valleys of these four Front Range commonwealths. Thus, agricultural organizations, such as the Farmers' Alliance, had a broad and varied base from which to draw support. In a similar vein, this Front Range region had a widespread mining industry which provided a labor base for organizations such as the Knights of Labor. This region, therefore, contained the building blocks of Populism. In addition, both state and territorial forms of government existed in the Mountain West. Colorado, Wyoming, and Montana had state governments by 1890, as had Idaho and Nevada; New Mexico along with Utah and Arizona, on the other hand, were administered under the territorial system.

An historical outline of the chronology of the movement in this region is provided for each of the four states or territories with an emphasis on those emotional issues that dominated the elections held before silver became preeminent. This study, using the particularly important sources contained in the platforms and campaign literature for the state or territorial elections held prior to the mid-1890s, carefully analyzes the political, economic, and social circumstances conducive to reform in the four selected commonwealths. These primary materials for all three parties will be systematically examined to see if there were significant political issues before the silver question became all-encompassing.

In addition to delineating the issues of the Front Range region, the author attempts to ascertain whether Populism had a regional character in this area. Earlier students of the movement, the same historians who organized Populism around the silver theme, have perceived one, but one based on the single theme of silver production and free coinage.

In addition to ascertaining common characteristics of Populism in this region, its differences must also be examined to insure an accurate and well-rounded assessment. The often dramatic topographical and climatic variations in this region that extends from the 49th parallel to the Mexican border produce the most obvious differences. Differences in agricultural and mineral resources are very important from an historical standpoint because the resulting economic development in each western state largely determined the direction of change and reform in that state. The ethnic composition of populations drawn to each commonwealth (particularly during the late nineteenth century) produced important differences too. Many of those who peopled the eastern plains, for instance, were native-born Anglo-Saxon Protestants. There were, however, large numbers of foreign-born drawn to the mining camps of the area. They included Cornish, Irish, and Welsh miners as well as those from southern and central Europe. There were also the Chinese, who were often viciously persecuted, and the native Spanish-speaking New Mexicans, whose ancestors had settled this part of the West almost three centuries ago. This study considers the influence of this racial, ethnic, and religious mix on protest and third party activity in the Mountain West. Even the differences in government had their impact on Populism. New Mexico was the only Front Range territory during the Populist Era. Because the territorial system imposed certain restraints, third party activity took a different form in New Mexico. The consequences of these restraints are also examined.

In the face of all these differences it is obvious that silver is not the only issue that binds these states into a cohesive region. The prime objective of this study is to determine whether one or more issues do, in fact, unify Populism in this region through a systematic examining of anti-monopolism as well as of the other issues already alluded to. Perhaps two or more issues intertwined like the strands of a rope provide a regional Populist bond. If that is the case, then the movement in the Mountain West is, indeed, multi-dimensional. Such a conclusion would put this branch of Populism in the national mainstream—it could no longer be regarded as simply a product of the crusading fervor for bimetallism so evident throughout the West during the late nineteenth century.

Two

Colorado

The Origins of Protest

Colorado is probably the logical state to start with in this analysis of Populism along the Front Range. If, as Hicks and Goodwyn believed, Populism in the Mountain West was a one-issue movement, then Colorado, as the leading silver-producing state in the nation, should be their prime example since it should be easiest to prove their case in this state.

Ironically the discovery of gold on Dry Creek near the confluence of Cherry Creek and the South Platte in 1858, not silver, led to the settlement of the Centennial state. The rush launched by that strike during the following year, however, soon sputtered as the placer diggings in what is today greater Denver did not yield enough of the coveted yellow metal to maintain a major gold rush. John Gregory's strike along Clear Creek in the mountains west of Denver in the spring of 1859, however, gave permanence to the newest mining kingdom. The output of gold soared after that: the average production figure for the years 1862 and 1863 was $3,400,000 per year.[1]

Colorado proved to be a treasure chest; indeed, it had some of the most varied mineral resources of any state or territory in the West. Gold and silver, of course, were the original attractions. In time, base metals such as lead, zinc, and copper assumed major importance. Of the two precious minerals mined, gold was the one that dazzled the imaginations of the earliest prospectors, and brought thousands of eager goldseekers to the Rockies in 1859. By 1860, according to the census of that year, there were 34,277 souls in Colorado—a remarkable growth when one considers that the only non-Indians in the area before the rush were a handful of Spanish-speaking people living in the San Luis Valley in the southernmost part of the state.[2]

The terrain of the central Rockies, however, provided major obstacles to the extraction of Colorado's mineral wealth. Transportation was difficult. The distinct metallurgical combinations found beneath the state's steep mountainsides needed certain technology to unlock them; and, obviously, there was the need for capital to extract, process, and transport on a large scale the mineral-rich ores of the New California. These obstacles particularly hindered the kind of low-cost mining engaged in by the scores of small prospectors who had scurried westward in search of quick fortune. Once the more accessible placers were exhausted, these obstacles stood like herculean barriers in the path of progress. Because of the formidable nature of these problems, mining in Colorado reached a low point in the mid-1860s. Indeed, the federal census of 1870 counted only 2,200 miners in what had been since 1861 the Territory of Colorado.[3] Farming on the eastern plains adjacent to the Front Range was probably more important that year than the mining activity of the mountainous two-thirds of this fledgling territory.

Several factors were responsible for the reinvigoration of Colorado mining. Eastern and foreign capitalists were enthusiastic about the developing economy of the central Rockies. (Colorado relied on outside help as early as the Civil War, and continued to do so during the years following that struggle.) The processing of Colorado's rich ores was another important breakthrough. Nathaniel P. Hill, a chemistry professor from Brown University who was backed by New England industrialists, applied the techniques of smelting he had learned while on trips to Britain and the Continent. He established the famous Boston and Colorado Smelter at Black Hawk in 1868, not far from where Gregory made his famous strike. Although the costs of refining ore at that smelter were so high that only the richest ores could be worked, the trend toward more sophisticated processing was unmistakable.[4]

Capital and technology from the East and abroad were also important. Hoisting machinery and tramways were two of the fruits of this type of assistance. Experienced miners from Ireland and Cornwall also helped in the reinvigoration of the territory's mining economy.

The establishment of railroads, such as the one built by the Colorado Central to connect Denver and "the Little Kingdom of Gilpin" where Hill's smelter was located also restored confidence in Colorado's future.

But help from the outside, as important as it was, proved to be a mixed blessing. Soon bankers and entrepreneurs from the East controlled a significant portion of the territorial economy; there were even capitalists from abroad demanding a quid pro quo for their investments. Operating through bankers and businessmen in growing Front Range communities such as Denver and Colorado Springs, these absentee capitalists began to exercise an increasing influence in the political as well as economic life of Colorado. If laws based on laissez-faire economics are any indication, absentee owners and investors had an immense influence on the legislators of the mining commonwealth. With statehood in 1876, Colorado had the distinction of being one of only twelve states without legal restrictions on usury.[5] Although a one-man railroad regulatory commission was established, the state legislature appropriated no money for it. Railroad interests, which outside capital largely controlled, minimized what little authority the commission had. The state's courts had the reputation of being partial to the interests of creditors. While this made Colorado attractive to those seeking sound and conservative investments, it caused the expected frustration among borrowers, who were always numerous in a developing economy.[6]

By the 1880s, certainly, Colorado had become what modern historians and social scientists call a "colonial economy." Earlier scholars, however, employed harsher terms. Leon W. Fuller, writing during the Great Depression, for example, excoriated the "sinister influence of private monopoly" in Colorado during the Gilded Age, concluding that the state had become "little more than a pocket borough of the corporate oligarchy."[7] Nevertheless, this outside capital did invigorate the territory's ailing economy.

Still another factor that stimulated mining in Colorado was the remarkable expansion of silver production. Silver had been discovered as early as 1864 in Clear Creek County, south of Gilpin. There was little serious effort to extract and process it until 1869, after which interest in the metal resulted in the discovery of silver lodes at a number of other sites in the mountainous territory. By 1874, silver production had surpassed $3,000,000, exceeding the output of gold for the first time. A silver boom in 1877 at Leadville, near the highest point of the American Rockies, caused silver production to soar. By 1880, Leadville with 14,820 citizens was the second largest community in Colorado, ranking just behind Denver. The annual silver output at Leadville alone soon exceeded that of any foreign country except Mexico; its lead production was almost equal to that of England's.[8] The ranks of Colorado miners swelled from 2,200 in 1870 to 28,970 in 1880 because of these renewed opportunities for riches.[9]

As the last decade of the dying century was reached, however, the glowing promise of Colorado's booming economy began to fade. Fuller insisted that a downward trend in the business cycle was perceptible as early as 1889.[10] It was undoubtedly aggravated by the crisis which resulted the following year when an Argentine revolution imperiled Baring Brothers and Company, the leading financial firm of England.[11] This development threatened the supply of foreign capital and caused panic among eastern creditors, who began to liquidate their capital holdings in the West. The resulting restriction of credit was a serious setback to a colonial economy such as Colorado's where prosperity was geared to ever-expanding growth. The credit restriction and liquidation that had occurred in the early 1890s, therefore, had an exceptional impact. According to Fuller, "No longer could the entire burden of fixed indebtedness be serviced out of earnings; liquidation of assets (often depreciated) was necessary."[12] Colorado was like an improvident debtor accustomed to living well above his means, who was suddenly asked to meet his obligations and was told to expect no more help until he did.

A byproduct of the state's economic slowdown was the development of serious negative attitudes. Wright, in his thorough analysis of Colorado Populism, stressed the disillusionment that accompanied the state's economic decline. The frontier exuberance of Colorado's pioneer miners, for instance, began to waver as mining operations passed from the hands of individual prospectors to corporate enterprises. For example, a few restless, independent-minded miners from the silver mining camp of Aspen laid claim to properties in what was expected to be "the greatest silver camp in the world"; yet, few of these prospectors could hold on to their claims. By 1885, four years after the first major strike in Aspen, an estimated 700 of the camp's 1,000 miners were wage employees. A concentration of control in the hands of fewer and fewer corporate enterprises accompanied the shift from individual to corporate ownership. In 1880 when the state's economy was sharply on the rise, there were 126 gold and silver mining corporations in the state. Twenty years later that number had swelled to 822, but 64 of them accounted for as much as 80 percent of the mining product of the state.[13] Needless to say, this trend toward intensification of control diminished the frontier dream of individual success that such western historians as Carlos Schwantes have stressed.

The concentration of mining ownership in the hands of a few is just another example of the degree to which Colorado was becoming a colonial economy. Many of these mining companies were also owned by absentee capitalists. The response among many of the once hopeful miners was to unionize. It was a slow process. In 1870, there was only one union, despite the fact that most miners were wage earners. But strong, even militant, unions were organized in time. Of the 109 strikes among all laborers in Colorado from 1881 to 1886, 46 of them occurred in the mining industry. In 1892, workingmen in the state belonged to 206 labor organizations. A greater percentage of Colorado's citizens belonged to unions than of those in any other state.[14]

The Knights of Labor, the blue-collar group that later participated vigorously in the formation of the national People's party, was one of the labor organizations that played a key role in the state's union activities. First organized in the coal fields north of Denver, the union became prominent in 1884 when it won a major regional strike against the Union Pacific.[15] Joseph R. Buchanan, editor of a radical Denver workingman's newspaper the *Labor Enquirer*, was responsible for this stunning success. He became one of the most prominent labor leaders of the region; Buchanan's reputation was accurately capsulized by the popular sobriquet "Riproarer of the Rockies."[16] As one of three members of the national executive board of the Knights of Labor, he played a leading role in the union's activities in the central Rockies, which included a major strike in the coal fields of southern Colorado during the late 1880s. Buchanan was also interested in radical politics and supported such controversial minor party candidates for the presidency as Benjamin Butler in 1884 and Henry George in 1888.[17] Although Buchanan had a great following, a large segment of organized labor in Colorado preferred the much more moderate stance of the Knights' national leader, Grand Master Workman Terence V. Powderly—at least those in the mines did when the economic slowdown of the 1880s appeared to be no more than just another short-term development in an industry accustomed to wild fluctuations.

Farmers and stock grazers also became disenchanted with the once-glowing future of Colorado. Agriculture had grown along with mining since farmers were needed from the very beginning to raise foodstuffs for the busy camps in the newly discovered goldfields. Small irrigated plots around Denver had soon produced enough food to feed the aspiring Fifty-Niners. Colorado, in time, led the way in developing large-scale irrigation based on the water law system of appropriation rather than riparian rights, whereby water was equitably divided rather than giving the lion's share to those upstream; indeed, such a system would bear the name of the young territory as it spread to many parts of the arid West.[18]

Colorado needed cattle grazers for the same reason that it needed farmers—to feed the hastily transplanted population brought to the region because of the mining boom. In a relatively brief time, the cattle industry was creating an unusually good balance of trade for the colonial economy of Colorado. While Coloradans were sending $1.3 million outside the territory in 1874 to buy food because local farmers could not raise enough, Colorado's stock grazers were making up the trade deficit by selling beef to northern and eastern buyers. In 1872 alone, they sold two million dollars worth of beef outside the territory.[19] The profits in the cattle industry were enticing. In 1882, the Denver *Tribune*, criticizing the state's obsession with mining and railroad investment, insisted that a 15 or 20 percent return could be made by investing in cattle.[20]

Even the high plains of eastern Colorado were being peopled by optimistic farmers. Coming during the exceptionally wet years of the mid-1880s, these farmers, part of what Wright called the "Kansas-Nebraska frontier spill," moved into a region once designated as the Great American Desert. Attracted by land laws that provided them with larger acreage than they could have expected in the East, these newcomers homesteaded, took advantage of the old Preemption Act, and qualified under the provisions of the Timber Culture Act. Believing that good rainfall was a permanent feature of the green prairie, they cultivated cereal crops, such as corn and wheat, in time-tested ways in defiance of the area's climatic imperatives. They had a remarkable faith in the future of what they called the "rain belt"—a faith that was tempered by periodic droughts such as those that disrupted normal life during the years 1888 and 1890. Since there was little water for irrigation in much of this region, these dry seasons were disastrous. They often caused an exodus of settlers where there had been an explosive influx of newcomers only a short time before. In Baca County, in the southeastern corner of the state, for example, the population plummeted from an estimated 3,000 in the spring of 1888 to only a thousand in 1890.[21]

Thus, there was a sharp decline in the confidence of farmers in the rain belt during the late 1880s to match that felt by the miners of this region. Adverse weather conditions, however, tell only part of the story. Many complaints and grievances, real or imagined, must be understood to comprehend the disenchantment of the three main groups—cattlemen, irrigation farmers, and nonirrigation farmers—in developing the eastern third of the state.

Cattlemen, for instance, felt that sheepmen were encroaching on their grazing land and ruining their pastures. Many of them correctly foresaw also that the days of the open-range cattle industry were numbered because of the increasing penetration of rain-belt farmers. A number of stock grazers wanted a national cattle trail along the eastern boundary of the state so that the Long Drive could continue, but Congress resisted the feverish lobbying of the Colorado Cattle Growers' Association and refused to act on that proposal.[22]

Irrigation farmers, who were the best organized of the agricultural groups on the eastern plains, had their alleged enemies too. They were particularly unhappy with the irrigation companies, which controlled the most valuable commodity on the Great Plains—water. The owners of these enterprising organizations often promised farmers in the important South Platte and Arkansas river valleys more water than the companies could deliver. The farmers especially resented the royalties that these companies added to the standard water rates. The fact that foreign capitalists owned some of these irrigation firms only increased the resentment against them. The Colorado Mortgage and Investment Company of London, a wealthy firm popularly known as the "English Company," for example, bore a double stigma: it was guilty of abuses commonly charged against water companies, and it was owned by foreigners.[23] These irrigation farmers had much at stake, for they were heavily capitalized with high farm-mortgage debts. When Colorado's economy began to falter in the late 1880s, however, their hostility was directed more against the water organizations than against the mortgage companies.[24]

Farmers in the rain belt, unwilling to blame all their troubles on the weather, had their adversaries too. In many way, the railroad corporations played the same role for the nonirrigation farmers as the water companies did for the irrigation ones. Colorado farmers regarded the rate structure of the railroads as inequitable because it placed them in

an unfavorable position to compete with wheat farmers and cattlemen outside the state. A drop in commodity prices about this time
exacerbated popular discontent.[25]

Consequently, before the silver crisis of the early 1890s crippled the
Colorado economy, burning issues had already aroused the working
people of the young state. They ranged from overdependence on capitalists and diminished prospects for economic success in the new
state to catastrophic weather conditions that aggravated Colorado's
already overextended agricultural economy. These issues produced a
variety of villains or scapegoats. To mine employees, there were the
indifferent mine owners with their close eastern and foreign connections. To irrigation farmers, there were the profit-hungry water companies, corporations more prone to renege on contracts with customers than to supply them with vitally needed irrigation water. To
rain-belt farmers, there were the railroads who were concerned more
with profit-and-loss statements than with the survival of their struggling customers. Even big cattlemen, who usually viewed themselves
as capitalists or employers, had their targets. Sheepmen and farmers
posed a very definite challenge to the proprietary attitude these stockmen had toward the miles of rolling plains in eastern Colorado.

To many citizens of the pioneer state, then, there appeared to be a
growing number of powerful or monopolistic interests arrayed against
them. Some kind of organized response obviously was needed to deal
with this threat. For the industrial or mining worker, it might be a
renewed and more militant unionism, such as that which had already
taken form in the mountainous two-thirds of the state. For working
people from both farm and city, however, it might be a political organization too radical for the nation's traditional two-party system.

Three

Colorado Populism

By 1890, the growing economic problems of the Centennial state had created a mood for action. A number of Coloradans were seriously casting about for solutions to the economic dilemmas that had become obvious during the 1880s. Certain channels for organized protest, of course, existed. Unfortunately, not all of them were universally applicable. The Knights of Labor, for instance, had been an appropriate vehicle for change and reform for the railroad workers and miners. But its relevance to farm folk was highly questionable. The two major political parties, traditional outlets for popular frustration, seemed more concerned with historical questions or cultural differences than with the knotty economic issues caused by industrialism.

From the very beginning, the Republican party had dominated the region's politics because Colorado had been made a territory and proclaimed a state under Republican rule. In truth, many of the successes that had been achieved by the Democrats were merely the result of factional struggles involving the leaders of the G.O.P. In most cases, the Republicans prevailed by exploiting to their advantage such time-tested issues as the patriotism of the Democratic party, the immigration of unwanted Chinese, and the prohibition of alcoholic spirits. The Civil War and its aftermath provided support for the historical issue. Following Colorado's admission to the Union, the bloody shirt was waved with remarkable success. A partisan Denver newspaper, for example, even questioned the loyalty of the Democratic presidential candidate, former Union General Winfield S. Hancock, in 1880.[1] Ethnocultural differences were also grist for the political mill. Republican support was very strong among the native-born pietistic Protestants of Colorado as evidenced by the strength and popularity in the party of the native anti-Catholic American Protective Association. Democrats, on the other hand, had more appeal among Catholic cultural groups, although they occasionally gained the support of certain Republican factions. In the 1880s, for example, Democrats introduced the prohibition issue into a political campaign and split the temperance Protestants from the other elements of the Republican party.[2]

In one area, both parties stood on common ground. They both reflected the virulent hostility of workingmen toward the Chinese in the 1880s. Of all the immigrant groups in Colorado, Coloradans reviled the Chinese the most. They feared their competition and abhorred their influence. Coloradans rioted against the Chinese in Denver in 1880. Other miners brutalized the Chinese in such mining camps as Leadville and Rico.[3] Politicians did little to protect them. Both major parties, as a matter of fact, took a strong national stand against Chinese immigration during the 1880s, a position that took little political courage. It seemed necessary, however, to attract or retain labor support in Colorado and elsewhere throughout the West.[4] Although negative attitudes also existed toward blacks and Spanish-speaking Coloradans, they were insignificant when compared with the anti-Chinese bias. Wright has argued, moreover, that this hostility toward the Chinese ultimately developed into an overall antiforeign bias by the year 1890. Many workers affected by the economic slowdown of the 1880s conveniently used unrestricted immigration to explain the cause of industrial disruption.[5]

The two parties only grudgingly came to grips with the economic issues caused by America's industrial transformation. Democrats supported labor issues, while the Republicans emphasized tariff protection. Both the Republicans and Democrats were concerned with the issue of silver coinage following the demonetization of silver in the so-called "Crime of '73." Both parties naturally worked diligently to encourage silver mining. The Republican state convention in 1888, for example, demanded the "free and unlimited coinage of silver."[6] Although the more traditional economic issues, such as the tariff, gave way in importance to those generated by the new politics of the 1890s, this issue would at least remain in the background.

Curiously, the farmers rather than the miners raised the issues that brought into question the laissez-faire politics that had dominated Colorado since the gold rush. Even though their aspirations were not as grandiose as the early argonauts, the farmers, particularly those on the eastern plains, were among the very first to look seriously at the system of rewards and incentives found in Colorado's colonial economy. (Miners would later join, and eventually dominate, the third party movement when it became the People's party in name as well as in substance.) In the beginning, third party action took the form of the Independent or Farmers' Alliance party organized in 1890. Disenchanted agrarians made up the bulk of the new party's rank and file.

Agrarian discontent in Colorado had manifested itself in protest movements as early as the mid-1870s. The Grange, the farm organization that had achieved such striking successes in coping with railroad abuses in the Midwest, was organized in the state in 1874. By 1875, there were sixty-nine Grange lodges; by 1888, there were eight-five with a membership of 2,390. At first, the Colorado Grange was concerned with such issues as the prohibition of margarine and liquor and the upgrading of the state agricultural college. But as the agricultural boom began to lose some of its momentum, many farmers in the state, both in and out of the Grange, started to adopt militant stands on more controversial issues. Wheat growers in northern Colorado in 1885, for instance, began to organize in order to defend their interests against the "millers' syndicate."[7]

Many farmers, at this time, became defensive. They felt their welfare was being threatened by large monopolistic enterprises. Rural newspapers were replete with allusions to monopoly power; articles referred to flour trusts, coal trusts, and trusts of almost every other description.[8] Farmers in the San Luis Valley of southern Colorado organized against the "eastern aristocracy" because of their acute awareness of the inordinate influence of absentee capitalists from the East and abroad.[9] Even though political action seemed imperative if the growth of monopoly was to be stemmed or friendly laws were to be enacted, the Grange, which was especially strong among the irrigation farmers of northern Colorado, was reluctant to move aggressively into politics.

The more recently organized Southern Alliance, however, had no reluctance to assume the reformist role that the Grange had declined. In the spring of 1888, the National Farmers' Alliance and Industrial Union, to use its official name, sent R. W. S. Overstreet into Colorado to organize local alliances. Irrigation farmers in the southern part of the state were especially receptive to the appeals of the persuasive Overstreet. In the meantime, one of the Southern Alliance's major rivals in the farm protest movement, the Northern Alliance or the National Farmer's Alliance, began a drive to enroll members. Although it made considerable headway in 1889 in the eastern rain-belt counties, the Southern Alliance prevailed. On December 17, 1889, the recently recruited Colorado alliancemen formed a state organization under a charter granted by the Southern Alliance. Growth of the new movement was greatest in the southern and eastern counties, where Alliance activity had begun; however, the gospel of cooperation, the trademark of the Southern Alliance, soon spread northward. There, in the irrigation counties of northern Colorado, farmers' impatience with the Grange created a receptive environment for the newer, more aggressively political farm organization. Because the Southern Alliance was willing to confront the issues of monopoly and monetary policy in a forthright way, it became dominant in northern Colorado in a remarkably short time. By 1891, the statewide membership of the organization was estimated at 15,000.[10]

The election of 1890 provided an unmatched opportunity for aroused farmers to test their new-found organizational strength. Not only were they united, but the political climate was also right. For one thing the powerful Republican party was engaged in a self-destructive intraparty struggle. The corruption of the state's Seventh General Assembly, which the G.O.P. controlled, was so flagrant that the legislature earned the nickname "the Robber Seventh." The Republicans had divided into two warring factions allegedly to reform their party. Each of the two rivals, known as the "Gang" and the "Gang Smashers," proclaimed its intention to revitalize the party and improve its tarnished image. The rivalry somehow got out of control, however, and degenerated into a power struggle.[11]

This serious schism in the state's dominant political organization presented Colorado's disenchanted elements with a chance they could not ignore. On July 4, 1890, two years to the day before the Populists met in Omaha to make their national challenge, reform-minded spokesmen for dissatisfied farm and labor organizations gathered in Denver to consider taking independent political action. They included representatives from the aggressive Southern Alliance, the labor-based Knights of Labor, and the Grange. Alliance leader E. H. Benton of Greeley, an agricultural town in the irrigated South Platte River Valley, was one of the more prominent figures. W. A. Wilson, a Denver Knight, was there as was Granger Ben Honnett and R. Q. Tenny, a former Granger and now an Alliance leader. B. A. Wheeler, who had organized irrigation farmers to fight the water companies, provided representation for his aroused constituency. The result of this gathering was the organization of the previously mentioned Independent or Farmers' Alliance party.

The new party met in Denver the following month. There were approximately 150 delegates representing many of the organizations that would form the national People's party two years later. The dominant delegates were, of course, from the Alliance. Knights were also present as well as Nationalists, the latter representing the Nationalist clubs that were inspired by Edward Bellamy's Looking Backward, the utopian novel that extolled the virtues of a cooperative society. Members of the United Order of Anti-Monopolists, a group dedicated to counteracting the excesses of monopolistic enterprise, were also present. And, not surprisingly, subscribers of the quantity theory of money were in attendance—with prices as low as they were in 1890, inflation schemes obviously had a great attraction. As a matter of fact, Benton who presided over the opening session was a former greenbacker, as were a number of other people who played key roles at the new third party convention.[12]

The gathering was basically an antimonopoly and anti-Republican affair—silver coinage was only of secondary importance at this time. The distinctive element in the platform drawn up by the new party was its hostile tone toward corporate power in Colorado. These delegates obviously were most dissatisfied with the state's colonial economy. Their most controversial action called for outright government ownership of railroads and telegraphs.[13] The Independent party, as a consequence, became an early advocate of nationalization. It went well beyond a resolution drafted that same year by a convention of the Colorado Farmers' Alliance, in which the creation of an effective railroad commission was the extent of railroad control. The newly constituted Independents also advocated state ownership and management of the ditches and reservoirs of Colorado. Foreign-owned companies, such as the English Company, were put on notice with a plank calling for the prohibition of alien landownership. (This was two years before the Populists, in effect, declared war against foreign owners in their Omaha platform.)

Although Colorado's Independent party was primarily a manifestation of agrarian protest, both for irrigation and nonirrigation farmers, it also appealed to labor by advocating reforms similar to those made at the national Populist party convention in 1892. The party made the familiar demand for an eight-hour day, a goal of much of the working class during the Gilded Age and one that the two major parties had done little to achieve. It also made such prolabor demands as the enactment of an employers' liability law and the creation of a labor arbitration board. The new party obviously made a real effort at the gathering to create a farm-labor coalition.

Other demands made by the Independent party reveal a variety of concerns on the part of the delegates. The call for the institution of the Australian secret ballot anticipated the Populist efforts two years later to cleanse the electoral process. Delegates advocated the free coinage of silver, although the recommendation was by no means central to the party platform. A few of the suggested planks were quite divisive and became the subjects of heated debate. Although a majority of the delegates were probably from a pietistic Protestant background, they did manage to defeat a highly controversial proposal which would have eliminated in Colorado one of the country's more venerable institutions, the saloon.[14] Considering the composition of this convention and its geographical representation, this action indicated a strong desire on the part of the new party to win at the polls. The Independents had to attract support form the state's laboring classes, a substantial number of whom were foreign-born, Roman Catholic, and decidedly not temperance-minded. The victory over the hard-line temperance forces made the new party more acceptable to outside elements; the fact that a debate was necessary, however, did not bode well for the untried farm-labor coalition.

To draw attention away from divisive ethnocultural differences, the Independent party, both in the convention and on the stump, railed against the Republican party and its close ties with the corporate community. To take advantage of the strong public sentiment against the G.O.P. and its "Robber Seventh," the third party nominated two disillusioned Republicans: John G. Coy and J. D. Burr. Coy of Laramie County was the party's gubernatorial candidate. His credentials were impeccable: an honest farmer, Coy had been a Granger and an Alliance member during his career, and had flirted with greenback principles. The party chose Burr of the rain-belt county of Yuma to run for a seat in the national House of Representatives. Burr gave credence to Leon W. Fuller's thesis that anticapitalism was a major political sentiment at this time when he told convention members that they were "not slaves of any class of men on God's earth."[15]

This strong assault against the Republican party came at the right time. Although the "Gang," which had gained control of the Republican state convention, styled itself as the reform element of the party, it nominated some of the same state officials who had been accused of corruption. The Republicans did, however, feel compelled to respond to the changing tides of public opinion caused by the economic slowdown: they advocated a railroad commission that could fix rates and irrigation laws that could abridge the powers of the controversial water comapanies. Thus, the G.O.P. was not indifferent to the sensibilities of irrigation and nonirrigation farmers.[16] As for the Democrats in 1890, they too responded to the new political currents by declaring that the state's railroads should operate without discrimination against any shipper.[17] They also exploited the corruption issue at the expense of their embattled Republican rivals.

The formation of a coalition known as the "Citizens' " ticket dashed Democratic and third party hopes for success. Although primarily the result of an accord to benefit the two major parties, this new alliance had the support of some of the state's most prominent agrarian reformers, including Herbert George, a Denver journalist who later became an important spokesman for the state's Populist party. Heading the slate organized by the coalition was the gruff old Republican veteran John L. Routt, who was selected as the candidate for governor.[18] The choice for lieutenant governor was a Democrat. The two major parties shared the rest of the slots on the ticket in such a way that the influence of the agrarian reform element in the state was minimal; for example, not one Allianceman was chosen by the reform coalition.

The work of the coalition was a boon to Routt, who won the 1890 election by the narrowest of margins—his majority barely exceeded half the popular vote cast. Most Democrats were also delighted with the results: the two offices they won because of participation in the Citizens' effort marked their best political year since 1886. But to the Independent party, the success of the coalition spelled disaster. The new party's share of the vote for the gubernatorial race was a mere 6.23 percent. Independents carried only two agricultural counties on the Western Slope: Montrose and Delta. Although the mining counties in the mountains remained predominantly Democratic, the Independent showing in Lake and Fremont counties was respectable. The large number of foreign-born in the mining labor force, however, was not attracted by the native Protestantism of the new party. Farm counties in the northeastern corner of Colorado, including Weld, Larimer, and Yuma, gave Coy and the new third party candidates strong support.[19] Wright, as a matter of fact, speculated that the Citizen's coalition may have neutralized the strength of the Independents among irrigation farmers, who seemed ready to terminate old political ties. He also concluded in his analysis that the issues being pedaled by the Independents, both economic and ethnocultural, did not have an appeal beyond the farm regions of the Centennial state. "Protestantism, wheat, corn, pigs, and the mortgage" simply did not have much attraction for miners and urban laborers, notwithstanding the support the Knights of Labor gave the Independent movement.[20]

Despite the disappointing results of the 1890 election, the Independents did raise a number of economic issues that were not easily forgotten. Eventually these issues would undermine the old loyalties based upon history, religion, ethnicity, and traditional party doctrine that Republicans and Democrats enjoyed. But the Independent effort in 1890 was premature. Miners, who still enjoyed a three-dollar-a-day wage, did not relate to the issues deemed so important by the state's farmers. Railroad abuses did not particularly affect them; indeed, as railroads were built to connect new mining camps with the outside world, transportation costs went down. Alleged irrigation or food-processing monopolies had even less relevance, and the prohibition issue evoked only negative responses. Inflationary schemes, with the possible exception of free silver, were not appealing. If food prices went up, real income for Colorado's miners and urban laborers could only go down. Even mortgage problems were minimal since a farm mortgage was almost always greater than one for a small urban homestead.[21] When these economic differences are added to the ethnocultural ones, the failure of the agrarian reformers in their quest for political unity in 1890 becomes more understandable.

Nevertheless, the efforts of the Alliance-dominated Independents continued. Following the organizational meeting of the national Populists in Cincinnati on May 19, 1891, Independents gathered in Denver on September 9 of the same year. Jackson Orr, chairman of the state central committee of the Independent party, called for another convention to restructure the Independents into the new People's party. The Alliance had a strong influence in these proceedings since thirty-one of the ninety-four delegates were alliancemen.[22]

Although the new party still retained its pronounced agrarian bias and had representatives from fewer than a third of the state's counties present, it was apparent from the beginning that the year-old political movement intended to become a major political force in Colorado. Elected to chair its proceedings was a steely-willed editor from the silver-mining camp of Aspen Davis Hanson Waite. Undoubtedly Colorado Populism's most fascinating figure, Waite has been described by historian Karel D. Bicha as a man obsessed with the monopoly question. He saw the intrusion of monopoly in practically every field of human endeavor: land, money, transportation, liquor and trade. He wrote in 1891, the year of Colorado Populism's genesis, that monopoly "is the great dragon whose breath withers and destroys the fleets of commerce—paralyzes the arm of industry—and arrays every person against his neighbor." By 1898, after he had served one term as a Populist governor, he still maintained the same opinion. To him, monopoly remained a dreadful monster who was "sucking the lifeblood of the prosperity and liberty of a nation."[23]

The selection of Waite to chair the first convention of the People's party reflected the control that the more radical members of the new party had. It was also evident in the rhetoric of the man the Populists nominated for a seat on the state supreme court Judge J. H. Croxton of populous Arapahoe County. He not only was willing to support the party's platform, which had unequivocally condemned the state court for its incompetent and corrupt conduct,[24] but he also delighted convention delegates with a campaign oratory that was in harmony with that angry platform. In the strongest of terms, he warned them that the railroads controlled the country: "They hire assassins to shoot down women and children who are demanding their rights under the constitution." His bitter words were, no doubt, reassuring to farmers on the eastern plains, particularly those in the rain-belt region where many felt they had been victimized by high freight rates and railroad abuses. But the old Independents, now Populists, had not neglected industrial workers in their platform either. A strong demand for a potent employers' liability act symbolized this commitment to continuing reform in the mines and urban workshops.

Croxton's forthright appeal to the voters was just slightly more persuasive than that of the Independent candidates of 1890. Although Croxton's total of 6,384 was only 1,185 votes better than that polled by candidates of the Alliance-dominated party one year earlier, there was strong evidence that the two major parties were starting to take the third party movement more seriously. For instance, to prevent agricultural Montrose County from being lured into the new political movement, Republicans and Democrats fused in order to deny electoral success to the emerging Populists.[25]

It was the fortunes of silver, however, which really shattered traditional party politics and gave the Populists their best opportunity. The value of silver in the United States had dramatically declined as the production of the metal continued to rise. The output in Colorado had reached the astonishing level of 24 million ounces in 1892. Unfortunately for silver producers, the governmental market in the United States was limited by the Sherman Silver Purchase Act to only 4.5 million ounces a month. The overseas market was primarily a commercial one since the major nations of Western Europe had moved to the gold standard. Consequently, because of the overproduction of silver in Colorado and throughout the West and because of the subsequent decline of the market, the price dropped to $.87 an ounce in 1892, more than $.115 less than the previous year and $.45 less than the price in 1872.[26] An increase in the production costs because of the necessity to mine lower-grade ores accompanied this alarming price decline. By 1892, the health of Colorado's mining economy was becoming seriously imperiled.

Both major parties had broken with their national bodies over what was becoming known as the Silver Question. Indeed, the economy of the Centennial state was so dependent on a healthy silver industry that the free coinage issue was in many ways a nonpartisan one. Naturally, the temptation to exploit a compelling issue, like free silver, was irresistible. Democrat Thomas Patterson, part owner of Denver's *Rocky Mountain News*, for example, insisted on resurrecting the old issue of silver demonetization—the emotional "Crime of '73"— and blaming the Republicans for it. He could not resist joining his Republican counterparts, however, in castigating Grover Cleveland for his "goldbug" views on the currency issue.

As declining silver prices and the hostility of the Harrison administration appeared more and more to jeopardize silver, clubs and political organizations began to organize in Colorado and elsewhere to promote the precious metal. In 1889, for instance, the Denver Chamber of Commerce called for a state convention to convene in the Queen City. It resulted in the formation of the Colorado Silver Association with silver mogul Horace Tabor as its president. In March of 1892, a state Silver League took over the activities from the moribund

Colorado Silver Association. The new Silver League soon boasted of fifty-eight silver clubs with a membership of 25,000.[27] Political action was the next logical step. As the state's majority party with its national organization decidedly lukewarm toward increased silver coinage, the Republicans were especially reluctant to see this happen. Obviously, the party that would profit the most from the politicalization of silver was the newly organized People's party. It had no negative performance to haunt it at the polls. Republicans and Democrats in Colorado had to explain their role in the enactment of such pieces of silver legislation as the Bland-Allison and Sherman acts to the electorate in such a way as to make their party look good. The brief life of the People's party provided no such embarrassments for its members. The 1890 stand for free silver by the party's predecessor, the Independent movement, was, if anything, an asset.

The Populist movement achieved national status for the first time in 1892. The election of that year would have been a replay of the 1888 election with the two conservatives Harrison and Cleveland facing each other once again, if it had not been for the dramatic emergence of third party politics. The July gathering of Populists in Omaha to nominate a national ticket was an exciting event for those who had become disenchanted with the two-party system as well as for those concerned about silver. Colorado's Silver League and the potent Denver Silver Club had representatives who focused almost exclusively on silver in attendance at Omaha. There were also Coloradans present at the convention who cared about the other issues that were emphasized in the new party's forthright platform. Davis H. Waite and Jackson Orr were among the delegates representing the state's Populist organization. More conservative Populists in Colorado probably would have preferred reform-minded Walter Q. Gresham, the Republican-appointed federal circuit judge from Chicago, as the new party's standard-bearer, but the delegates instead nominated the Greenback presidential candidate for 1880, former General James B. Weaver to fill this role.[28] Although many delegates were concerned with only one issue, the party, as an entity, adopted a multi-issue platform. In addition to the call for the free coinage of silver, the delegates at the convention demanded government ownership of the railroads and telegraphs, direct election of United States senators, a graduated income tax, and a host of other controversial proposals.[29] It was unknown whether single-issue delegates would support these other planks of the tough platform.

Three weeks after the Omaha convention, Coloradans who were demanding a fundamental change gathered at Denver. The powerful Silver League and the new Populist party had arranged to convene their conventions at the same time and in the same place to coordinate their strategy for the coming November election. Heading the Silver League was the prominent Democrat Thomas Patterson and the almost equally influential Republican M. H. Slater, who was also the league's state president. Both men had reservations about the national Populist platform and the party's presidential candidate General Weaver. Most of the Populists who attended the party convention, however, were strongly influenced by the doctrines of the Alliance movement, the first reform group in Colorado. In both organizations, different men emerged as persons who could best represent the divergent viewpoints. Silver Leaguers, for instance, backed former Republican Julius Thompson, a silver mine owner from Dolores County on the Western Slope. He attempted to persuade hard-line Populists that he wholeheartedly embraced their party doctrines. These Populists, however, preferred Davis Waite, who had been active in the third party movement for at least a year.

Waite's selection over Thompson at the state convention was a clear triumph for those agrarian leaders most responsible for Populism. The essence of the Colorado movement, at this time, was not "simply silverism." As a matter of fact, Thompson's support came from those delegates representing the mining counties of the state, whom committed agrarian Populists rightly suspected of being one-issue political participants. The *Denver Republican* obviously sensed this division when it emphasized that those nominated with Waite were largely from Farmers' Alliance and Populist backgrounds: "The ticket is a weak one and will secure no recognition outside the purely People's Party ranks. The candidates are of the calamity howler order and fitted to follow the Weaver obsequies."[30] Nevertheless, both sides were reconciled to make the fight together: the Silver League was able to surmount its reluctance and support the ticket headed by Waite with the necessary enthusiasm.

Beginning in 1892, the central focus of Colorado Populism began to shift toward an emphasis on free coinage. During the campaign in Colorado, it became evident to party leaders that there were many uncommitted votes in the economically depressed mining counties where the plummeting price of silver had created disaster. The state Populists at the Denver convention were obviously aware of that fact;

in addition to putting planks in their platform that would satisfy the struggling agrarian entrepreneurs and the silverites, they also had planks specifically directed toward urban and mining wage earners. For instance, the 1892 platform called for an eight-hour day, a child labor law, and the state operation of coal mines. (The demand for employers' liability was also reaffirmed.)[31] Armed with these politically attractive commitments to workingmen as well as with those made in behalf of the agricultural community, Waite using a strident antimonopolism and prosilver stance appealed for votes to the downtrodden of both the mountains and plains. But of the issues that he advanced, the one that really struck a common chord was free silver—a price rise for that metal would both reinvigorate the mining economy and hike the price of farm produce.

The result of the Populist campaign in 1892 was a stunning victory. Benefiting from a Democratic fusion movement led by Patterson, Waite defeated his Republican and Democratic rivals with a healthy plurality of the votes cast.[32] Weaver did even better; he received 57 percent of the popular vote. (Evidently, more Democrats voted for him than they did for Waite.) The entire Populist state ticket was triumphant. The infant party came within four votes of gaining outright control of the state senate and within seven of winning a majority in the state assembly. Two fusionist candidates Lafe Pence and John Bell gained a voice for the new movement on the national scene; both men won seats in the House of Representatives. It was a remarkable feat for a third party movement that had polled less than 7 percent of the state vote in 1890.

Silver was certainly a substantial part of the answer to surprised queries about this Populist success. Waite carried almost the entire mining portion of the state. County after county in the mountains of Colorado backed him, but he also drew support from agricultural areas. He won in Laramie, Weld, and Boulder, three irrigation counties in the shadow of the Front Range.[33] He outpolled his two gubernatorial rivals in Yuma and Sedgwick, two nonirrigation counties on the northeastern plains. The party's Alliance origins still had an appeal. He even carried two counties in the Arkansas Valley, Bent and Otero. These successes were probably due more to the discontent caused by a grasshopper plague than to any appeal the Populist platform might have had.[34]

Silver was still only one of several compelling issues facing the Colorado voter, but its rapid ascendancy would soon change the entire nature of the state's politics. The new party movement was already being influenced by that change. Indeed, Colorado Populism in 1892, like the third party movement in the South and Midwest, was beginning to drift into what Lawrence Goodwyn called the party's shadow movement. O. Gene Clanton noted in his study on Kansas Populism that it was "the issue of free silver that relegated the other Populist reforms in Kansas to a secondary position."[35] Hicks himself admitted that the free coinage issue invariably received a more enthusiastic response among the farmers who voted Populist in 1892 than any of the other issues.[36] Thus, the pattern that emerged in Colorado, the prevalence of a number of reform issues in the beginning with a shift toward free silver around 1892, was characteristic of other Populist strongholds, including those troubled agricultural areas east and south of the Mountain West. The repetition of this pattern in the Mountain West, therefore, suggests that the third party in this region was part of the Populist mainstream.

Despite this emphasis on the silver issue, Waite, when he became governor, did not exploit the coinage issue to its fullest potential. His inaction was not surprising: Waite was an antimonopolist and social reformer who favored free silver—not a silverite. He proved his commitment to other reforms during the first session of the state legislature, which convened in Denver in January of 1893. At that gathering, Waite pushed for a number of reforms including tougher railroad controls, employers' liability, an eight-hour workday, a stringent child-labor law, and an anti-Pinkerton measure that would eliminate the controversial private detective agency as an important factor in industrial strife.[37] His record of success was a poor one. Part of the problem was a lack of unity within his own party, which was common in other states where Populists had gained at least partial control. Another was the poor cooperation achieved between Democrats and Populists. In the end, almost all of the Populists proposals supported by Waite were defeated. The governor, who had favored a more effective railroad commission with rate-fixing powers, was compelled to witness a remarkable regression in the status of railroad regulation. Over Waite's veto, the Ninth General Assembly passed a bill to repeal the 1885 statute that had established the existing railroad commission.[38] Since Waite had made railroad regulation his first item of business, this setback was especially painful.[39]

There were a few achievements about which Waite and his fellow Populists could boast. The legislature passed an eight-hour-day law, but it applied only to government workers. A woman suffrage measure supported by Populists made it through the legislature and was approved by voters throughout the state in November. Although this reform was not included in the Omaha platform, it was in the spirit of equality and Direct Democracy so clearly embraced by almost all Populists. As Waite put it: "I favor woman suffrage because of its justice. Suffrage should be based on intelligence, not accident of birth, sex or wealth."[40] More important, perhaps, Colorado was the first state after Wyoming to provide a general suffrage law for women. Changes were also made in the election laws so that the Australian ballot could be administered more effectively. Nevertheless, the Populists were disappointed by the extent of the important reform legislation which was successfully enacted.

Following the adjournment of the Ninth General Assembly, the state was hit by the devastating Panic of 1893. To Colorado a debtor state with a colonial economy, the national economic decline, which began in May, was especially serious. But its worst effects were not felt in Colorado until June. During that month, Britain closed the mints of India to silver coinage, thus eliminating the last of the important silver bullion markets of the world. The impact of this development on the Colorado silver industry was an expected one—almost all of the state's silver mines were forced to shut down, including the fabled ones in the Leadville area.[41]

Waite's response to the depression was to call a special session of the Ninth General Assembly. Again, the steadfast governor did not concentrate solely on free coinage in his legislative agenda; instead he came up with an elaborate program to treat the diversity of ills caused by the panic. For general relief, he recommended a usury law and legislation to exempt homesites from the execution of debt. He also wanted to amend the attachment laws. However, Waite directed a large number of his proposals specifically toward one or the other of the party's voting blocs. For irrigation farmers, for example, he proposed legislation that would prevent private irrigation companies from collecting more than a third of their annual rates before they delivered the water. He also hoped to appeal to the traditional antimonopoly sentiments of most farmers by supporting legislation that would prevent any concentration of control in the coal industry.[42] As for miners and urban workingmen, many of whom were becoming his vigorous supporters, he again recommended familiar labor legislation including an eight-hour day for private industry, a more effective employers' liability act, and a child-labor law. In addition, the governor called for the elimination of

sweat shops and proposed a one-hundred-dollar-exemption from gar-
nishment. But as was the case with the regular session, the special
session did not net the governor and his party much success. There was
legislation to modify garnishee, foreclosure, and attachment laws, but
these measures fell far short of Waite's expectations.[43]

Curiously though, it was Waite's handling of the silver question
that brought him the notoriety that is still associated with his name.
Indeed, his reputation for radicalism developed well before he made
his sweeping recommendations to the special session. It started with
a highly controversial speech in Denver on July 11, 1893, following
the collapse of most of the state's silver mines. In this speech, Waite
attacked the "money power" for its insistence that bimetallism—
coinage of both gold and silver—could only come about through
some sort of international agreement. "Another revolution may be the
answer to the crippling silver crisis," he contended, "for it is better,
infinitely better that blood should flow to the horses' bridles than our
national liberties should be destroyed." For this remark, he became
known as "Bloody Bridles" Waite in much of the national press.[44]

This white-bearded state chief executive, however, was hardly an
anarchist. Despite his sometimes profane language, he had a dignified
appearance; his expression was often as solemn as that of an Old
Testament sage. Nevertheless, Waite made a proposal during his
gubernatorial term that dwarfed much of the criticism he received for
calling a special session. He recommended that the state send its
silver to Mexico to be minted into Mexican dollars, which would be
declared legal tender in Colorado. This proposed "fandango dollar"
plan was a bizarre one and brought the governor much ridicule. (It
might have been legal if the courts read the Constitution the way
Waite did: Although the Constitution prohibited the states from coin-
ing money, it also stated that no state could make anything but gold
and silver coins as legal tender in the payment of debts.[45])

Waite's problems mounted during the second year of his term of
office. The so-called City Hall War in early 1894 was a case in point.
The governor's removal of two of his appointees from the Denver Fire
and Police Board for allegedly condoning corruption precipitated this
confrontation, which brought Denver to the edge of violence. The two
refused to abide by Waite's decision and armed city employees were
deputized by the sheriff of Arapahoe County to protect the City Hall.
Fortunately, Waite called out the state militia, but the state supreme
court intervened before bloodshed occurred. It upheld the governor's

right to remove the two but disapproved of his methods.[46] Waite's handling of the Cripple Creek Strike later that year was even more controversial. He successfully used the state militia to prevent a mercenary army of 1,300, headed by the sheriff of El Paso County, from breaking a strike waged by the Western Federation of Miners in the Cripple Creek area.[47] The governor also endeared himself to many of the state's miners by negotiating in behalf of the union so that Cripple Creek miners would have to work only eight hours a day instead of nine.[48] Such a gubernatorial position on labor issues at this time was almost unthinkable.

As politicians prepared for the election of 1894, many Republicans and Democrats had their strategy clearly planned. They would make "Bloody Bridles" Waite the issue. He and his party would be particularly vulnerable because of the controversies that had surrounded him while in office. Moreover, the old agrarian and labor attack against absentee capitalism was losing its effectiveness. Conservatives knew it and had a strategy for using it: they would simply turn the once-potent issue against their opponents. As the *Denver Republican* bluntly put it:

> Let the Populist party triumph in the approaching election and capital will shun Colorado as people avoid a city stricken with plague. . . . Colorado men will appeal in vain to Eastern and European capitalists for money with which to develop any of our natural resources or to embark in new industries.[49]

The G.O.P. especially saw an unmatched opportunity to regain its political dominance. Its strategy was to convince the voters that it alone could protect the state from the forces of confusion caused by the governor and his party. It proposed to maintain law and order and make Colorado an attractive place for investment once again. It also guaranteed that capital along with labor would respect the law.

Another issue injected into the campaign that also hurt the Populists was the anti-Catholic one advanced by the American Protective Association (A.P.A.). Since some historians have tended to see Populism as a nativistic movement, it is somewhat ironic that it was the Republican party that offered the A.P.A. its most congenial home in Colorado. The chief targets of this one-issue organization were the Catholic immigrants in the labor and mining work force, who comprised perhaps the most dependable segment of the new third party's political base. Consequently, even though Governor Waite had said some indiscreet things about Catholics and the pietistic agrarian Protestant element of his party was most critical of the Catholic Church, any successful exploitation of this issue in the 1894 campaign would hurt the Populists more than the Democrats and Republicans.[50] When it was reported that the Republican gubernatorial candidate Judge A. W. McIntire of Conejos County had applied for membership in the Denver branch of the American Protective Association, a fact that was to be kept a secret until after the election, the anti-Catholic issue assumed a new importance during the election campaign.[51]

In the final analysis, it was Waite's record that led to the defeat of Colorado's only Populist governor. Judge McIntire associated his name with socialism and his controversial actions as governor received widespread attention. The voters were apparently convinced: they gave Waite only 41.38 percent of the vote, while McIntire won slightly more than half of the 180,983 ballots counted.[52] The differences between the 1892 and 1894 gubernatorial races were significant. A county-by-county tally, for instance, revealed that Waite lost much of the support he received in the state's agricultural counties in 1892. Of the seven counties which he lost in 1894, all but one were agricultural. He managed to win only three of ten counties that had been regarded as strongholds of the Farmers' Alliance in 1891. The governor had obviously outdistanced many of the party's agrarian backers with his social philosophy. Waite did, however, retain much of the support he won in the mining counties in 1892.[53] The miners had not forgotten the governor's benevolent intervention in the Cripple Creek Strike nor the prolabor measures he urged upon a reluctant legislature during the special session.

The 1894 election was the last one of the decade that would not feature silver as the preeminent campaign issue. In 1896, for instance, silver brought about a major party realignment. Colorado Senator Henry Moore Teller bolted the Republican party in that year because of William McKinley's negative stand on bimetallism.[54] The two major gubernatorial candidates Alva B. Adams, who was the choice of the Democrats and Silver Republicans, and Morton Baily, who was the choice of the Populists and National Silverites, won an overwhelming majority of the votes cast, with the victorious Adams receiving the most. Even Waite, who ran as the candidate of the radical Populists, endorsed free coinage. Although he received only several thousand votes, his tally was greater than that of the regular Republican gubernatorial candidate who supported McKinley. As for the presidential race, William Jennings Bryan dispelled any doubts about how important the free coinage issue had become in Colorado when he buried McKinley by a six-to-one margin.[55]

The elections of 1898 and 1900 followed a similar pattern although the results were not as dramatic. During both elections, Populists collaborated with Democrats or Silver Republicans in putting together triumphant fusion slates. Democrats won the governorship on each occasion; and the Populist party, according to Wright, was in the process of becoming "an election-year appendage to the Colorado Democracy."[56]

By the late 1890s the influence of the Populists in Colorado had been largely spent. During its heyday, the third party movement in the Centennial state had achieved some remarkable electoral successes including the election of a governor. He was a true Populist, not a silver one, such as the state of Montana elected in 1896. The party's performance in the 1892 election, as a matter of fact, was one of the most impressive in the Mountain West. The People's organization, working closely with the Democrats in a fusion arrangement, swept the elections for state office and won the state's two seats in the national House of Representatives. Moreover, it achieved these victories when silver was just one of many campaign issues, albeit an exceedingly important one.

Nevertheless, the silver question was indisputably important—it had to be in Colorado, the state with the nation's largest silver industry. Through 1894, however, the silver issue in Colorado was largely neutralized. All the parties in the state were for bimetallism, the Republican party having pledged itself to work for free coinage in 1888. Consequently, other issues could vie with silver in importance. Antimonopolism, workingmen's issues, direct legislation, and by 1894 the governmental response to the Panic of 1893, along with "Waiteism," were as much in the forefront of Colorado politics as free silver. These were all important issues to the Populists. The third party movement in Colorado, therefore, was a multi-issue one. It remained so until the great Battle of the Standards in 1896 when silver became the monomania of electoral politics throughout the nation. Thus, familiar trademarks of Colorado's third party movement, such as the cry against absentee ownership and against the formidable irrigation and rail monopolies, predated the crusade for free and unlimited silver coinage by at least six years. In all fairness, then, Colorado Populism cannot be categorized simply as a silver movement.

Four

Wyoming Populism

The free coinage issue did not dominate Populism in the state north of Colorado either. Indeed, it was a celebrated range war, the Johnson County War, which gave Wyoming Populists what power and influence they enjoyed during the troubled 1890s. Nevertheless, both before and after this war had erupted on Wyoming's northern plains, Populism was a multi-issue movement supported by both rural and urban workingmen.

In the summer of 1890, the first rural activity of any note occurred: a local Farmers' Alliance was organized in Crook County in the northeastern corner of Wyoming. During the following year, approximately seven Alliance clubs were formed at such far-flung places as Lander and Tie Siding. One was even started in Johnson County where, despite the kinds of tensions that could spur significant protest, little organizational success was achieved.[1] The growth of the Alliance movement was generally slow throughout the state, because of the limited amount of arable land available in Wyoming. Wheat production in the state, for instance, was less than one-fifteenth of one percent of the total national output. In 1890, there were only 4,584 acres of wheat cultivated in Wyoming and 14,607 of oats. Hay was the most important crop with nine times more acreage devoted to it than wheat and oats combined.[2]

As far as urban workingmen were concerned, most of them lived in communities strung along the Union Pacific railroad, which bisected the lower half of this rectangular state. Here in railroad towns such as

Cheyenne and Laramie were active and politically minded Knights of Labor. Two of them in particular would become prominent in the state's Populist movement: Henry Breitenstein and Shakespeare E. Sealy. Both men worked for the Union Pacific and became third party organizers. They both were staunch antimonopolists and articulated their suspicions of capitalistic enterprises in a manner reminiscent of Colorado's Populist governor Davis Waite. Breitenstein, for instance, who became the ideological leader of Wyoming Populism, once likened bankers and bondholders to "ticks that fattened on the body of the laboring honey bee."[3]

Miners were also in Wyoming just as they were in Colorado. They did not, however, play as important a role in third party politics as their brethren to the south because Wyoming lacked mineral resources and, therefore, tended to have a small mining labor force. Francis E. Warren, among Wyoming's more astute leaders, was acutely aware of that fact. While serving as the state's last territorial governor, he acknowledged Wyoming's mineral deficiencies in his report to the Secretary of the Interior in 1889. He reported that with the "exception of coal . . . the mineral wealth of Wyoming can hardly be said to be developed."[4]

The paucity of Wyoming's mineral wealth gave the silver question a different dimension in this state than elsewhere in the West. How was Wyoming Populism a simple case of silverism when little of the precious white metal had been discovered in the state's vast terrain? It is tempting to discredit the silver interpretation of mountain Populism in Wyoming. In fairness to Hicks, Hofstadter, Goodwyn, and other historians who view Populism in this region as a single-issue movement, however, one has to acknowledge that early settlers in Wyoming did not know their state contained very little silver. During the 1890s, there were reports of silver finds in places like the Powder River country, the area near Rockdale in Carbon County, and the mountains west of Laramie, but none of these finds led to the great strikes that made the Mountain West so famous as a mining region.[5] Nevertheless, these reported discoveries did manage to fuel expectations for the future. There were many who predicted that Wyoming, too, would one day have bustling silver camps dotting her landscape.

Notwithstanding this state's great optimism for the future, Wyoming was different from the other states along the Front Range. Her scanty precious mineral resources, modest farm acreage, and limited industry separated her from the rest; indeed, these factors in combination were to have a decided effect on her development. They had already discouraged migration to the state of the kind of people who would build a strong and enduring Populist movement. Consequently, even though there were Knights in the south and a scattering of Alliancemen throughout the rest of the state, their numbers were hardly sufficient for the development of the classic farm-labor coalition that was important in those states where Populism did become a major political factor.

Obviously another larger occupational group would have to be politicized if any popular reform were to be achieved in this state. Wyoming's small stockmen seemed to have the best potential in this regard. For one thing, by virtue of nature's bounties (or lack of them to be more exact), the livestock industry had flourished almost from the beginning. Only the construction and maintenance of the Union Pacific offered any real competition. Majestic cattle spreads rapidly occupied mile upon mile of rich prairie landscape, symbolizing the preeminence of this characteristic Wyoming industry. By 1890, stock growers ranked second in size among the state's listed occupational groups. This high ranking, however, does not do stockmen justice because the census reports identified the largest occupational group statistically by the very vague label of "Laborers (not specified)." It included a wide variety of workers categorized under the general heading "Domestic and personal service."[6] Its members were scarcely part of a cohesive group such as the small stock grazers.

Moreover, staunchly individualistic stockmen were hardly promising recruits for reform. Their marked independence made them poor candidates for the kind of group movements necessary to achieve change. Indeed, the nature of the cattle industry by 1890 dictated against small grazers having much success as reform leaders. Large cattlemen dominated stock grazing in the state. They had the power to control the range and make life impossible for small stock growers who might wish to challenge their authority. Their control had been perpetuated for twenty years through a remarkably effective organization, the Wyoming Stock Growers Association. This organization could not only draw from its substantial economic resources, but in 1888, it also acquired a governmental ally the Board of Live Stock Commissioners, a supervisory body established during territorial days and given new life in 1891 by Wyoming's first state legislature. This board exercised extraordinary powers. It could, for example, place inspectors at railroad terminals and provide them with a list of brands allegedly used by rustlers. Shippers, consequently, had to prove ownership before their beeves could be transported to market. Moreover, the association's members, operating through the board, could decide which brands belonged to rustlers and which did not; state courts were excluded from such crucial decisions.[7] With such close cooperation between the state and its largest industry, it is little wonder that Wyoming became known as the "cattlemen's common-wealth."

The power arrayed against Wyoming's small stockmen was impos-ing. How could these people, as capable and self-reliant as many of them were, do anything but accept the all-prevailing economic order that had been effectively imposed upon them? The cattle association was, in short, a conspicuously successful monopoly, one formidable enough to control almost every aspect of grazing on Wyoming's seem-ingly boundless range. These powerful and influential cattlemen, however, failed to reckon with that one intangible element of the American frontier: the independence of a pioneering breed. Deter-mined to make a living raising cattle, many small growers were will-ing to take extraordinary measures to survive. Some supplemented their small herds by rounding up and branding mavericks. Others posed a more serious threat: they rustled the stock of the larger opera-tors. What really threatened the hegemony of the stock growers asso-ciation, however, was a decision on the part of small stockmen on the northern plains of Wyoming to organize during the winter of 1891—92 in Johnson County. At Buffalo, seat of the large cattle-grazing county that sprawled eastward from the Big Horns, a group of small stock-men organized a rival group the Wyoming Farmers and Stock Grow-ers Association. To emphasize that its goal was to challenge the cattle-men's association, the new organization boldly announced that it would hold its own roundup on May 1, one month before the of-ficially sanctioned roundup of the Board of Live Stock Commission-ers.[8]

The reaction was swift. Members of the Wyoming Stock Growers Association, who had gathered in Cheyenne on April 4, 1892, for the organization's twentieth annual meeting, were in a sullen mood. They left no doubt about their support for the embattled Board of Live Stock Commissioners; indeed, they passed a resolution commending one of the board's more controversial policies, the withholding of proceeds from the sale of beeves believed stolen.[9] Enthusiasm for the resolution symbolized the large cattlemen's belief that small grazers were going into business using stolen cattle to get established.

The strong convictions of association members set in motion a much more ominous response to the defiant activities in Johnson County than angry resolutions. The cattlemen recruited twenty-five Texas gunmen to deal with this first really coordinated threat to the longstanding dominance of the Wyoming Stock Growers Association. On April 5, the day after the big cattlemen convened their annual meeting, these gunmen in the company of certain local stockmen left Cheyenne for Casper, southern gateway to Johnson County. According to T. Alfred Larson, whose *History of Wyoming* has become the standard work on this area, none of the local people with the group were below the rank of foreman, which gives the Johnson County invasion at least one feature commonly associated with class warfare. Moreover, Larson speculated that the Union Pacific, which provided the six-car special train, had to have some inkling of the goal of this clandestine expedition.[10] (If there was such an awareness, the Johnson County War is replete with the kind of evidence that makes conspiracy theories thrive.)

Since the story of the Johnson County invasion is a familiar one, only a brief recapitulation is necessary. The mercenaries and trusted lieutenants of the association were to head for Buffalo upon their arrival in Casper. They decided, however, to detour to the KC Ranch first to investigate a rumor that fourteen of the rustlers they sought were there. Almost an entire day was spent at the KC trying to capture two alleged rustlers Nate Champion and Nick Ray. Champion, before he was killed, managed to hold off fifty of the invaders singlehandedly after Ray had died of his wounds. The long delay allowed the sheriff of Buffalo Red Angus to organize an impressive force of small stockmen to intercept the invaders. Fearful that they were outmanned, the invading force decided to seek shelter at the friendly TA Ranch, thirteen miles south of Buffalo, where they were soon surrounded by Angus's enraged posse. Amos W. Barber, a friend of the association who had been appointed governor when Warren was elevated to the United States Senate, wired President Harrison asking that army troops stationed at Fort McKinney near Buffalo be sent to put down the "insurrection."[11] (There is even a tale that Wyoming's two United States Senators Warren and Joseph M. Carey got a sleeping president out of bed in order to save the lives of the beseiged Johnson County invaders.[12]) In the end, federal troops rescued the mercenaries, who were never convicted of any crimes, not even the murders of Champion and Ray.

T. Alfred Larson has called the Johnson County War the "most notorious event in the history of Wyoming," and much controversy still surrounds it.[13] The objectives of the invaders have never been clear. Some accounts said there was a list of small stockmen, ranging from twenty to as many as seventy, who were marked for elimination. Other accounts reported that the Wyoming Stock Growers Association hired the band to intimidate small grazers in the area from further defiance.[14] Confusion over the role of some of Wyoming's most prominent figures has continued. The evidence, however, is circumstantial. Acting Governor Barber, for instance, waited until the invaders were trapped at the TA Ranch before wiring for help, and preferred federal troops to the National Guard unit stationed at Buffalo. There is a question whether Wyoming's two national senators were involved in the plot. The case against Carey seems almost foolproof: his foreman was assigned to cut the telegraph wires to Johnson County during the invasion. On the other hand, Lewis L. Gould has presented some convincing evidence that while Warren devoted significant time to helping the invaders after the violence, he was not one of those association members in on the planning.[15]

More germane to Wyoming Populism were the political repercussions of the entire affair. Before the invasion, the third party movement in the state had enjoyed little growth; it lagged far behind Colorado in its electoral activities. Laramie's People's party club, the first one in the state, had not been organized until January of 1891. These newly organized Populists, in 1891 and 1892, entered the municipal elections and won several seats on the Laramie city council in the earlier contest. Other local party clubs were formed throughout the state that same year. A state central committee was finally organized during the summer of 1891. Breitenstein attended two important organizational meetings for the national third party movement: one in Cincinnati in May of 1891 and the other one at Saint Louis on February 22, 1892. There was little in the way of activity, however, that would impress or concern the state's Republican or Democratic leaders.[16]

Even the focus of the new party was not designed to win maximum attention. The Populist organization in Laramie, for instance, drew up a platform in 1891 that concentrated on national rather than local issues—certainly not the wisest strategy for a new party struggling to exist in a largely underdeveloped and isolated frontier state. The Laramie platform, in fact, reflected the national issues of the third party at the time. The Wyoming Populists included such familiar planks as the government ownership of railroad and communication facilities, a taxation system in which one class would not benefit at the expense of another, the abolition of national banks, and, yes, the free coinage of silver. Indeed, this local platform was almost an exact duplicate of the one drawn up in Saint Louis in 1889 by Southern Alliancemen and Knights of Labor (and was probably much more relevant to that gathering than the one in Wyoming). Besides free coinage, one of the platform's catch-all planks contained the only issues in the Laramie document which dealt directly with the local scene—the prohibition of alien landownership and the return of all unused corporate land to small settlers. Of greater significance, was the omission of any critical reference in the platform to the Wyoming Stock Growers Association or the Board of Live Stock Commissioners.[17]

Platforms and party strategy, however, changed after the Johnson County War. The Populists realized immediately that the invasion of the Powder River Country by the cattle association's mercenaries would be a boon to the new party and a liability to the two established ones. There were the important switchovers that occurred as outraged Republicans and Democrats left their old parties to become Populists. In Johnson County, for example, the entire Republican county committee resigned, because such prominent members of the G.O.P. as Carey, Warren, and Barber were implicated in the invasion. Joseph DeBarthe, who had chaired the Johnson County Republican committee, not only joined the People's party, but later edited a Populist newspaper in Buffalo *The Free Lance*. In Converse County, Democratic editor E. H. Kimball changed the Douglas *Graphic* from a Democratic to a Populist journal. One prominent Wyoming couple Mr. and Mrs. I. S. Bartlett of Cheyenne left their respective parties to become Populists. Mrs. Bartlett had been a lifelong Republican; her husband, a Democrat.[18] The Johnson County War provided the Populists with an issue that was far more important to Wyoming residents than such national issues as the abolition of national banks or the free coinage of silver.

Vigorous attacks against the big cattlemen accompanied these party switchovers. As a Methodist minister wrote in a letter to the *Daily Boomerang* of Laramie: "If things go on as they are, none but the cattle barons and range lords can live in . . . [the] state, save those who may be poor enough to be compelled to become their menials." Shakespeare Sealy, the Populist leader from Laramie, lumped the cattle

association with the Republican party because of the close association of these two bodies in the past. He accused the G.O.P. of plotting
to depopulate Wyoming "in order to make room for steers, cows,
horses, and sheep."[19] The increasingly bitter criticism of the Johnson
County invaders, however, spread well beyond the state's boundaries
and commanded national attention. When they gathered in Omaha
for their national convention three months after the invasion, the
Populists used the Wyoming event to dramatize all their criticisms of
the established order. In their platform, they characterized the Johnson County affair as an "invasion of the Territory of Wyoming by the
hired assassins of plutocracy, assisted by federal officials."[20]

The political impact in Wyoming of the invasion, however, was not
a positive one in favor of Populism, but a negative one against the
G.O.P. Populists among other critics accused Dr. Amos Barber, the
affable Douglas physician who had served as acting Republican governor during the Johnson County War, of doing nothing to stop the
invasion. He was also criticized for failing to turn the invaders over to
Johnson County authorities after they had been caught by the sheriff's
posse. Carey's and Warren's alleged complicity in the raid was another negative for the Republicans. As United States senators, they
were undoubtedly two of the so-called federal officials named in the
Omaha platform who assisted the "hired assassins of plutocracy" in
their invasion of Johnson County. Moreover, because both were from
the Cheyenne area, opponents increasingly referred to the state G.O.P.
as the Cheyenne Ring in the barrage of political attacks that followed
the infamous affair.[21]

Although they participated in the invasion in a limited way, the
Democrats managed to disassociate themselves with great deftness.
At their state nominating convention in Rock Springs on July 27, state
party chairman Walter R. Stoll, one of the defense lawyers of the
accused stockmen, found it expedient to resign. Moreover, the party
nominated John E. Osborne of Rawlins as governor, another physician but unlike Barber, an outspoken foe of the stock association.[22]

Populists, when they gathered in Laramie on June 29, 1892, to elect
delegates to the Omaha convention, were fully aware of the new
political climate created by the Johnson County affair. In their platform, they concentrated on state issues rather than national ones; they
focused on the Johnson County War, the cattlemen's association, and
the Board of Live Stock Commissioners. As a matter of fact, the longest
plank in the Laramie platform was a blistering denunciation of the

Wyoming Stock Growers Association "for introducing an armed force" in the state which killed citizens, burned homes, and confiscated property. Another plank demanded the repeal of all laws "relating" to the association; a third wanted to remove all laws conferring "possessory rights on the public domain" from the association's grasp. The Populists strongly challenged the special legal status of the association and the livestock board. They condemned even the congressional bill sponsored by Senator Warren, which allowed arid federal lands to be transferred to the state for reclamation purposes. The Warren measure was looked upon as just another land grab, the kind that could be expected from that "corrupt, venal, and damnable . . . organization known as the Cheyenne ring."[23]

When the Populists assembled for their first state nominating convention in Douglas on September 21, the intensity of their attack against the association and the Republican party had not subsided; but they were confronted with a new issue which they had to resolve before they could begin their political crusade. Democrats, who had launched their own spirited offensive against the G.O.P., wanted to fuse with them in order to ensure a November victory. They had already nominated Dr. Osborne, whose negative views of the stockmen's association were well known, and they were willing to throw their support to the Weaver-Field ticket if the Populists would not nominate candidates for state office. They also advocated Democratic and Populist cooperation in both the county and state legislative races.

As wisely expedient as the Democratic offer appeared to be, many of the more committed members of the young party, including Breitenstein and Sealy, bitterly opposed it. The most promising of the party's new leaders, Lewis Cass Tidball, a rancher from the Sheridan area joined these two Knights in their opposition.[24] They were dead set against fusion and loudly proclaimed their opposition at every opportunity. Accounts vary dramatically as to the size and disposition of the Douglas meeting, but if the *Daily Boomerang* is to be believed, the struggle between the fusionists and antifusionists dominated the proceedings. Fusion was fought "to the bitter end by every means possible. Not a straw that could possibly prove an advantage against the other fellow was overlooked by either side." The struggle spilled out into the streets near the convention hall, where outsiders serving the "oligarchy" (presumably the cattle association or the Cheyenne ring) tried to convince antifusionists that they were being "sold out to the democratic party." Money was allegedly exchanged. Fusionists were accused of receiving illicit Cheyenne money, while antifusionists were accused of taking bribes from wealthy Laramie banker Edward A. Ivinson who had been nominated by the Republican party for the governorship just two weeks earlier.[25] Obviously, many of the state's economic and political factions considered the role of the People's party in the 1892 election to be crucial.

Whether the accounts in the *Daily Boomerang* were exaggerated or not, the debate over fusion engendered the kind of harsh feelings that lingered. When a vote was finally taken on the issue, an angry minority of the delegates was unwilling to accept the twenty-seven-to-seventeen count in favor of fusion; those from Albany, Crook, and Sweetwater counties stalked out.[26] More might have followed if they had not feared what the stock association might do if the Populists did not remain united.[27] Consequently, the remaining delegates worked out an acceptable fusion arrangement: Populists agreed to support the Democratic nominees for governor, for the national House of Representatives, and for the state supreme court. In return for this strong commitment, Democrats pledged themselves to vote for the Weaver-Field presidential electors.

The platform of the Douglas convention, almost a carbon copy of the one drawn up in Laramie, included a recommendation that the state constitution be amended to include the initiative and referendum and proclaimed that the "purity of the ballot" was the best safeguard for the exercise of political rights. Its major thrust, once again, was a denouncement of the Johnson County War. The planks in the Douglas platform directed against the Wyoming Stock Growers Association were not only scathing, but constituted the heart of the Populist indictment against Wyoming's established leadership.

A broader theme noted in the platform was the harsh disapproval expressed throughout of the monopolistic nature of the state's economy. The platform not only characterized the cattlemen's association as being determined to dominate Wyoming's range lands, but it also denounced Warren's plan to turn federal lands over to the states for reclamation as "fraudulent." The alarmed Populist delegates undoubtedly envisioned more corporate and plutocratic control of the state's lands.[28]

This platform and the one drawn up in Laramie curiously lacked any direct reference to silver. Wyoming residents widely supported the free coinage issue since they believed their state was potentially rich in silver. The closest that both Populist platforms got to the currency question, however, was a vague denunciation of President Harrison's "unpatriotic act in soliciting foreign interference in revising our monetary system."[29] Despite this jab at international monetary cooperation, the Populists failed to suggest any alternative to the single standard—even the possibly acceptable one of worldwide bimetallism. This Populist stance on the money question contrasted sharply to the Democratic call for the unlimited coinage of silver in their 1892 Rock Springs platform. Even the Republicans, handicapped by the lukewarm attitude of both Warren and Carey toward free coinage, endorsed bimetallism which they reluctantly supported since 1890.[30]

The issues raised in the Douglas platform determined the election battle that followed in the autumn. The fusionists in both the Populist and Democratic parties made certain that the invasion of Johnson County was the main issue. Senator Warren's arid land bill also generated a surprising amount of controversy which, no doubt, was a testimony of the degree to which antimonopoly sentiment had taken hold in Wyoming. The fusionists characterized this measure as part of a colossal land theft planned by powerful individuals or corporations.[31] Silver played a secondary role. Again the Republicans proved vulnerable. Warren and Carey had both voted against an amendment introduced by Nevada Senator William M. Stewart in January of 1891 which would have provided free coinage and the remonetization of silver. To keep their antisilver record fresh in the minds of the public, they took the same stand a year later.[32] The opposition to free coinage by Wyoming's two senators gave Republican Edward A. Ivinson few favorable issues for his gubernatorial campaign. There was little he could say about silver and even less he dared say about Johnson County. The tariff protection theme, which historically had been advantageous to Republicans, was not helpful either in 1892.

Consequently, the election results came as no great surprise. The three fusionist nominees from the Democratic party won. Osborne was elected to the governorship; Gibson Clark, to the state supreme court; and Henry Coffen, to Wyoming's lone seat in the national House of Representatives. Populists and Democrats also carried the lower house of the state legislature, winning twenty-one seats to the Republicans' twelve. Nevertheless, some significant losses tempered the victory of the fusionists. The two parties, for example, failed to win one seat in the state senate.[33] The most disappointing loss, however, was the defeat of the Weaver-Field electors by 828 votes out of 16,450 cast.[34]

Some Populists felt betrayed by what they perceived as a lack of support by the Democrats for the fusionist candidates in the presidential race. Although the Democrats might not have shown as much enthusiasm for the Weaver-Field ticket as the Populists did, the major cause for the defeat of the Populist presidential slate was the support of Republicans for their party's national ticket in the northern counties. Although they did not forgive their own state party leadership for its involvement in the Johnson County War, they did separate the policies of the Harrison administration from those of the state organization in their 1892 vote.[35]

Another disappointment suffered by the Populists was the low percentage of popular votes. The party, a poor third, received from 11 to 13 percent of the votes cast—they even lagged behind the largely discredited G.O.P. Apparently the prominent converts to the new party did not bring with them the necessary numbers of ordinary voters to make their support really count. As a result, only five of the fusionist candidates who won seats in the lower house of the Wyoming state legislature bore the Populist label. Even so, this small delegation did hold the balance of power because there were only sixteen Democrats and twelve Republicans elected to that body. Consequently, to acquire full Populist cooperation in the coming legislative session, Democrats in collaboration with Populists elected Sheridan Populist Lewis Cass Tidball as speaker.

Tidball's selection may have been a mistake. He certainly had some serious drawbacks for a coalition leader: he was as far to the political left as Sealy and Breitenstein.[36] He was also a forceful politician who aggressively sponsored legislation that was most controversial in a fundamentally conservative state such as Wyoming. For example, Tidball introduced a bill in the house to create a board of railroad commissioners with the power to fix both passenger and freight rates. He also moved to amend the state constitution to include the initiative and referendum. Both of these efforts were in the mainstream of national Populism, but neither came even close to success in Wyoming. The Sheridan speaker was not alone in pushing for reform during the state's second legislative session. Dudley A. Kingsbury, one of two Populists elected to the lower house from Johnson County, presented a bill that had been inspired by both the Laramie and Douglas party platforms. It would have guaranteed equal use of the public domain for both large and small settlers. As idealistic and solidly American as this proposal sounded, it too failed to pass.[37]

Tidball tended to blame the Democrats for the disappointing legislative performance of the fusionist coalition he presumably headed. In one speech, he accused them of a complete turnabout in their critical attitude toward the Board of Live Stock Commissioners, an organization which many people in Wyoming correctly believed served the state's large cattlemen.[38] Other topics of disagreement, including the choice of a candidate for United States senator, also existed between Populist and Democratic legislators. Democrats refused to cooperate in the Populist effort to elect the popular Republican convert Mrs. I. S. Bartlett as Wyoming's second senator. Although only a historical footnote in a state with an enviable feminist record, the support for Bartlett may have been the first effort on the part of a legislative caucus to nominate a woman to the United States Senate.[39] Bartlett's bid failed, but so did that of incumbent Francis Warren. The powerful Laramie County Republican was denied re-election, and for two years the Cowboy state had only one United States senator Joseph M. Carey.

Even the Democrats, dominant in the coalition in terms of numbers, failed to achieve most of their objectives. They had wanted to revise the state's election laws and develop better efforts to encourage state immigration, but failed in both endeavors. Many of them, at the behest of Governor Osborne, did work to abolish the controversial Board of Live Stock Commissioners, an effort that was doomed because Republicans controlled the state senate. The governor, however, accomplished his objective by vetoing the $12,000 appropriation for the board, thus forcing the Wyoming Stock Growers Association to fund the activities of that body until the next session.[40] Many Democrats looked at the young state's second legislative session as a frustrating holding operation because only thirty-three laws were passed. Populists, however, voted enthusiastically in behalf of two of the six memorials that the Wyoming state legislature presented to the Congress: one was for free coinage; the other, for the direct election of United States senators.[41]

Populist strength in Wyoming, as it turned out, would never be greater than it was in 1892, a fact that party leaders refused to acknowledge for some time. Even though only one Populist was elected to office from a full slate of candidates in the Laramie municipal elections in 1893, for instance, the Populists tended to discount this political disaster. The realities of their poor electoral performance in such Wyoming communities as Cheyenne, Rock Springs, Evanston, Green River, and Newcastle were also ignored.[42] One reason for their surprising equanimity in light of these setbacks was a strong conviction on their part that the Panic of 1893 had vindicated the harsh

Populist critique of the capitalistic system. Evidence that this system had failed was becoming increasingly obvious. Property valuation in the state had dropped from $32,356,801.96 in 1893 to $29,198,041.20 in 1894, a significant loss in a state that depended almost exclusively on the property tax for its revenue. The bankruptcy of the Union Pacific railroad in 1893, followed by the forced receivership of the Warren Livestock Company in 1894, provided further evidence that the nineteenth century system of laissez-faire capitalism was collapsing.[43]

Members of the state's People's party were eager to exploit the difficulties caused by these adverse economic conditions. As a matter of fact, their activities outside the legislature drew more attention to them than those in the statehouse. Wyoming Populists, for instance, were conspicuous in their support of the many protests that erupted throughout the country as a result of the nationwide panic. They tended to show great sympathy for Coxey's ill-fated march on Washington. One Wyoming leader even claimed that the march was no different than the familiar trips of prominent business leaders to Washington to lobby for government handouts. The Albany County Populist organization went so far as to provide public support for the Coxeyites, as these unemployed protestors were commonly called. The highly publicized Pullman Strike of 1894 also received Populist support in Wyoming. Two Populist leaders, for instance, were very much involved in the American Railway Union's highy controversial boycott of trains hauling Pullman cars. Sealy, who was president of local number 19 of the American Railway Union, (A.R.U.), and Breitenstein were both active strike leaders and received strong backing from most Wyoming Populists.[44]

In truth, state Populist leaders had grown so confident that the panic was a winning issue that they rejected fusion with the Democrats in 1894. At their August meeting in Casper, they not only came up with their strongest prolabor platform to date (a politically smart move at a time of high unemployment), but they also nominated their own independent candidates for state office. In many ways, they were following the course of the successful Colorado Populists, but they were doing it as strict middle-of-the-roaders, members of a completely autonomous political organization. Their tough platform reflected this independence. It called for compulsory arbitration and condemned the federal administration and the courts for their "unjust and un-American" attitude toward the Pullman strikers. It blamed the seriously depressed

conditions of the country "entirely" on what is called "vicious legislation." It also re-endorsed such typical Populist planks as government
ownership of railroads, free coinage, and the incorporation of the
initiative and referendum as part of the law of the land. Moreover, the
Populists did not forget their dominant rural stock-grazing base. They
called for the repeal of all laws that might benefit the Wyoming Stock
Growers Association and urged federal retention of the state's arid
lands, a response no doubt to the recently enacted Carey Act, which
had incorporated many of the features of former Senator Warren's
proposed legislation.[45]

Even their choice of candidates underscored this new independence
on the part of the state's Populists. They nominated Tidball as governor. Sealy, fresh from his controversial involvement in the Pullman
Strike, was chosen for Wyoming's seat in the national House of Representatives. The determined Casper delegates also nominated a full
slate of candidates representing those middle-of-the-road sentiments
so popular with the state People's party in 1894.

In November, however, surprised Populists discovered how seriously they had misgauged the temper of Wyoming's electorate. Tidball, Sealy, and the entire People's ticket went down to inglorious
defeat. Thomas A. Krueger, in his history of Wyoming Populism,
estimated that Populist candidates polled just about the same vote
that they did in 1892.[46] The Wyoming party could take little comfort
from that fact since in that same election, Populists throughout the
rest of the country increased their popular vote by nearly 50 percent.[47]

The lackluster performance of the Populists during the seemingly
favorable depression year of 1894 was nearly lethal to the party's
future in the state. Their setback was particularly devastating because
the defeat of their state ticket was matched by substantial defeats in
the other races in which they competed. For example, the party's
effort to win in Laramie County ended in disaster—the six Populist
candidates nominated lost by margins of six-to-one. Worse yet, only
one candidate with Populist connections was elected to the state
legislature. The party's dwindling strength was even more dramatically emphasized by its failure to offer candidates. In ten counties,
there were no Populist nominees at all.[48]

Because of the painfully disappointing results of the 1894 election,
most Populists were willing to try fusion again in 1896. When party
delegates arrived in Cheyenne for their state convention in July, most

were ready to cooperate closely with the Democrats. A fusion ticket similar to the one in 1892 seemed like an excellent strategy. The bargaining power of the fading Populists, however, had greatly diminished from the almost commanding position of strength that they had enjoyed four years earlier. With only five counties sending delegates to the Cheyenne gathering, there was a real question as to whether the Populists had anything substantial left to offer their old allies. More important, the venerble planks of the Omaha platform had lost much of their appeal; the all-encompassing silver issue had largely shunted them aside. Consequently, there was no great rush on the part of the Democrats to fuse, unless such an arrangement was on their terms. This angered some Populists, notably John W. Patterson of Sweetwater County, the party's current state chairman. He insisted that in any fusion arrangement Democrats should support Populist William Brown for Congress instead of the party's popular ex-governor John Osborne.[49]

Wyoming Republicans, uncomfortable in 1896 because they had to hedge on the silver issue, saw in Patterson's dissatisfaction an excellent opportunity to exploit what looked like a split in the People's party over the question of fusion. The letterbooks of Frances E. Warren show that this astute Republican, elevated again to the United States Senate in 1895, provided free railroad passes, plus $250 in expense money, for Patterson so that Patterson could muster support for Brown's bid for Congress as well as for two independent Populist electors whom the antifusionists wanted to keep on the ballot. Warren even provided railroad passes for Brown so that he could carry on his campaign throughout the state.[50]

In the end, however, the antifusionists were not able to make much of an impact on the 1896 race, despite this covert Republican help. Bryan, the great silver candidate, carried Wyoming, but his margin of victory was fewer than 600 votes. It was the closest presidential race in the West. Although Warren regarded the narrow margin as a moral victory for the state's Republican party, a more significant reason was the lack of any important silver discoveries by 1896.[51] In the state's other major race, the contest for Wyoming's congressional seat, Osborne defeated his Republican rival Frank Mondell by a vote of 10,310 to 10,044. Brown, the obstinate Populist from Big Horn, received only 648 votes, despite the assistance he received from Warren and other G.O.P. leaders. Support from fusionist Populists proved crucial in the extremely close presidential and congressional races of 1896.[52] As for the two antifusionist Populist electors supported by Patterson, they netted only 2 percent of the vote, polling fewer than 500 votes apiece.

Fusionist successes in the statewide races, however, were not matched in the electoral struggle for control of the Wyoming legislature. There the G.O.P., which had been severely damaged by the Johnson County War four years earlier, made a remarkable recovery. It managed to win twenty-three seats in the state house of representatives as compared to only fifteen for candidates with fusion support.[53] Four Populists were among those elected in the legislative balloting: three from Sheridan County (including Tidball) and one from Crook, where the Farmers Alliance got its start.[54]

Populist activity would continue in Wyoming until 1916, but only on a token scale.[55] Eighteen ninety-six was the last year that the party had any real influence on the state's political direction. One could argue that the third party movement lost much of its authority after 1892. Its showing in 1894 was a poor one and if the 1896 vote had not been close, its influence in that election would have been slight. T. Alfred Larson has concluded that Populism "never amounted to much in Wyoming," giving as his two major reasons the small number of crop farmers and the state's inadequate silver resources. He also mentioned the manipulation of the small party by both Democrats and Republicans.[56] Democrats, for example, were able to steal much of the protest vote away from the Populists; while Republicans plotted, with mixed results, to widen the Populist split over fusion in 1896.

Certainly, Larson's analysis discounts the one-dimensional interpretation of Populism. With virtually no silver, Wyoming Populism could hardly have flourished as a silver movement. Moreover, it is very clear that the growth of the movement was due more to the panic caused by the Johnson County invasion than to any other single factor. Besides this reaction to Wyoming's famous range war, antipathy to bigness attracted a portion of the state's voters to this aspiring new political organization. After all, the Wyoming Stock Growers Association, the organization that monopolized most of the state's grazing land and menaced many of its small users, sponsored the notorious invasion of the large northern cattle-grazing county. Indeed, it seems evident that at least in Wyoming, the essence of opposition to the status quo was antimonopolism. Consequently, many who voted for the fusion ticket in 1892 were casting a negative ballot. They were voting against the Wyoming Stock Growers Association or against its compliant tool, the Board of Live Stock Commissioners. The threat of bigness, however, was not confined to the cattle industry alone. The controversial arid land bill sponsored by Senator Warren (later incorporated in the Carey Act) also fell into the monopoly category.

As long as the Johnson County War remained fresh in the minds of uneasy Wyoming voters, there was a role for Populism or at least a role for some kind of third party or fusion movement. But as time passed and the immediacy of the threat to small grazers or ordinary citizens subsided, Wyoming voters began to change. The radicalism of the early 1890s dissipated; it was slowly replaced by the conservatism evident in the young state's political origins. Once this transition gained momentum, the decline of Wyoming Populism was irreversible.

Davis H. Waite, Populist governor of
Colorado. As reproduced in Karel D.
Bicha, *Western Populism: Studies in
Ambivalent Conservatism*
(Coronado Press, 1976) facing p. 65.

Chinese hard-rock miners in Idaho Springs, Colorado. As reproduced in
Robert G. Athearn, *The Coloradans* (University of New Mexico Press,
1976) 184.

Robert Burns Smith, Populist
governor of Montana. Courtesy of
Montana Historical Society.

Henry M. Teller, Colorado silver
senator considered by Populists as a
presidential candidate in 1896. As
reproduced in *The Parties and the
Men* (© 1896, Robert O. Law) facing
p. 357.

Will Kennedy, Populist editor of the
Boulder *Age*, Boulder, Montana.
Courtesy of Montana Historical
Society.

Francis Emroy Warren, powerful
Republican and target of Wyoming
Populists. As reproduced in T. A.
Larson, *History of Wyoming*
(Lincoln: University of Nebraska
Press, 1978), following page 306.

Ella Knowles Haskell,
prominent Populist. From Miller,
History of Montana, courtesy of
Montana Historical Society.

Coxey's Army in camp at Forsyth, 1894. Courtesy of Montana Historical Society.

Coxey's Army group, 1894. Courtesy of Montana Historical Society.

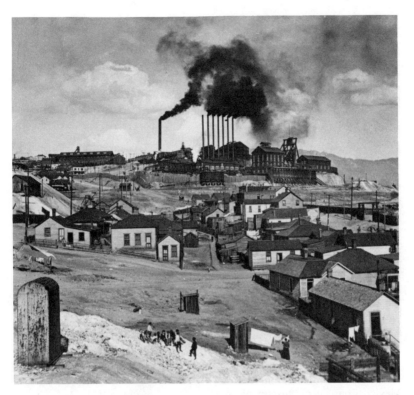

"The Richest Hill on Earth," Butte, Montana. Courtesy of Montana Historical Society.

L. Bradford Prince, temporary
Populist candidate from New
Mexico. Courtesy of Museum of New
Mexico (Neg. no. 50444).

Antonio Joseph, friend of the New
Mexico Knights of Labor. Courtesy
of Museum of New Mexico (Neg.
no. 9915).

Harvey B. Fergusson, Populist-
Democratic candidate from New
Mexico in 1896. Courtesy of
Museum of New Mexico (Neg.
no. 7211).

Theodore B. Mills, territorial
legislator from New Mexico,
territorial candidate for delegate to
U. S. Congress. Courtesy of Museum
of New Mexico (Neg. no. 10297).

The Herrera brothers, Juan Jose, Pablo, and Nicanor, founders of the night-riding *Gorras* from San Miguel County, New Mexico. As reproduced in Robert Kern, ed., *Labor in New Mexico* (University of New Mexico Press, 1983) 36.

William M. Stewart, prominent silver senator from Nevada. As reproduced in *Servant of Power: A Political Biography of Senator William M. Stewart* (University of Nevada Press, 1983) facing p. 260.

William "Buckey" O'Neill, Arizona
Populist and candidate for territorial
delegate to U. S. Congress. As
reproduced in Jay Wagoner, *Arizona
Territory, 1863–1912* (University of
Arizona Press, 1970) 341.

Peter Breen, Idaho labor leader.
Courtesy of Montana Historical
Society.

Threshing wheat in the upper Great Plains in the 1880s. As reproduced in Gilbert C. Fite, *The Farmers' Frontier*, 1865–1900 (University of New Mexico Press, 1975) 99.

James B. Weaver, Populist
presidential candidate in 1892. As
reproduced in *The Parties and the
Men*, 175.

William Jennings Bryan,
Democratic-Populist presidential
candidate in 1896. As reproduced in
The Parties and the Men, 455.

Five

Montana

The Origins of Protest

The Populist movement at the top of the tier of Front Range states was one of the most distinctive in the nation. Nowhere else in the country was the voice of labor so audible in third party protest as it was in Montana. For this reason, Populism's historian for the Treasure state Thomas A. Clinch entitled his monograph *Urban Populism and Free Silver in Montana*. The fact that he chose to place urban Populism before free silver in his title is significant. The essence of the movement was shaped in mining communities such as Butte and Anaconda rather than in the state's scattered agricultural areas. Its chief spokesmen were labor leaders or journalists from the western mountains of the state rather than Alliance organizers from its plains and valleys.[1]

As was the case with Colorado to the south, the lure of mining riches first drew settlers to this part of the Rockies. Gold was discovered in Montana almost at the same time as it was in Colorado. In 1858, James and Granville Stuart were returning to Iowa from the gold fields of California with Reese Anderson when they located traces of the yellow metal on Benetsee Creek (now known as Gold Creek), but they did not have the necessary tools to do serious prospecting until 1862. Even then the gold mined around the community of American Fork at the mouth of Gold Creek was not sufficiently impressive to trigger a major rush. It took a strike on Grasshopper Creek to the west in July of 1862 to bring an influx of argonauts that qualified Montana as another New California. Within two years, bustling mining camps such as Bannack on Grasshopper Creek and Virginia City and Nevada City along the course of the Alder Gulch were centers of frenzied mining activity.[2]

These early strikes produced a period of placer mining that extended well into the next decade. The yield was impressive. The value of gold placers in the state from 1862 to 1875 was close to $134,000,000. Montana, like Colorado, was rich in its variety of metals; the Treasure state is an appropriate nickname for this immense commonwealth. The two most important minerals, other than gold, were copper and silver. Of the two, copper is most often associated with Montana history; yet, copper production was sluggish at first because of a destructive price war with the rich copper mines of Upper Michigan in the 1880s. The disruptive efforts of a French syndicate to corner the world market did not help either. Silver, on the other hand, achieved an early importance in Montana. By 1880, it had surpassed gold in production and by 1892, the output of the state's silver mines was more than seven times that of gold.[3]

Both copper and silver, however, were much more difficult to mine than gold ore. From the very beginning, mining operatives used expensive quartz-mining methods because each of the two minerals was found far below the surface of the earth. More capital than local investors could provide was required. Many of the state's mining enterprises, therefore, had sought outside money, often from more than one financial source. The famous Anaconda Company, for example, got its start because of San Francisco capital. When the company was forced to reorganize during the Panic of 1893, many of its shares were sold in England, a leading source for foreign capital, and later in Boston, the nation's copper headquarters.[4] Outside investment in the mining industry followed a pronounced pattern of dispersion. The East and the Pacific Coast as well as Western Europe were among the most conspicuous sources of mining capital, but investment money also came from such midwestern locales as Saint Louis and Indianapolis.[5] It was only a matter of time before Montana faced the same problem of absentee capitalism that Colorado did.

Human resources were needed as well as financial ones; Montana's mineral wealth acted as a powerful magnet, just as it did in other mining states. Hard-rock miners were attracted to Montana from such western states as California, Nevada, and Colorado as well as from

Michigan's upper peninsula, an early rival in the production of copper. There were also experienced miners from abroad. Cornish and Irish miners, for instance, added to the state's diverse and growing labor force. An extraordinary ethnic mix, therefore, characterized a number of Montana's important mining communities. Italians and Poles inhabited some; Slavs and Finns, others. Most had, at least, a sprinkling of native Americans. All of them nurtured some hope of becoming one of the major urban centers in the state's mountain domain.[6]

Unionization of this heterogeneous labor force occurred quite early. The previous contact that some miners had with the union movement in Nevada was certainly one catalyst for organization. The depressing results of no union activity in Michigan provided yet another. Appropriately, the earliest effort to unionize occurred at Butte, the largest urban mining center in the state. There on June 13, 1878, a small group of miners organized what eventually became the Butte Miners' Union.[7] Miners formed similar labor organizations in a number of other towns during the 1880s, so that by 1891 the state's union movement counted 4,000 members. Until the Western Federation of Miners was organized in 1893, however, the largest and most important union in Montana was the familiar Knights of Labor. The Knights, the behemoth of American unionism during the Gilded Age, got their start in the Treasure state in 1882. During that year, a group of workingmen organized the Pioneer Assembly at Butte. A total of twenty-two assemblies were formed throughout Montana during the subsequent decade. All but two of them operated under one umbrella organization District Assembly No. 98.[8] Ironically, the labor organization in this predominantly mining state comprised surface and craft laborers, workingmen who were not permitted to join underground unions.[9]

By 1893, there were 9,000 workers organized in Montana, a figure that does not include the Knights of Labor. Union objectives undoubtedly varied because the unions included bricklayers, carpenters, cooks, stationary engineers, clerks, and boilermakers as well as miners; however, they all shared important common goals.[10] All unions, for instance, wanted recognition. This was especially significant in the dominant mining industry, where mine owners had the advantage of enormous economic strength. The eight-hour-day and mine-safety legislation were also important goals. Problems such as blacklisting, child labor, convict labor, and harassment by the Pinkertons commanded attention too.[11] Some successes undoubtedly were achieved: the average daily wage of a miner and smelterman was $3.50, one of the highest in the nation.[12] There was enough frustration over the failure to achieve an eight-hour day and other coveted union objectives, however, to make some members good candidates for popular protest.

There was also agrarian activity in the sprawling northern state; not surprisingly, it first developed where mining developed. Farmers, sensing a market, moved into the Gallatin and Bitterroot valleys as early as 1863 to grow vegetables for the miners of Virginia City and the other recently organized camps. Irrigation was one of their early passions, but diverting water in many of these river valleys was a slow and frustrating process. The first legislature following Montana's organization as a separate territory on May 26, 1864 instituted the doctrine of riparian rights, a largely unworkable policy that was not reversed until prior appropriation was adopted a decade later. Consequently, progress was slow. The privately financed and owned irrigation system that developed did not satisfy the needs of most farmers.[13] Although the inadequacies of the system discouraged a proliferation of monopolistic water companies, such as those in Colorado, it also failed to produce an irrigation system similar to Colorado's much emulated one. Nevertheless, despite the disappointments connected with the development of the state's water resources, agriculture in Montana continued to grow. Of the 20,000 inhabitants in the territory in 1870, 2,000 were farmers.[14]

Stock grazing also became important in Montana as the open-range cattle industry spread northward. The grazing of both cattle and sheep assumed economic significance in a comparatively short time. In 1880, there were 274,321 cattle and 249,888 sheep grazing in the northern territory; three years later, that number had nearly doubled. According to an estimate made by the Department of Agriculture in 1883, there were 600,000 cattle and 500,000 sheep. Moreover, the majority of these stock animals were located on the eastern plains rather than in the western and central parts of the state. Not only was this shift due to the Texas drives, but it was also the result of overcrowding. Stockmen had grazed too many animals in the central ranges of Montana.[15]

Just as they did in Wyoming, cattlemen felt a need to organize from the very beginning. In 1885, they formed the Montana Stockgrowers Association. It was never to enjoy the special privileges of its Wyoming counterpart because mining, not stock grazing, was the favored industry in Montana. Throughout the entire territorial period, farmers and sheepmen as well as cattlemen labored unsuccessfully against the most coveted privilege enjoyed by mine owners—tax exemption.

When Montana became the forty-first state in 1889, the industry's favored treatment continued: only the net proceeds of mining were taxed.[16]

Wheat farming also became significant in Montana. Because of mining's dominance and the state's great distances, however, this industry grew slowly at first. Like other agricultural endeavors in Montana, wheat raising was largely confined to the western two-thirds of the state during the nineteenth century. For the most part, farmers did not cultivate the arid plains of the east until the twentieth century. The Missouri and Gallatin valleys were particularly noted for their good wheat crop, but the market was primarily a local one.[17] The completion of the transcontinental railroads through the state revealed the full potential of this crop, which by the 1880s had become very important to the economy of Montana's neighbors to the east. For example, the construction of the Northern Pacific, finished in 1883, provided an outside market that had not been accessible before. James J. Hill's Great Northern, which entered the state later that decade, strengthened the importance of this agrarian enterprise by creating even more outside markets for Montana wheat.[18]

Despite improved rail connections, the wheat industry did not flourish east of Billings because of the aridity of the Great Plains. Development of this country waited for more generous federal land legislation such as the Enlarged Homestead Act of 1909 which allowed wheat farmers to cultivate 320 acres of land instead of 160. Consequently, many "honyockers," as settlers of eastern Montana were called, came during the wet years from 1910 to 1917, only to suffer during the subsequent droughts. Because of their small numbers, wheat producers in Montana were not as influential in the protest movements of the Populist era as the rain-belt farmers of Colorado had been. When the agricultural population engaged in wheat production finally became significant during the twentieth century, it too turned to a new generation of farm organizations for help. The Non-Partisan League or the Montana Society for Equity, rather than the Grange or the Farmers' Alliance, then articulated agrarian views. The agricultural contribution of wheat farmers during the Gilded Age was great even if their protest role was minor. Their wheat production—a little less than two million bushels in 1889—still exceeded Wyoming's miniscule output.[19]

Railroads played an important role in the development of all of Montana's industries. The large distances between communities in much of the state made this mode of transportation essential. The mine owners were the first, and undoubtedly, the strongest voice demanding the kind of efficiency that only rail transportation could provide. Not only did they need to ship processed ores eastward and abroad, but even before the early 1880s they needed to have cuprous ores from the copper mines smelted elsewhere. The first railroad to provide the mine owners with these necessary freight services was the Utah and Northern, the brainchild of some enterprising Salt Lake City businessmen eager to link Montana's mining wealth with the Union Pacific. But this railroad, which was a narrow-gauge one until 1888, was too small to serve the entire state.[20] Montanans eagerly awaited the coming of the great transcontinental railroad, the Northern Pacific. It provided them with the kind of transportation necessary to benefit all segments of the state's economy.

The Northern Pacific Railroad was especially fortunate; it received the most generous land grant of all the subsidized transcontinentals. Congress eventually committed a total of 38,916,338.61 acres for the construction of this railroad, which was to connect Lake Superior with distant Puget Sound at the edge of the Pacific.[21] The grant, made in 1864, included ten alternate sections on each side of the track for each mile of track laid in the states and twenty for each mile laid in the territories. In Montana, this gave the Northern Pacific an incredible fourteen million acres of land to sell or develop. Of later significance, however, was the provision that excluded all mineral lands from the grant, except coal and iron.[22]

This extraordinarily generous subsidy, of course, produced envy. Robert N. Sutherlin, founder and editor of Montana's pioneering farm journal *The Rocky Mountain Husbandman*, wrote apprehensively in the newspaper's January 27, 1876 issue: "We feel its need and importance, but we do not know of a single case upon record where the people have subsidized or loaned their credit to private corporations, that, sooner or later, they have not regretted." Nevertheless, Sutherlin demonstrated the usual ambivalence toward railroads found in any developing frontier country. If a "continuation of the land grant is the only means by which the road can be secured," Sutherlin wrote, "it would be preferable to seeing the project fall to the ground."[23]

This ambivalence is understandable, for although railroads brought problems by virtue of their formidable economic power, they were vital to the growth of a new region. The mine owners initially welcomed the Northern Pacific. Cattlemen and sheepmen favored this new force in the state's economic affairs. Cattlemen were happy because the Northern Pacific encouraged their industry to meet the great demand for beef in the Midwest and East; sheepmen, because there was no apparent rate discrimination against them. Despite the historic antipathy between farmers and railroads, most of Montana's farmers even were excited about the new markets that were available to them because of the Northern Pacific.

Trouble between the railroad and the citizens of Montana Territory began in 1884 when the Northern Pacific selected mineral lands in western Montana on the pretext that they were agricultural. The railroad's owners stirred even more controversy by insisting on a new interpretation of the railroad's 1864 charter. Mineral wealth had to be known at the time the charter was granted, they maintained, if the restrictions against mineral development were to apply. The brewing crisis took on an alarming immediacy when lodes of gold and silver ore were found on the western outskirts of Helena in June of 1888 on the odd-numbered sections of land claimed by the Northern Pacific. Concerned Montanans resisting the railroad's claims convened a second time in Helena in the year following this discovery; they had been equally vocal in their opposition to the Northern Pacific at an earlier convention held a few months before the discoveries in the same city.[24]

By the late eighties, most segments of the state's economy viewed the Northern Pacific quite differently. The Northern Pacific's controversial assertion that it was entitled to all the mineral land on its grant not known in 1864 had dissipated much of the earlier good will enjoyed by the railroad. Mine owners and workers alike were both fearful of and angry at the prospect of having the Northern Pacific as their most powerful and aggressive competitor. Stock grazers were less disturbed by this possibility, although their attention was undoubtedly distracted by the adverse weather conditions that marked the latter years of the 1880s. Farmers, despite a certain appreciation of the importance of railroad transportation, had the usual reservations that result from an unequal relationship, such as the one that existed between the state's carriers and them. Their suspicions, however, paled in comparison with those harbored by Colorado's dryland farmers. Even so, it was only a matter of time before a remarkably large and diverse cross section of the state's population regarded the Northern Pacific as Montana's most threatening monopoly.

Although miners and mine owners felt more menaced than farmers by the Northern Pacific, agricultural discontent, nonetheless, surfaced in Montana. As a matter of fact, the two major farm organizations of the Gilded Age the Grange and the Farmers' Alliance experienced surprising growth in the state, considering the extreme isolation and small numbers of Montana farmers. The first local Grange was founded near White Sulphur Springs in 1873, three years before the Battle of Little Big Horn was fought in Montana territory. The person most responsible for the success of this early effort was Robert N. Sutherlin who, besides being editor of the *Rocky Mountain Husbandman*, was also National Deputy for the Grange. Largely through his efforts, the organization spread rapidly throughout the sparsely settled territory. By 1874, in addition to twenty-three local groups, members of the organization had established a territorial Grange in Helena.[25]

In 1875, however, the Montana Grange got involved in a dispute with the War Department. It disappeared shortly thereafter and did not re-emerge in Montana until 1912. The fateful confrontation resulted from the Grange's inability to deliver grain to army posts according to the terms of a contract the Grange had negotiated with the government. The Patrons of Husbandry (to use the Grange's other name) had wanted to bypass both grain merchants and regular post contractors by selling oats directly to the army at $1.29 per hundred.[26] When grasshoppers destroyed much of their crop, however, the farmers were unable to fulfill their contract. Only the intervention of the territorial delegate Martin Maginnis saved these Grange members from financial ruin. Under a new agreement he helped to arrange, the War Department released these farmers from their original contract and entered into a new one in which they paid the farmers $2.25 per hundred. The War Department, however, issued an order that no more grain contracts would be made with the Grange. At least one agricultural historian has attributed the rapid decline of the Grange during the mid-1870s to this unfortunate episode.[27]

The Farmers' Alliance was to replace the Grange as the voice for many Montana farmers. The first local Alliances were apparently formed in the Bitterroot Valley, as early as 1885. In time two Alliance organizations came to dominate the movement: the Missoula Farmers' Alliance No. 3 and the Gallatin County Farmers' Alliance, both of which were organized toward the end of the decade. Each organization attempted, without much success, to form cooperatives in the best traditions of the Alliance movement. The Missoula organization, however, was able to publish a newspaper the *Missoula Alliance*, which eventually became a feisty Populist organ. In time, some twenty-seven local Alliances were organized, extending from Glendive and Miles City in the east to the Bitterroot Valley in the west.[28]

The organization of a state Alliance, however, did not occur until 1892 when the Montana Farmers' Alliance was organized at a convention in Missoula. The gathering, which was convened on February 26, was a small one; only twenty-five delegates were present. The new organization must have had some potential: D. F. Ravens, president of the National Farmers' Alliance, as the Northern Alliance was officially called, addressed the new state Alliance at the Missoula meeting. The delegates responded to Ravens's spirited message by passing a resolution that called for a union of farmers and laborers to coordinate a protest movement. They also enthusiastically backed the growing effort for free coinage and resolved to give their wholehearted support to the cause.[29]

The radical politics evidenced at the Missoula meeting was not an instant development among the state's agricultural population. The pages of the popular *Rocky Mountain Husbandman* show that there was substantial discontent on the part of many Montana farmers as early as the Granger period. Sutherlin reflected the views of some of his readers, for instance, when he joined stock grazers in condeming the tax exemption enjoyed by the mining industry. His attack on the enormous Northern Pacific land grant in early 1878 was also indicative of agrarian concern. His assaults on the unfair profits of the middleman and speculator, made as early as 1875, as well as his views on monopoly were typical of the rhetoric associated with so many nineteenth century agrarian reformers. Indeed, because of the power of the mining and rail corporations in Montana, Sutherlin urged miners and farmers to band together and fight monopoly in his January 20, 1876 issue of the *Husbandman*.[30]

Sutherlin was not an irresponsible radical. Otherwise, his newspaper would not have lasted for sixty-seven years. Moreover, when the Grange disappeared from the Montana scene, the farm editor lost much of his ardor for activist agrarian movements. He even warned the state's Alliance organizatons in 1890 to be wary of political involvement.[31]

Participation by some groups in state politics, however, was inevitable by the last decade of the century. Urban laborers in western Montana had pretty clear ideas of what they regarded as essential to their welfare. They perceived free coinage as vital because of its significance to the state's silver industry. Other issues such as the eight-hour day, union recognition, and mine inspection were also important to them. These workingmen were also suspicious of the corporate giants of the state's mining industry, many of which were controlled or unduly influenced by outside capital. Yet by 1890 the threat posed by the Northern Pacific's claims to mineral lands exceeded all other issues. Miners, of course, were most affected, but farmers were not indifferent to the railroad's aggressiveness. After all, the power and influence of the railways was a major cause of the radical agrarian movement of the late nineteenth century, and both the Grange and the Alliance had already established themselves as part of the state's agricultural history. Because of their small numbers, however, farmers could not take the initiative to bring about political reform, though one of their most respected leaders, Sutherlin, had suggested a farm-labor coalition to fight monopoly as early as 1876. Workingmen from the mountainous portion of the state would have to take the lead if there were to be an independent third party movement in Montana. by 1890 a segment of the state's laboring force seemed both ready and prepared to launch such a movement.

Six

Montana Populism

In 1890, Montana was admitted to the Union; however, the exuberance that usually accompanied statehood was diminished by the unhappiness of much of the new state's laboring force. In fact, the failure of the 1889 constitutional convention to include a provision for an eight-hour day in the state constitution was a major cause in the growth of Montana's third party movement. The shorter workday was an important objective for labor reformers throughout the United States and Montana's working population was no happier with the standard ten-hour shift than were their counterparts elsewhere. Because of this dissatisfaction, many elements of Montana's largely unionized work force were prepared to support a controversial move to call into session an Independent Labor convention in 1890 at Butte. Butte was an ideal location because one-third of this mining community's population was working class and many of the delegates, who arrived for the opening session on August 14, 1890, were of the same background. Other elements of the population also attended the Butte gathering, and thus, formed a coalition. A scattering of the delegates were spokesmen for the Farmers' Alliance. A determined band of Henry George's disciples were also present to push for his widely publicized Single Tax.

Nevertheless, the major purpose for this convention was to protest the inadequate provisions in the new constitution to protect labor. The constitutional convention, with labor's approval, had prohibited convict labor and established a Bureau of Agriculture, Labor, and

Industry. Along with the eight-hour day, however, it had rejected demands to ban blacklisting, to restrict the activities of Pinkerton detectives, to exclude Chinese employment, and to eliminate child labor. Almost all the delegates at the Butte convention wanted to incorporate more labor safeguards in the constitution. To some, however, such changes did not go far enough; they wanted to start a third party.[1]

The free-swinging platform adopted by the convention reflected the independent mood of the delegates at Butte. The delegates gave the eight-hour day a high priority, along with demands for a mine inspection law and equal pay for both sexes. They continued to favor a child-labor law. They also anticipated the Omaha platform of 1892 by pledging their complete support for bimetallism. Their approach to silver coinage was from a labor standpoint; it was primarily to guarantee full employment rather than to raise farm prices or to provide a market for silver producers. The delegates also advocated government ownership of the nation's rail and communication facilities as well as the restriction of Chinese immigration. (The Chinese seemed to have unjustifiably won disfavor throughout the Front Range country.) The plank that had the most immediacy about it, though, was the one that dealt with the ominous threat posed by the Northern Pacific's attempted mineral-land grab. The delegates roundly condemned the railway corporation for this effort.[2]

The Independent Labor convention rejected the Single Tax. With all the concrete issues facing labor in Montana in 1890, it seems ludicrous that George's panacea for the economic ills of society should have generated such emotion. But it did, and it left the Independent Labor movement sharply divided as an unexpected aftermath of the Butte convention. The three leading Single Taxers in the state at this time were Will Kennedy, editor of the Boulder *Age*, Samuel Mulville of the Butte Blacksmiths' Union, and Caldwell Edwards, who represented the Gallatin County Farmers' Alliance. These three ably represented the numerous Single-Tax associations that had materialized by 1890, most of which were located in the western part of the state.[3] Of the trio, Kennedy had the most prestige. As a senator from mountainous Jefferson County, he successfully sponsored a bill to legalize the Australian secret ballot in 1889, three years before the Populists advocated the secret ballot at Omaha.[4] For this significant accomplishment, he became known as the "father of the Australian system of ballot."[5]

Kennedy took the lead in pushing the Single Tax at the Independent Labor convention. But the Single Taxers encountered surprisingly stubborn resistance. Later, after George's theory had been rejected, the Boulder editor assumed a statesmanlike posture, blaming the defeat on a lack of knowledge about the virtues of the Single Tax. Clinch, however, felt that the decision of the delegates was motivated by a fear of what the mine owners would think.[6] The industry's long history of tax exemption probably benefited employees as well as employers; and if mining revenues were to be taxed under George's scheme, all those involved in mining would be hurt. Whatever the reasons for the rejection, Single Taxers were embittered, notwithstanding Kennedy's philosophical explanation of the defeat.

The convention also gave the state's voters a choice for public office. Since the 1890 election was an off-year one, there was really only one important state office to fill: Montana's new seat in the national House of Representatives. The delegates chose William T. Field, a locomotive engineer from Livingston, and A. P. Flanagan, a representative from the Miles City Farmers' Alliance in the eastern part of the state for the nomination. Field won over his agrarian rival, yet another reminder that in Montana the third party movement would be dominated by labor. Field's selection was a good one. As a Democratic labor delegate at the constitutional convention the previous year, he was able to speak from personal experience about labor's disappointment with the new constitution.

In many ways, the election of 1890 was a strange affair for the newly christened Independent Labor party. Field ran as its congressional candidate, while many of those who attended the convention or identified with the new political movement ran for local office as Single-Tax candidates, notwithstanding the issue's rejection. Kennedy, for instance, made his bid for re-election to the territorial council using the Single Tax as his political label. The results of the election were a disaster for the Independent Labor movement. Field ran last in a field of four. He received only 160 votes of the 31,000 cast; a fact rivaled only by his place in the race behind the Prohibition candidate—no mean feat in a state whose large ethnic population considered drinking alcoholic beverages almost as normal as eating. The entire effort seemed premature. The Single-Tax candidates lost, and even the popular Kennedy was defeated for his council seat.

This conspicuously ineffective bid for power, however, caused an unusual amount of anxiety for both major parties. The prospect of a separate party for Montana's working people produced apprehension.

Democrats, for instance, saw the new political movement as an unfortunate one because the party of Jefferson and Jackson was labor's truest friend. The strongly Republican *Daily Inter Mountain* of Butte, on the other hand, condemned the Independent Labor convention as a gathering of foolish idealists who hoped to make over the world.[7]

Apparently, these nervous critics had overlooked some important drawbacks for the new political venture. Peter Breen, the popular prolabor Democrat and a major leader of the Knights of Labor, for example, had some serious misgivings about the fledgling party—as a matter of fact, he refused to join it. But Breen's reluctance may have been symbolic of something besides a fear that the new party was too fragile. The Democratic party in Montana, like the one in Wyoming, was always ready to siphon off the protest vote from the left. Most dissidents would eventually return to the party fold; perhaps the Democrats were content to wait their turn. There were other political problems for the Independent Labor movement, too. Some elements of the state's agrarian population acted with extreme caution. In an editorial a week after the convention, Sutherlin wrote that the Farmers' Alliance might go the way of the Grange if it got too deeply involved with the newly launched party. Like the Grange, the Alliance is "nearing the breakers," he warned, "and there are grave doubts as to its riding safely through the whirlpools ahead." The farm editor then added cynically that there was "little hope for reform from the new political party. Its leaders will be corrupted just as the old ones."[8] Finally, there was the divisiveness caused by the zealous Single Taxers: their separate bid could only damage what slim chances the Independent Labor party had.

The young party's defeat in 1890, however, triggered a chain of events. Because of the division in the ranks of labor caused by the new political organization's bid for power, the Second Legislature had fewer labor representatives present when it convened in 1891. Consequently, with labor's voice diminished, the chances for the enactment of prolabor legislation were adversely affected. In fact, the legislature failed to enact an eight-hour-day law. This did more than anything else to push Montana's laboring people toward another independent political effort.[9]

By the following year, labor's disenchantment with the two older parties had reached a critical point. By January of 1892, labor representatives planned to hold a convention in Anaconda. The gathering followed a Knights of Labor district meeting in the same city. Peter

Breen, who had been elected as District Master Workman for the Knights at that assembly, was chosen to preside over the labor convention.[10] Again it appears that the once reluctant Breen's role was symbolic, for organized labor this year was much more serious about an independent labor course than it had been in 1890. The wide representation of union groups at Anaconda was evidence of labor's new commitment. The groups were from such mining or smelting communities as Butte, Anaconda, and Helena with the largest union representation from Billings in south central Montana.

Farmers' Alliance delegates as well as Single Taxers were among the nonlaboring people in attendance. Both of these groups were considerably stronger than they were in 1890, although the Single Taxers were further ahead. As previously mentioned, the Farmers' Alliance would not be organized statewide until February 26 of that year, while the disciples of Henry George had organized as a statewide group called the Montana Single Tax Association by January 17, the day the Anaconda convention convened. Their unquestioned leader was now Will Kennedy.[11]

When the 230 delegates gathered in Anaconda for their first meeting, there was considerable confusion, which was reflected in contemporary newspaper accounts of the meeting. The question of organizing a third party haunted this conclave, just as it had the one in Butte two years earlier. The *Butte Mining Journal* reported on the day the convention adjourned that the delegates had not decided to form a third party; yet clearly, the *Journal* wanted Montana's laborers to break with both older parties. It was "high time the laboring men in this country should begin to pull together at the polls," it editorialized.[12] The Republican *Semi-Weekly Inter Mountain*, on the other hand, proclaimed with joy that the convention had displayed "commendable wisdom in leaving the organization of a third party in abeyance."[13] Earlier, the Butte newspaper roasted the convention delegates as a group of "disgruntled 'outs' who wished to get 'in'."[14] Sensing that the members of the Anaconda convention were inching toward the Populist party, it argued strenuously that the Republican party was "distinctively and preeminently the people's party and if there are any needed reforms the people have but to bring them about."[15]

Whether Montana's Populist party actually organized itself in the shadow of Marcus Daly's huge copper smelter in Anaconda is still unresolved. According to Clinch, who believed it had, the Anaconda delegates formulated a detailed statement of principles as part of the party program.[16] The *Butte Mining Journal*, which reported on January 24 that a committee of five was appointed, gave his contention some credence. The committee's purpose was to select an executive committee authorized to choose subcommittees that could organize politically in those counties where two-thirds of the local union men were in support. These subcommittees could raise money and call county conventions—surely strong evidence that a new political party was being organized. But if these intricate plans were not proof enough, one of the resolutions adopted by the convention called upon all delegates to accept appointment as part of a committee of one "to pay the expenses of our new party."[17]

The rousing preamble adopted at Anaconda contained further proof that a new party had been formed. Its militant spirit was much in harmony with the one written by Ignatius Donnelly. Reminiscent of that Populist leader's fiery rhetoric, it proclaimed the following:

> There . . . [was] a widespread and constantly growing sentiment among the laboring, wealth producing people of the state, in common with that held by the masses in the United States, that the burdens and benefits of government are unequally and unjustly divided, and that such unjust distribution imposes upon the laboring classes of the country an undue proportion of such burdens and deprives them of their rightful share of the produce of labor. . . .[18]

The resolutions or principles approved by the convention harmonized with that preamble in both tone and intent. Not surprising, the familiar demand for free coinage headed the list in this silver-producing state. Its advocacy, however, was not the sole method suggested for currency reform. The delegates deemed an expansion in the volume of money, with $50 per capita as the goal, as essential. Unfortunately, the convention's call for currency expansion was rationalized by an anti-Semitic remark: ". . . an insufficient volume of money means Shylocks and money sharks dictating the price of labor's product and property." The principles also contained significant prolabor resolutions including the familiar call for an eight-hour day, the demands for Chinese exclusion, abolition of child labor, election of a state mine inspector, prohibition against the use of Pinkertons, and the elimination of company stores. In an approach more reminiscent of agrarian states, the delegates called for the reform of railroads. They wanted the establishment of a state railroad commission which would cooperate with a

greatly strengthened Interstate Commerce Commission and the appointment of a state inspector of transportation authorized to condemn
dangerous roads, trestles, and bridges. The strong antirailroad bias
evident here was due to the Northern Pacific's attempted mineral-land
grab, which the delegates condemned in another part of this so-called
statement of principles.

The convention's resolutions were curiously modern. Several of
them called for reforms that would not be successfully implemented
until the Progressive Era. At least three of them were consumer-ori-
ented and would be relevant even today. For instance, one of the
resolutions opposed the use of adulterated food: "If articles contain
artificial matter they should be so branded before being allowed to be
placed on sale." Another called for the appointment of a state chemist
or food inspector as a method of policing the restricted use of impure
food. Two resolutions dealt with banking and lending practices. One
asked for a state bank inspector who could "examine all affairs of all
banks and . . . compel all banks to publish quarterly statements," and
the other called for a gradual reduction of all interest rates above one
percent per annum.[19]

If the birth of Montana Populism occurred at the Anaconda meeting
(and the evidence seems overwhelming that it did) then the movement in the Treasure state was unquestionably a multi-issue one. Free
silver was undoubtedly of paramount importance—even as early as
1892—but there were a host of other significant demands. Some dealt
with labor's needs and aspiraticns, while others addressed those important questions related to railroad regulation and consumer protection. Clinch has concluded that while the Sherman Silver Purchase
Act was the most important national issue in Montana in 1892, the
eight-hour day was the most important local one. He also believed
that the urban nature of Montana Populism created the emphasis on
regulation and protection for the benefit of workers and consumers.[20]

During the spring months, the course charted at Anaconda began to
develop. A place was chosen for a state nominating convention and a
date set: the new political party would launch its challenge against
the Republicans and Democrats at Butte on June 14. The organizers
optimistically thought that the gathering in Butte would rival in numbers and enthusiasm the meeting in Anaconda. But the weather did
not cooperate. One of those late spring storms typical of this mountain country swept across much of the state. It washed out railroad
beds and destroyed bridges. The entire Missoula delegation was un-

able to attend. Consequently, only thirty-five delegates were present at the Caplice Hall in Butte on opening day, despite the elaborate strategy devised at Anaconda for the systematic organization of a strong state party.[21]

Undiscouraged, those in attendance immediately set about to draft party resolutions for a forceful state platform. The document was shorter than the statement of principles adopted at Anaconda, but very similar in nature. Free Silver again headed the list; it was the first plank. The delegates argued again for the eight-hour day. They justified it not only as a way to shorten the workday but also as a method to increase the number of industrial and mining jobs in the mineral-rich state. The Northern Pacific received its usual critical attention; the plank dealing with it was the harshest yet. The delegates demanded that the controversial railroad's land grant be "forfeited by reason of the failure of the company to build the road within the time specified in the charter." The plank which called upon the federal government to "establish and maintain reservoirs for the irrigation of arid lands" indicated the suspicions of Montana farmers and their disappointment with private irrigation ventures. Montana farmers had no more faith in state-initiated irrigation projects than did the farmers from Wyoming. The substance of two other planks included in the platform dealt with issues of immense common appeal for the newly formed national party. One urged the popular election of the President and Vice-President and the United States senators; the other, that the nation's railroad and communication facilities be "controlled and managed" by the federal goverment. To dispel any doubts about the intention of this gathering, the delegates enthusiastically included a separate endorsement of the February 22 Saint Louis platform.[22]

The plank directed against the Chinese (although it does not mention them by name) revealed a darker side of third party activity in the Mountain West. In this plank, the convention favored the "restriction of immigration to such classes as will make good citizens."[23] Most Montanans had long believed that the Chinese had no real potential for exemplary citizenship. Even though these Far Eastern immigrants numbered only 2,532 in a state with a total population of 132,159 in 1890, they had aroused fear and animosity from the beginning. Curiously, they rarely competed in new mineral strikes, reworking only abandoned gravel fields. They were, however, formidable competitors in those urban areas where they were concentrated. They often successfully operated laundries and restaurants.[24] The delegates at Anaconda had already opposed making any Montana community that employed Chinese the new state capital.[25] Montana workingmen, however, were not alone in displaying hostility toward Chinese immigrants. In Denver, there was the previously mentioned Chinese race riot of 1880. Even more shocking was the massacre of Chinese at Rock Springs, Wyoming in 1885, in which the Knights of Labor were involved.[26] It seems that wherever Chinese immigrants concentrated in appreciable numbers, persecution or violence occurred.

The popular issue of Chinese exclusion, however, did not generate the most emotion at Butte. Free silver, the eight-hour day, and the Northern Pacific mineral-land grab caused more passionate concern. In fact, the machinations of the state's most feared monopoly, the Northern Pacific, ignited almost instant emotion. As one newspaper reporter wrote, "The reading and adoption of the section relative to land grants of the Northern Pacific railroad occasioned tumultous [sic] applause. . . ." Delegates also greeted calls for an eight-hour day and free coinage with enthusiasm, particularly the demand for a shorter workday: "There could be no mistaking the feeling of the assembled delegates toward the eight hour clause in the platform. Every reference to it was loudly applauded. Several delegates spoke on the question."[27]

Following the adoption of the platform, the Butte delegates turned to the question of nominations, which produced a divisiveness similar to that of the Independent Labor convention of 1890. One controversy concerned time. Some of the delegates wanted to wait until after the Republicans and Democrats nominated their candidates before selecting their own. The Republicans had not scheduled their state convention until September 6 at Great Falls; the Democrats, not until September 12 in the same city. Such a delay would have required a wait of three months. Consequently, the convention ignored the wishes of these more cautious delegates.

Another controversy involved the Single Tax, which had created such acrimony during Montana's first third party effort. Although Henry George's much publicized theory was not included in the 1892 platform either negatively or positively, Single-Tax proponents played a prominent role in this Populist convention. The Butte gathering, for example, nominated Single Taxer Caldwell Edwards for the state's seat in Congress. The nomination of Single Taxer Will Kennedy for the governorship was even more controversial; his selection divided the convention. Ex-Democrat Breen, armed with the reassurance that the

Democrats would probably endorse his choice when they met at Great Falls, had confidently expected to receive the gubernatorial nomination by acclamation. When the votes were counted, however, Kennedy received thirty votes to Breen's four. (Samuel Mulville of the Butte Blacksmiths' Union received one.) Kennedy's choice embittered some delegates. They alleged that the Kennedy-controlled convention failed to seat delegates such as those from Deer Lodge who supported Breen. This action, they believed, plus the failure of the Missoula delegation to arrive because of bad weather had clinched Kennedy's victory. Expressing a common viewpoint, some Silver Bow delegates charged that organized labor had received a "slap in the face" by Kennedy's controversial nomination.[28]

Despite the anger that it generated, the choice of Kennedy was good for the struggling young party. As it turned out, Kennedy, along with the Populist nominee for attorney general Ella Knowles, did most of the campaigning for the People's party in 1892. Breen spent much of his time during the election campaign in Idaho, where he was deeply involved in the violent Coeur d'Alene Mining War. The other Populist nominations were wise ones too. Harvey Collum, a mining foreman from Butte, was nominated for lieutenant governor, and Samuel Mulville was the party's choice for United States senator. Considering the almost exclusive labor composition of the Independent Labor party in 1890, the delegates' nomination of only two laboring men such as Collum and Mulville was a strategically sound move.

Two other important nominations were William Y. Pemberton of Butte for chief justice, a man who later received the Democratic nomination, and the previously mentioned Miss Knowles.[29] Ella Knowles represented a growing feminist movement in this part of the Rocky Mountains. (In 1892, Colorado passed a woman suffrage law, while Wyoming was the first state to grant women their franchise.) Knowles, the "Portia of the People's Party," was an able lawyer who worked diligently in 1892 for the entire Butte ticket.[30]

The Populists were deeply involved in the campaign long before the two older parties had made their September nominations. The twelve delegates chosen to attend the Populist national convention in July had already made their choice. They had supported James H. Kyle of neighboring South Dakota on the first ballot but later seconded Weaver's choice to make his presidential selection at Omaha unanimous. The victorious Weaver, along with blunt-talking Populist Mary Elizabeth Lease, the "Kansas Cyclone," campaigned in Montana in mid-August even before the Republicans and Democrats of Montana had chosen their state tickets. A surprising amount of publicity, both good and bad, accompanied Weaver's arrival in Montana since he was the first major presidential candidate to campaign in the state.[31]

The Republicans and Democrats convened in Great Falls the following month after their parent parties had nominated Harrison and Cleveland respectively for the presidency. The platforms of each party showed a deliberate effort to keep the state's large laboring population from drifting toward Populism. Both endorsed free silver. The Democrats, however, were determined to make more political capital out of the issue. They condemned the Sherman Silver Purchase Act as being directly responsible for the decline in the price of silver. Nevertheless, the silver issue was largely neutralized in 1892 because all three parties endorsed bimetallism. The two major parties also attacked the Northern Pacific's mineral-land grab, but not with the uncompromising directness with which the Populists had launched their attack. The Republicans, for instance, did not even mention the Northern Pacific by name. Both parties joined the Populists in demanding Chinese exclusion. Aware of labor's distrust, the Republicans, moreover, went even further to win over Montana's workingmen: They condemned the use of Pinkertons and advocated the establishment of boards of arbitration in labor disputes. Undoubtedly, the G.O.P. would have been much more convincing if it had supported the eight-hour day. Only on the high McKinley tariff did the two parties take diametrically opposed stands, with the Republicans unquestionably having the advantage on this issue because of the popularity of wool protection.

As far as candidates for 1892 were concerned, the Republicans nominated the incumbent lieutenant governor John E. Rickards for the gubernatorial post and Charles S. Hartman for the state's lone seat in the national House of Representatives. Hartman's selection stirred some controversy. He was a Bozeman attorney who had to promise the delegates that he would renounce his close legal ties with the Northern Pacific. The Democrats nominated Timothy E. Collins, an Irish immigrant lawyer from Great Falls, as their candidate for governor and renominated incumbent William W. Dixon for Congress.[32] Another popular Democratic nomination was William Pemberton for state chief justice; the Populists had already nominated Pemberton for the same position.[33]

With candidates from all parties now on the hustings, the campaign became more intense. Kennedy and Knowles, representing a new approach in Montana politics, attracted an unusual amount of attention. As a matter of fact, because the Democrats knew that most of the Populist support would come from their party's more progressive ranks, they organized so-called truth squads to follow the ubiquitous twosome around the state. As for the Republicans, gubernatorial candidate John Rickards, a man with some populistic ideas of his own, carried most of the campaign burden for his party.[34] When the votes were cast on November 8, Rickards realized the fruits of his effort. He outpolled Collins and Kennedy for the governorship. The vote was close, however. His margin over Collins was a scant 547 votes. Balloting was close in most other races, too. Harrison carried the state by a plurality of only 1,270 votes. Although the Republicans lost control of the state senate to the Democrats, each party elected twenty-seven members to the lower house.

The Populists had done well in their first bid for office—sensational if one compares their successes with the candidates associated with the Independent Labor movement in 1890. The Weaver-Field ticket had won the support of 7,334 Montanans, 16.55 percent of the popular vote cast.[35] Kennedy did better, polling 7,738 votes. He even outdistanced his Democratic rival Collins in populous Silver Bow County, where Butte is located. Ella Knowles garnered 11,465 votes of 43,448 cast in her three-way race for attorney general. Caldwell Edwards, the Alliance leader, was shy by only 2 of a 7,000-vote tally. Pemberton, with combined Democratic and Populist support, defeated his Republican rival by 6,088 votes.[36] Pemberton's solid victory and the closeness of Rickards's gubernatorial success are convincing proof that, if the Democrats and Populists had fused in 1892, they would have easily won in Montana.

One unexpected Populist advantage occurred in the contest over control of the state legislature. Since Republicans and Democrats both had twenty-seven seats in the lower house, Democrats agreed to cooperate with Populists to gain control of that body. Three members of the People's party had been elected to the state House of Representatives: Thomas F. Matthews and Absalom F. Bray from Silver Bow County and D. F. Beecher from Cascade County. To win their allegiance, Democrats agreed to support Matthews as Speaker and Bray as Speaker Pro Tem. Both choices were popular. Matthews was from the influential Butte Miners' Union and Bray, a progressive merchant, was an ardent silverite.

The popularity of both Matthews and Bray soon waned, however, because of the ineffectiveness of Montana's Third General Assembly. For one thing, because of evenly divided party strength, the legislature failed to elect a United States senator. Despite their energetic lobbying for that post, Republican incumbent Wilbur F. Sanders, Democrat William A. Clark, and Populist Samuel Mulville all fell short of the necessary majority.[37] Consequently, a situation reminiscent of Wyoming's developed. Montana was represented by only one senator Thomas C. Powers from 1893 to 1895, just as Wyoming was by Joseph M. Carey during that same period.

This stalemate in the selection of a United States senator seems to have adversely affected the legislature's entire performance; they failed to enact significant legislation of a progressive nature. The eight-hour day, for instance, was not enacted into law except for stationary engineers.[38] A law to restrict the activities of Pinkertons and two futile memorials to Congress calling for free silver and the direct election of senators fell considerably short of expectations.[39] Because Matthews and Bray played such prominent roles, Populists were forced to take some of the blame for this lack of productivity.

There were, however, two important developments outside the legislature which were to affect the course of Montana politics significantly. One was the Supreme Court's decision against the Northern Pacific in the case of *Barden et al. v. Northern Pacific Railroad Company*, and the other involved the disconcerting results caused by the Panic of 1893. The high court's decision against the much publicized mineral-land grab naturally caused much elation throughout the state. The court, by a reassuring six-to-three vote, had reversed a lower court decision in behalf of the railroad when it decided that the Northern Pacific could not recover mineral lands under its 1864 charter even though the existence of such minerals was not known until 1888 (the year of the Helena gold and silver strike). Republican Congressman Hartman later introduced a bill which required the examination and classification of the Northern Pacific's lands in Montana and Idaho to avoid further disputes over mineral rights.[40] The Barden case was good for the state, but not for the Populists. It had removed the monopolistic threat of the Northern Pacific, but it had also eliminated one of the Populists' most visible targets.

The Panic of 1893 had the same crippling impact on Montana as it did in Colorado. The experiences of both states were similar because their economies were so much alike. Each was a major silver producer; each was blessed with great mineral diversification. Both were significantly dependent upon outside capital and vulnerable to decisions by out-of-state investors to liquidate their holdings. According to Clinch, the liquidation of British investments caused by the failure of the Baring Brothers banking enterprise in 1889 hurt Montanans in much the same way as it had Coloradans. As a result, almost four years before the national panic reached the area in May of 1893, the economies of both states were weakened. Another similarity involved labor. Both states had large urban and mining work forces which were vulnerable to unemployment when outside financing faltered. When many businesses did fail during the Panic of 1893, unemployment soared to one-third of Montana's entire labor force by the end of that year.

In one important respect, however, Montana was worse off than Colorado. During the depression the Treasure State did not have the large agricultural sector to provide balance to its ailing mining economy (an unfortunate development because of relative health of rural Montana). Farmers and grazers from sparsely populated eastern Montana were affected by the dismal panic which began in 1893 but not to the same degree as those involved in mining. Grain and beef prices, for example, were not so vitally affected as were the prices of metals. Moreover, wool protection seemed as good a depression medicine to some as free silver did for the majority of workers in the urban and mining sections of the state.[41]

The same forces of discontent unleashed in Colorado were unleashed in Montana. Even before the mints of India were closed, miners and other trade unionists started to organize branches of the militant Industrial Legion of the United States.[42] With silver mines failing throughout the state because of the closure of Indian silver mints in June and the repeal of the Sherman Silver Purchase Act in October, more radical labor organizations sprang up. On May 19, 1893, the Butte Miners' Union and Peter Breen of the Knights of Labor, playing major roles, organized the tough Western Federation of Miners.[43] In April of 1894, one workingman's organization the Butte Industrial Union fathered one of the most controversial of the numerous Coxey armies organized that year. Its leader was William Hogan, a jobless teamster from Butte. Hogan and his desperate army of unemployed seized a Northern Pacific train to join Jacob S. Coxey's 500-man army on its way to Washington to seek relief. This contingent of Coxeyites got as far east as Forsyth before their train was stopped by federal troops from Fort Keough near Miles City.[44]

Aggressive action to seek relief accounted for a miniscule part of the total effort. The vast majority of stricken Montanans agitated for free silver to bring an end to their depression woes. Populism, along with almost all political "isms" in the Treasure state, became absorbed in the growing silver movement; this development was evident in 1894 and was even more so in 1896. Much of this prosilver activity took a nonpartisan form during the early years of the depression. The Montana Free Coinage Association is a particularly good example: it was composed of bimetallists from almost every occupational calling and from almost all shades of political opinion.[45] There were miners and mine owners who had political views that ranged from Populism on the left to silver Republicanism on the right. Even silver-thumping Prohibitionists were active. The effort provided convincing evidence that fusionism was feasible whenever the forces of silver were ready.

Montana Populists, however, were not prepared to fuse in 1894, although it was obvious to the more astute that if the Democrats and Populists had cooperated in 1892, they could have won both the gubernatorial and congressional races.[46] Populists in the state may have believed that the Panic of 1893 had vindicated their indictment of the country's laissez-faire economy or that their unsullied record on silver gave them a substantial advantage over the other parties. Whatever their motives, those who gathered at Deer Lodge on June 25 for the state convention nominated their most prominent convert Dillon attorney Robert Burns Smith for Congress. Smith had left the Democratic party in March of 1894 in protest over the repeal of the Sherman Silver Purchase Act.[47] The party platform was almost identical to the one of 1892 with perhaps a greater emphasis on silver. An especially strong legislative slate was nominated and, as was the case in 1892, the People's party began its campaign for office two months ahead of the other parties.[48] To ensure political success, the chairman of the Populist state central committee J. H. Calderhead, a leader of the militant American Railway Union from Butte, conducted a vigorous canvass of the state. He organized Populist clubs and publicized inconsistencies in the silver stands of both major parties.

Smith lost during the November balloting, but only because the Republican incumbent Charles S. Hartman had won such favorable publicity fighting against the repeal of the Sherman Silver Purchase Act.[49] Republicans also won solid control of the legislature. The Populists, however, had improved their position. They outnumbered Democrats in the lower house thirteen to three; they still had three members in the state senate. Their biggest disappointment was the surprise loss of Silver Bow County to the Republicans. The mining county had been regarded as a Populist stronghold before the election. A riot in Butte provoked by the American Protective Association on the Fourth of July may have been the principal cause. The A.P.A. was apparently successful in consolidating the Republican vote by inciting anti-Catholic sentiments, while Irish Catholics in Silver Bow County divided their strength between the Populist and Democratic parties.[50]

The Populist refusal to fuse with the Democrats in 1894 proved that the new political organization was a serious contender; after all, it had done better than the Democrats in that off-year election. Its decision to field a second separate slate of candidates resulted in another victory for the Republican party. Moreover, by helping the Republicans to gain control of the Fourth Assembly, which convened in 1895, it allowed the G.O.P. to choose the state's two new United States senators Thomas H. Carter and Lee Mantle. Consequently, when the Battle of the Standards began in 1896, the state was largely under Republican control.[51]

The silver issue was so popular in Montana in 1896 that before the election was over, some of the state's confident prosilver candidates were campaigning for Bryan and Sewall in the Midwest and border states. The pressure on Montana Populists to fuse had never been greater. Prominent Republicans and Democrats were making major sacrifices for the cause. Montana Congressman Hartman even bolted the Republican national convention with Teller because the G.O.P. rejected free silver. Although he did not leave the convention floor with Hartman, Senator Mantle eventually broke with his national party to become one of the state's leading silver Republicans. This year was clearly not the time to put party above principle. Besides, there was a growing feeling among local Populists that the nation had to restore silver to its rightful place as a legitimate currency before the country could tackle the other reforms advocated in the Omaha platform.[52] As a result of these irresistible pressures to fuse, a meeting of Populists, Democrats, and silver Republicans was held in Butte on August 19. The Populists had a single requirement for their full cooperation: one of the state's three presidential electors had to be a Populist. This stipulation presented no major problem; Montana Populists overwhelmingly supported the Bryan and Sewall ticket, having little interest in Tom Watson's vice-presidential candidacy.[53]

When the Populists gathered for their state convention in Helena on September 2, they agreed to appoint a committee of five to attend the Democratic convention in Missoula the following day. At Missoula, it was agreed that Populists would be nominated as fusionist candidates for governor, lieutenant governor, secretary of state, and superintendent of public instruction. A Populist would also be chosen as one of the presidential electors. Robert Burns Smith proved the popular choice for the state's gubernatorial post, while Populist Daniel Brown was nominated as one of the presidential electors. Because of Congressman Hartman's widely approved stand on silver coinage, neither the Populists nor the Democrats wanted to challenge him for his seat.

The Republicans in 1896 faced the same bleak dilemma that the other G.O.P. parties in the Mountain West faced. McKinley's stand on gold destroyed any advantage gained by the party's popular position on wool protection. When the Republicans convened at Helena on September 9, they adopted the so-called Butte report. It stated that the full party would nominate all candidates, except the one for Congress and the three presidential electors. To attend to the latter nominations, the convention would then separate into bodies authorized to take independent action. The entire convention at Helena chose Alexander C. Botkin for governor. Following the plan, the silver Republicans nominated Hartman for Congress in a separate action, while the gold Republicans chose O. F. Goddard for the same position. Although the silver Republicans failed to place one of their own on the prosilver Bryan-Sewall fusionist slate, the gold Republicans nominated three electors pledged to McKinley and Hobart.[54] The election results were a foregone conclusion. Bryan outpolled McKinley by a convincing vote of 42,537 to 10,494; McKinley carried only two counties.[55] Smith's margin over Botkin was more than 21,000 votes, while Hartman's over Goddard exceeded 24,000. The fusionists also swept the state legislative races. Democrats won forty-two seats; Populists, eighteen; while the hapless Republicans had to content themselves with only eight.[56]

Smith, Montana's only Populist governor, proved to be a much more moderate chief executive than Waite. His state-of-the-state message was downright cautious when compared to Waite's first one. But times had changed—four years had elapsed since Waite's inauguration in Colorado—and Democrats in the Montana legislature outnumbered Populists by a margin of two-to-one. Even so, the practical Smith recommended the creation of a railroad commission, a more effective means to regulate other businesses, and not forgetting the party's rural constituency, better implementation of the Carey Act. He also urged Montanans to adopt the initiative and referendum through a constitutional amendment. The Fifth Assembly only gave him some labor legislation legalizing the eight-hour day for hoisting engineers and improving mine safety, plus some harmless memorials to Congress in behalf of a postal savings system and the direct election of senators.[57]

Following the adjournment of the Fifth Legislative Session, the Populist party went into a surprisingly decisive decline. The silver issue began to lose its clout shortly after Bryan's defeat. Copper and gold production were now more important to the economy of the Treasure State. Democratic mining magnate William A. Clark, as part of his persistent quest for a seat in the United States Senate, rejected fusion with the Populists in 1898. Democrats, meeting in Anaconda on September 21, decided to nominate a straight ticket—even rejecting Hartman as being too "populistic." Perhaps the most potent blow to the independence of the People's party was Governor Smith's return to the Democratic party. The governor, a purely silver Populist, justified his decision on the basis of the strong Democratic record on free silver.[58] In the end, the Democrats won everything. Hartman, after some hesitation, declined the congressional nomination of the Populists and silver Republicans, so the Democrats were able to add that seat to their list of successes. Democrat Andrew J. Campbell, a strident bimetallist from Butte, therefore, became Montana's new congressman.[59] In the legislature, the Populists elected only one member who disgraced himself and his party by supporting Clark for the Senate; Clark had allegedly bought his new seat for $431,000.[60]

By 1900, the Populists were reduced almost to helplessness, witnessing a titanic struggle between copper kings Clark and F. Augustus Heinze on one side and Marcus Daly on the other. Daly had threatened the competitive position of Clark and Heinze by selling his properties the previous year to Standard Oil; these became part of a gigantic holding company known as Amalgamated Copper. It was only natural that Populists would side with Clark and Heinze in this struggle: both copper moguls had instituted an eight-hour workday for their employees to win worker support. Also, Populists saw Clark and Heinze as fighting a great outside trust. Most fair-minded Montanans would have to concede that the People's party had been the most uncompromising of the state's political parties in resisting the land claims of that other outside-controlled monopoly the Northern

Pacific.[61] At any rate, the Populists accepted four places on a fusion ticket that the mercurial Clark now supported, and in 1900, they elected to Congress Caldwell Edwards, the Farmers' Alliance man who had unsuccessfully run for Congress in 1892.[62]

The election of 1900 was the last one in which the Populists had any significant role. In 1902 and 1904, the party fused with other political organizations without notable success. In 1906, the old Populist veteran and former American Railway Union leader J. H. Calderhead won only 261 votes in his bid for a congressional seat.[63] Despite the rapidity and completeness of its decline, Clinch did not see the Populist movement in Montana as a failure. A great deal of reform legislation that the party advocated was eventually passed; ironically, much of it was enacted after the Populists had passed their peak. For example, in 1901, the legislature enacted a state eight-hour-day law; in 1903, mine-safety legislation was extended. In 1904, they passed a child-labor law for the mines and in 1906, they approved constitutional amendments for the initiative and referendum. Clinch believed that early Populist agitation had at least something to do with these successes.[64]

Moreover, these substantive advancements far transcend the mere quest for free silver. Even before free coinage became an obsession in Montana, Populists were struggling for an eight-hour day and opposing the sweeping mineral-land claims of the Northern Pacific. They were working for mine safety and lobbying for a variety of consumer and producer reforms. And, unfortunately, they were adding their shrill voices to the cry for Chinese exclusion. Despite the movement's darker side and its perennial weakness of promising more than it could deliver, Populism seems to have left a deeper imprint on Montana than elsewhere along the Front Range. Perhaps this was because of the urban nature of the labor force which made up a large part of the state's third party movement. It also might have been a result of the movement's pragmatism; there were not nearly so many angry middle-of-the-roaders in Montana as there were in Colorado. Whatever the reason, for a party with an effective life of less than a decade, the People's party performed admirably well in the Treasure State.

Seven

New Mexico

The Origins of Protest

An interest in gold opened up New Mexico just as it did the other Front Range states. The first mineral exploration in the Land of Enchantment, however, occurred more than three centuries before the famous rush to the Rockies in 1859. When Coronado started northward from Mexico in 1540 at the head of a major expedition, one of his goals was to explore the mineral potential of the Southwest. Coronado failed to find the mythical Seven Cities of Cibola; but after a half of a century of neglect, the Spanish finally settled New Mexico during the last years of the sixteenth century. What ensued were more than two centuries of Spanish rule and a quarter of a century of Mexican rule before New Mexico and the remainder of the Southwest came under the authority of the expansionist-minded United States. In 1850, Congress passed an organic act creating New Mexico as an American territory, a status in which the historically rich southwestern state remained until 1912. New Mexico, consequently, differed from the other Front Range states in two important ways. In addition to an indigenous Indian population, it had a comparatively advanced European-based culture with which the Anglo-American civilization had to reckon. Also New Mexico was, and would remain, a territory throughout the entire period when agrarian frustrations were released as part of the Populist protest movement.

The settlement of New Mexico by Spanish-speaking people from the south was a slow process. By the middle of the eighteenth century, there were only 5,200 Hispanos living in this vast wilderness after more than one hundred and fifty years of settlement. In fact, the Pueblo Indian population remained larger than the Hispanic one for nearly two centuries. It numbered 13,500 in 1750, more than double that of the Spanish settlers. The next half century, however, saw important changes. Largely because of a smallpox epidemic from 1779 to 1780, the number of Pueblo Indians dropped to 10,000. The Spanish population, on the other hand, began to grow significantly. It rose to 24,000 by 1800 and then doubled in size during the next fifty years.[1] The first census taken under American rule in 1851 counted 56,984 New Mexicans with only a fraction of that number, a little more than 500, being Anglos.[2]

Throughout the years when the territory was governed from Mexico City, Europeanized settlers, most of whom had some Indian blood, dominated the developed parts of New Mexico. They cultivated the warm Rio Grande Valley, replacing the more primitive irrigation methods of the Pueblos with irrigation methods learned centuries earlier from the Moorish invaders of Iberia. Before long, corn, wheat, and pinto beans were the staple crops of Spanish New Mexico. Nevertheless, with 98 percent of New Mexico's land unfit for crop production, other industries were essential if this distant outpost of New Spain were to continue to grow.[3]

Stock grazing was an early pursuit that soon assumed major importance. From the time of their arrival in New Mexico with Don Juan de Onate in 1598, sheep would thrive in the arid, mountainous landscape of New Mexico. Mutton was the basic meat dish; garments made of wool, the most common form of wearing apparel. Many Indians in the area became sheep grazers and learned to weave blankets, finding such blankets a sought-after trade item in their exchanges with the Spanish. Sheep grazing almost became the monopoly of the wealthiest or most favored Spanish settlers in New Mexico. According to a tradition (which is probably exaggerated), one Spanish governor owned two million sheep. Even after the American conquest, there were those among the *rico* class of New Mexicans who owned flocks of sheep as large as a quarter of a million.[4]

Mining was also important. Prospects for gold had spurred the first efforts to explore New Mexico. To the Spanish, New Mexico as an El Dorado was a great disappointment; nevertheless, the quest for mineral riches never ended. The first mining claim for which there are records was filed in 1685. In 1804, the Spanish began working the copper deposits of Santa Rita, which one day would become very important to New Mexico's economy. In 1828, the gold that eluded Coronado was finally discovered in the Ortiz Mountains between Santa Fe and Albuquerque.[5]

By the end of the Mexican period, then, New Mexico was a surprisingly advanced area for a region widely dismissed as primitive by Anglo-Americans. There were some 50,000 non-Indian settlers who cultivated the Rio Grande Valley, raised sheep in the less arable land and mined copper and gold in the lonely mountain ranges. The problems in developing New Mexico were different from those in the other states of the Mountain West. For one thing, the assimilation of a relatively advanced Europeanized culture was a challenge that Anglo-Americans in Colorado, Wyoming, and Montana never had to face.

Another problem encountered by westward-moving settlers to New Mexico was its prolonged territorial status. This southernmost Front Range state was denied admission to the Union as part of the Compromise of 1850 and remained a territory for sixty-two years, a record for the contiguous states of the American Union. Territorial status did make a significant difference. It meant that the affairs of New Mexico were under the jurisdiction of the Department of State until 1873 and under the Department of the Interior after that year. All laws enacted by the territorial legislature had to be submitted to Congress for approval. All the important government officials, from the territorial governor on down, had to be appointed by the president with the advice and consent of the Senate. New Mexico had only one national representative, a territorial delegate whose authority was largely diluted by his nonvoting status.[6] In short, the territorial system gave New Mexico a decidedly subordinate status in relation to the full-fledged states of the Union.

Many western commonwealths on both sides of the Great Divide were territories when third party activity began in the United States. The territorial system was found in Montana, Wyoming, Idaho, Utah, and Arizona as well as New Mexico. By 1896, when Utah was admitted to the Union, only New Mexico and Arizona were left in this category. The political environment of both of these territories was probably the least conducive to reform of any of the commonwealths of the Mountain West. Under the territorial system, the citizens had no effective way to advance reform on the national scene because a territory did not have a vote in Congress. The ability to bring about reform locally was also hampered by this system because of the often imponderable role of the federal government. The cooperation of Washington was essential to the growth and development of any territory. Unfortunately, this need for growth often influenced reform adversely. To advocate change, particularly the kind associated with third party activity, tended to alienate those people a territory needed most—the congressmen and federal officials who oversaw territorial affairs. These included senators and representatives from the once-powerful congressional committees devoted to territorial administration as well as presidential appointees such as the governor and the members of the judiciary. Talk of reform to these people was counterproductive; even disagreement with them over purely political matters was dangerous. L. Bradford Prince, a New Mexico territorial governor and Harrison appointee, tried to dissuade his party allies from sending a delegation in opposition to Harrison to the Republican national convention because the Territory of New Mexico had "to depend so much on the National Administration that it would be foolish for it to act in an unfriendly manner even if there were some reasons."[7]

Because of the many cultural and economic differences, plus the liabilities of the territorial system, Populism in New Mexico underwent different experiences than elsewhere. Even so, the influx of Anglos, particularly after the Civil War, created situations that eventually led to organized protest. One reason for this development, of course, was the tendency of the Anglo-Americans to bring their politics with them. Another was the usual problem of rapid population growth found all along the Front Range. This was complicated by the distress experienced by many native New Mexicans who saw their way of life imperiled. The change seemed phenomenal; the population of the territory soared by 40,000 during the decade of the 1880s alone, bringing the number of New Mexicans to 160,282 by 1890. Ten years later, census takers would count 193,310 territorial inhabitants.[8]

These newcomers not only introduced new ideas and new ways to New Mexico, but new industries as well. A large-scale cattle industry, for instance, began in the territory when Charles Goodnight and Oliver Loving drove beeves up the Pecos into Colorado in 1866. During the 1870s, New Mexico had its first genuine cattle king John S. Chisum, who at one time grazed 60,000 head of cattle along 150 miles of the Pecos River. By 1890, there were 1,340,000 beeves grazing within the territorial boundaries. Cattle grazing differed from sheep grazing in one very important aspect: it was Anglo-dominated from the very beginning.[9]

Mining also grew with the arrival of more Anglo-Americans. With great gold finds occurring all over the West, Anglo settlers in New Mexico were eager for any news regarding new or promising bonanzas. The presentation of a beautiful "rock" by an ailing but grateful Indian who was nursed back to good health at Fort Union inaugurated a full-scale gold rush to that part of the territory in 1867. One discovery followed another during the post-Civil War years, until gold was being mined in twenty-three of the state's thirty-two counties. Classic gold rushes, like those that occurred in Colorado and Montana, did as much to open up remote parts of the territory as anything else. The two most important gold mining regions in New Mexico were in the Sangre de Cristos, particularly in the Elizabethtown-Red River area, and in the southwest corner of the territory.[10]

Silver strikes also involved Anglo newcomers. Magdalena and Socorro became burgeoning centers of silver mining as early as 1863, but Silver City in Grant County eventually became the hub of the territory's silver industry. Similar to the situation in Colorado and Montana, silver in time eclipsed gold in importance. Before the 1880s, gold production was three times greater than silver; but from 1885 to 1889, the familiar reversal occurred. Silver production reached $19,113,000, while the output of gold was only $3,808,000. Silver's increasing importance during the 1880s, however, was as tenuous as elsewhere. The price of the white metal was on that fateful decline which made the silver crusade of the 1890s inevitable. The value of silver dropped from $1.33 an ounce in 1885 to $1.05 in 1890. With this price decline came a slump in production; the output of silver dropped by 40 percent during the last five years of the 1880s.[11]

But the earliest protest in New Mexico did not occur in the silver-producing counties of Grant and Sierra in the southwestern part of the territory. It occurred on the eastern side, where the Anglo-dominated cattle industry had begun in New Mexico at the end of the Civil War. Moving into the extensive plains adjacent to the Texas panhandle, these Anglo newcomers began to erect fences to separate their herds from the flocks of sheep tended by native inhabitants. The effort was part of an enclosure movement, which was greatly accelerated by the introduction of inexpensive barbed-wire fencing after 1870. This movement had been so successful in Texas that by 1900, most Hispanos in the Lone Star State had been driven into the ranks of landless wage laborers. The same development might have happened in New Mexico if there had not been such large concentrations of native farmers cultivating irrigated areas such as the Rio Grande Valley.

Anglo migration increased remarkably after the Atchison, Topeka and Sante Fe Railway reached New Mexico in 1879. The arrival of the railroad, which followed the old Santa Fe Trail over Raton Pass, brought efficient transportation that greatly increased the territory's national trade. An eastern market for the wool, meat, and hides produced in northeastern New Mexico was now more accessible. It also provided an outlet for the mineral wealth being taken from the bordering Sangre de Cristo Mountains.[12] The coming of the railroad had some negative aspects, too. Large ranchers saw great opportunities for profit in New Mexico's seemingly boundless prairies. Having both the capital and determination, some of these wealthier cattlemen soon threatened the very existence of the territory's small grazers. Water was often the key. Stephen W. Dorsey, the former carpetbag senator from Arkansas who later became involved in the infamous Star Route frauds, established an enormous ranch in Colfax County by gaining control of scarce water resources. He owned "all the springs" on 160 acres, and control of this water affected the "whole 10,000 acres back of it."[13]

Corporate ranchers also posed a threat. By controlling the limited water resources in eastern New Mexico, the better-financed cattle companies monopolized the range. Some of these major cattle firms were also among the largest in the West. Included in this category were the Scottish-controlled Prairie Cattle Company plus such American-owned enterprises as the Illinois Livestock and Palo Blanco cattle companies.[14]

Because of the monopoly threat in eastern New Mexico, the National Farmers' Alliance and Cooperative Union of America, or Southern Alliance, established chapters in such counties as Lincoln, Colfax, and Dona Ana. In Lincoln County, which at one time incorporated the entire southeastern corner of the territory, small stock grazers felt greatly threatened by the activities of large cattle concerns. County assessment rolls for 1888, for example, show that Captain Joseph C. Lea's cattle company owned 16,500 acres of land. Again, the familiar pattern of controlling scarce water resources was evident in Lea's enterprise. He had purchased land from 1879 to 1885 all along the Rio Hondo to its juncture with the Pecos. Other large cattle enterprises in the county included the British-incorporated Carrizozo Cattle Ranch, Limited, and El Capitan Land and Cattle Company.[15]

The Lincoln County Farmers' Alliance honestly believed that these large cattle firms intended to gain control of the entire range and drive out all competitors. In the little town of Nogal, twenty-five miles northwest of the county seat at Lincoln, the Alliance not only established an active cooperative, but also published a little newspaper called the *Nogal Nugget*. The pages of the peppery *Nugget* were often devoted to warnings about the malevolent intentions of the cattle kings. It characterized a quarantine law passed by the territorial legislature to keep beeves carrying dreaded Texas fever out of New Mexico as a measure to prevent new stockmen from entering the territory to challenge large cattlemen in their "*monopoly of the public domain.*"[16]

Alliancemen to the north in Colfax County faced another kind of monopoly: the Maxwell Land Grant and Cattle Company. It is probably the best known of the large tracts of land granted either to individuals and communities during the Spanish and Mexican periods and provides yet another example of how New Mexico's uniqueness as a former Spanish and Mexican holding created different reform needs. Mexican Governor Manuel Armijo in 1841 awarded a grant of land, twenty-two square leagues in size, to Carlos Beaubien, an influential French-Canadian from Taos, and Guadalupe Miranda, Armijo's collector of customs. Following Beaubien's death in 1864, Lucien Bonaparte Maxwell, Beaubien's son-in-law, purchased the grant which became known as the Maxwell Grant. In 1870, Maxwell sold his grant to a group of land speculators (commonly called "land-grabbers" in the Territory of New Mexico). Included among the purchasers were Stephen B. Elkins, a former territorial delegate who later became a prominent United States senator from West Virginia, and Thomas B. Catron, who was the most powerful political figure during New Mexico's long territorial period. Eventually the grant was sold to some English buyers. As a part of this transaction, a group of Dutch financiers from Amsterdam agreed to a request by the new English owners to handle the mortgage of the ambitious land company.

Moreover, nearly every time the grant changed hands, it became larger. It had started as a tract of land 22 square leagues in size, or 97,000 acres; but by the time it became a Dutch concern, the Maxwell

Company claimed almost 2 million acres of valuable grazing and farming land in northeastern New Mexico and southern Colorado.[17] As a land monopoly of colossal size that was foreign-owned, it, like similar holdings, became the bane of western Populism.

The Colfax County Farmers' Alliance was not the first organized effort to resist the claims of the Maxwell Company. Miners in the crowded gold camp of Elizabethtown, which the Maxwell owners insisted was located on their grant, were disdainful of, if not defiant toward, the grant owners. Recently arrived stockmen, primarily from Texas, either ignored the Maxwell's claims or organized noisy squatters' clubs to oppose them in places like Cimarron and Raton. Violence was triggered in the so-called Colfax County War after a Methodist minister F. J. Tolby was murdered allegedly because he opposed the Maxwell Company.[18] Anglos in the Colfax Alliance even made common cause with poor Hispanos, toward whom they had shown scant sympathy before, because of the Maxwell threat. The *Raton Weekly Independent*, which often spoke for the Alliance, claimed in its February 16 and 23 issues of 1889 that territorial authorities were working against these "very poor" native New Mexicans to tighten the "iron band of that mighty land monopoly which is surely grinding their bones into flour that it may make its bread." In the end, however, the claims of the Maxwell Company were upheld by the Supreme Court in a controversial 1887 decision.

What especially upset Alliance members in Colfax County were the obvious ties between the Maxwell Company and a powerful political clique known as the Santa Fe Ring. For instance, the alleged head of this ring was "Tom" Catron, who at one time was part owner of the Maxwell Grant. According to one of its severest critics Cleveland-appointed Governor Edmund G. Ross, the Santa Fe Ring, also known as the Land Grant Ring, was one of a number of groups of scheming speculators operating in the territory. These included, to quote Ross, "Cattle Rings, Public Land Stealing Rings, Mining Rings, Treasury Rings and Rings of almost every description." The Santa Fe Ring was the "central head" for all of them, and the obsession of its members was land speculation on an unheard-of scale.[19] Catron provides the best example of successful land-grabbing. Throughout his long and complicated business career, he acquired a princely domain in New Mexico. He became part owner of the Mora Grant, south of the disputed Maxwell one, and sole owner of the immense 593,000-acre Tierra Amarilla Grant in northern New Mexico. By 1883, after he had been in the territory for fewer than twenty years, he was reputed to be one of the largest landowners in the entire nation.[20]

The Territory of New Mexico was part of what Professor Kenneth N. Owens has designated as the "no-party" system because both major parties were able to collaborate to such an extent that real partisanship was kept to an absolute minimum.[21] Consequently, there were prominent Democrats involved in the Santa Fe Ring as well as leading Republicans. For example, Democrat William T. Thornton, Cleveland's appointee as governor during the president's second term, and Antonio Joseph, the five-term Democratic territorial delegate, were both accused of being ring members and land-grabbers. The inordinate influence of the ring gave them opportunities for speculation and monopoly unrivaled along the Front Range.

The legality of the numerous Spanish and Mexican land grants became even more complicated as a result of the maneuverings of the Santa Fe Ring. The land-grant question, confused from the beginning, eventually became so perplexing that the federal government had to create the Court of Private Land Claims in 1891 to adjudicate the countless disputes over land titles. Although conflicting claims to 33 million acres of land in New Mexico were processed during the court's thirteen years of life, its decisions were even more controversial than the ones that usually result from prolonged litigation.[22] For one thing, Hispanos, whose land holdings were supposed to be guaranteed under the Treaty of Guadalupe Hidalgo, were at a decided disadvantage in proving their claims of ownership in an American law court. Often their only recourse was to hire a shrewd Anglo lawyer, who often took land as his fee and became a large landowner in his own right—Catron is a perfect example in this regard. Cultural confrontations by necessity, then, became an integral part of the overall settlement of New Mexico's land-grant question.

The controversy over the Las Vegas Community Grant was particularly significant. It involved land-grabbing and cultural confrontation on such a scale that it prepared the way for the territory's first Populist party. This grant differed from the Maxwell Grant in at least one important respect: it was a communal holding. Located in San Miguel County, the 500,000-acre grant traced its historical origins as far back as 1821, when Louis Maria Cabeza de Baca received the grant from the Mexican government. Because Cabeza de Baca failed to establish a permanent settlement, the Mexican government transferred the grant to thirty-one petitioners and their families in 1835. By 1841, more families had moved on the grant, which had become an enormous unfenced communal holding ajacent to Las Vegas, one of the fastest growing native settlements in the territory.[23]

Trouble for the inhabitants of this attractive grazing and agricultural area, where much of the land was cooperatively utilized, did not begin until increasing numbers of Anglo cattlemen arrived in San Miguel after the conquest. Many of these newcomers insisted on buying or taking land on the grant, which they believed was part of the public domain. Then they would fence their claims to separate their stock from the flocks of sheep tended by the descendents of the original grantees. Of course, the right of these people to sell their land was questionable; the Las Vegas Grant was, after all, a community one. Even if these purchases were legal, however, there was the controversial practice by Anglo cattlemen of stretching their land claims beyond the original boundaries.

The Noble and Holy Order of the Knights of Labor, which during the 1880s had established three active assemblies in East Las Vegas, West Las Vegas, and Tecolote, was the group most aware of these Anglo malpractices.[24] In 1890, three local Knights reported to Terence V. Powderly, the organization's national leader, that many Anglos had constructed fences on the public domain "without the shadow of a title," while those who did purchase land from native inhabitants more often than not "fenced in ten times as much as they bought."[25] The Knights of Labor in San Miguel were so sympathetic to the plight of the native grantees that they formed a support group as early as 1887 called the Las Vegas Community Grant Association.

The grantees on the Las Vegas tract did not have to depend on outside help. They had their own champion—a resourceful Hispano named Juan Jose Herrera. Herrera, a native New Mexican who had lived in San Miguel and Santa Fe counties, was a remarkable man. In 1866, he had abruptly left the territory presumably because of some scandal involving a woman. For approximately twenty years, he lived in Colorado, Wyoming, and Utah before he returned to New Mexico in 1886 or 1887 and settled on the Las Vegas Grant.[26] Shortly after his return, he had a serious altercation with an Anglo neighbor who had insisted on fencing off so much land that there was little room left for others to graze their stock. In anger, Herrera seized his greedy neighbor and shoved him into a rain barrel.[27] The strong-willed Hispano leader, however, was not content just to fight his own battle; he organized as many of his neighbors as possible into a band of night riders called *las Gorras Blancas* or the White Caps. Wearing masks to avoid detection, Herrera's new followers, themselves desperate victims of the Anglo enclosure movement, began to cut down fences and burn barns and haystacks.[28] Operating mostly at night, they managed to destroy a great many of the hated fences in a short time, but their actions aroused great opposition. Territorial Governor Bradford Prince even went so far as to ask the federal government to send troops to patrol the area between Las Vegas and Lamy, where White Cap raids had been especially serious.[29]

The infiltration of the Knights of Labor by White Caps particularly distressed Governor Prince. Herrera, having been involved in Knight activity while living in Colorado or Utah, became a district organizer for the San Miguel Knights in 1888.[30] The leader of the Colorado Knights was Joseph R. Buchanan, one of the most militant Knights in the country. Buchanan's influence may have accounted for some of Herrera's aggressiveness (or at least, for some of the tough tactics that Herrera presumably introduced to the local labor movement).[31] For instance, on April 3, 1890, the *Gorras* put posters setting the rates that workers should charge for cutting and hauling railroad ties in public places throughout Las Vegas. During the previous month, a gathering of armed men chopped in half approximately 9,000 ties which belonged to the Santa Fe Railway. Angry railroad officials retaliated by declaring on July 23 that they would no longer purchase railroad ties in the Las Vegas area—a decision that would cost the economy of San Miguel an estimated $100,000 a year.[32] These defiant tactics made the White Caps as controversial among some of the laborers in the county as they were among most Anglo ranchers.

The controversy in San Miguel County became political in nature as early as 1888. In that year, F. A. Blake, editor of the Las Vegas *News*, and a group of Knights organized a new party. Calling it the People's party to dramatize their commitment to the common man, the new party leaders assumed an idealistic stance similar to the one taken by their union: "principles first and men second." They promised that their new party would support public officials responsible to the "whole people" and that it would wage a determined fight against bossism, the long-time bane of San Miguel politics. Although the infant party polled only 140 votes in 1888, the accumulating "white-cap troubles" provided the Knights of Labor with an unprecedented opportunity to grow. Prior to the 1890 election, this active union organized "a large minority, if not a majority," of San Miguel voters into assemblies.[33] Moreover, in the fall of 1890, Herrera and some of his *Gorras* joined the new People's party.

By 1890, many territorial citizens were ready for political action, although it was not necessarily within the framework of a new political organization. The alleged cattle monopoly which threatened small grazers in the eastern part of the territory spurred this readiness. Other important reasons existed, too. The Maxwell Company jeopardized the claims of both the miners in the Sangre de Cristos and the small farmers and grazers east of that range. There were still millions of acres of New Mexico land in dispute. The legal questions surrounding the issue of land possession under the Treaty of Guadalupe Hidalgo only exacerbated the territory's cultural conflict. Shrewd Anglo lawyers in the Santa Fe Ring successfully exploited all the legal procedures involved in proving title to Spanish and Mexican land grants. On the other side of the territory, the production of silver was in a five-year decline, which adversely influenced the economic development in these silver-producing counties. Most disconcerting of all, however, was the aggressive nature of the enclosure movement in San Miguel County which affected the lives of scores of small grazers and farmers on the Las Vegas Grant.

Nevertheless, action to cope with these developments was already taking shape. Chapters of the Southern Alliance in Lincoln, Dona Ana, and Colfax counties actively opposed the efforts of big cattlemen to monopolize the range. Squatters clubs in Colfax County had resisted the determined owners of the Maxwell Company. A new native organization the White Caps had confronted Anglo ranchers on the Las Vegas Community Grant by destroying the fences which the ranchers had erected. And the Knights of Labor, sympathetic to the plight of the Las Vegas grantees, had formed a new political party in 1888 which many *Gorras,* including Herrera, elected to join in 1890.

In many respects the future of protest in New Mexico depended upon political activities in San Miguel County and the role of the Democratic party in the territory. In San Miguel, the newly organized People's party could acquire great importance. Because the county had the largest population in the territory, it could certainly become a weather vane for the future political direction of the territory. The Democratic party, which had already shown considerable sympathy toward the views of the vulnerable grazers and farmers, was also in a crucial position. It could capitalize on the antimonopoly views of ordinary New Mexicans. If, however, the party faltered in dealing with the widespread insecurities that were so evident by 1890, it would allow the territory's first Populist party to expand its activities beyond the boundaries of San Miguel and become a major force in New Mexico politics.

Eight

New Mexico Populism

Populism achieved its place in New Mexico politics as a primarily local movement. From the beginning, its greatest strength was on the county rather than the territorial level. The People's party made no effort to win control of a territorial-wide office because most major territorial positions, including the governorship, were appointive, and the occupants of these offices almost invariably reflected the views of the ruling party in Washington. Nevertheless, the party exercised its influence in the races for the territorial legislature and in the contests for county office. Moreover, while Populism would never have the same kind of impact in New Mexico that it had in Colorado or Montana, it did enjoy more grass roots support than in Wyoming. Also, it was active in a highly significant way in one or more counties or regions of the territory in the elections from 1890 through 1898—a fairly long tenure for such a transitory political movement.

San Miguel County, as has been argued, was a logical birthplace for territorial Populism. The distress caused by the aggressive enclosure movement on the Las Vegas Grant was more acute here than elsewhere because the movement was concentrated over a shorter period of time. (The controversy over the Maxwell Grant, on the other hand, smoldered for years; and as a consequence, its impact was probably less intense.) Also, the territorialwide publicity made the county a hot spot, a breeding ground for the kind of discontent that caused protest. Indeed, White Capism overshadowed another condition that usually generates protest: chaotic political factionalism. San Miguel was one of the most politically unstable counties in New Mexico, despite the one-party rule that had prevailed there for years. The animosity generated by its two rival leaders Eugenio Romero, the longtime party *jefe*, and Romero's upstart brother-in-law Sheriff Lorenzo Lopez divided the dominant Republican party.[1] Because the Democratic party was weak, the shaky political situation in this county was almost designed for the emergence of a new party.

On the eve of the 1890 campaign, Democrat Felix Martinez, a San Miguel politician, saw the People's party, organized by Blake and his associates, as a likely vehicle for the acquisition of political power. Although the Republican party was torn by the Romero-Lopez feud, his own party was not strong enough to fill the resulting void. Martinez had political experience—he had just completed a term in the territorial House of Representatives—and he had extraordinary political skills. Therefore, he was able, much to Blake's disgust, to get himself elected chairman of the party's convention and to win appointment to its exclusive executive committee.

Two Republicans also appreciated the opportunities that the new People's party provided. One was Sheriff Lopez himself, who, no doubt, was frustrated by his struggle with Romero. The other was Theodore B. Mills, who would one day become the most important leader of the territorial Populist movement. Mills, like Martinez, had political experiences that would make him valuable to the new party. He had served one term in the Kansas state legislature before coming to New Mexico in 1878 and one in the territorial house six years after his arrival. Mills also gained quick recognition; he was elected chairman of the party's key coordinating committee.[2]

An even more surprising recruit to the San Miguel People's party was Pablo Herrera, brother of Juan Jose, the White Cap leader. Pablo's decision to join was not an individual one because Juan Jose had also sought membership; as a matter of fact, Juan Jose was elected county probate judge on the People's ticket two years later.[3] The addition of the Herrera brothers to the ranks of the new party meant only one thing: the *Gorras* had switched from active resistance to politics as a way of dealing with the enclosure threat. The addition of the Herrera brothers also gave the People's party a controversial image since both Republicans and Democrats could now accuse that party of being in league with the White Caps.

The party convention of the San Miguel Populists was a lively affair.

The party nominated Mills, along with another Populist, to represent the county in the territorial council. (San Miguel was entitled to two seats in that body.) To the consternation of many, it also nominated Pablo Herrera with three other members to the county's important four-seat delegation to the territorial house of representatives.[4] Blake and the Knights who founded the fledgling party, however, were most concerned because ex-Democrat Felix Martinez seemed to be gaining the most influence in the new political organization.

The two older parties were alarmed by the political potential of the San Miguel People's party. They were most distressed because some of their prominent members had joined the new party, but they had to concern themselves with control of the entire territory as well as its most populous county. Consequently, both parties dealt with a variety of issues when they convened their territorial conventions during the early autumn of 1890. Republicans, who gathered in September, were clearly on the defensive. They had to counter the charge that the state constitution they had drafted the previous year was a land-grabbers' document. One Democratic newspaper the *Santa Fe Sun* later made an estimate that fourteen of the Republican leaders at the convention had amassed, through speculation or other means, a total of 9,457,166 acres in individual landholdings.[5] The Republicans also had to defend the Sherman Silver Purchase Act since that measure had not stopped the price decline of the territory's important silver product. The only positive development the Republicans could boast about was President Harrison's support of the Court of Private Land Claims. The G.O.P. delegates thanked the president in advance because he would not be able to sign the bill creating the court until March of the following year.

Democrats, who met in Silver City, not only lambasted the Constitution of 1889 as a land-grabbers' one, but also argued that the 1 percent limit on state taxes in the document was designed to shift the tax burden to the less able. (The maligned constitution, as a matter of fact, was defeated in a referendum in October, not necessarily because of Democratic opposition but because of the suspicions of the Roman Catholic Church toward it. The Church was apprehensive about the proposed tax-supported school system envisioned in the document.) The Democrats also took a strong stand on silver at their gathering; in 1890, even before the allegedly silver-obsessed Populists organized on a territorialwide basis, they came out squarely for free coinage.[6] The Democratic gathering at Silver City also addressed issues relating to the failing cattle industry. By 1889, cattle prices had dropped to only seven or eight dollars a head.[7] Many Anglo stock growers were distressed by this price decline, along with alleged cattle and land monopolies on the eastern side of the territory. Democrats took full advantage of the chaos; after all, small stock grazers as well as farmers were part of the party's natural constituency because the healthier native-dominated sheep-raising industry had traditionally been Republican.

The Democrats at Silver City also renominated Antonio Joseph as their candidate for territorial delegate. He faced a determined challenge from the Republican nominee, Mariano S. Otero, a successful Bernalillo businessman and banker. Joseph received his share of abuse during the subsequent campaign since the territorial Knights of Labor endorsed his candidacy. Since the *Gorras* had infiltrated this controversial labor organization, its support made Joseph vulnerable to the increasingly familiar charge of White Capism.[8]

Aggressive Republican attacks on Joseph in 1890, however, were to no avail. He won by a vote of 17,206 to 15,142, carrying twelve of the territory's sixteen counties. He won majorities in the embattled cattle counties of Colfax, Lincoln and Chaves (which had recently been severed from Lincoln). He carried the three major silver-producing counties of Grant, Sierra, and Socorro. His 1,478-vote margin of victory in San Miguel County gave him a major boost toward his 2,000-vote territorial edge.[9] Other Democratic candidates also did well. The party swept all the offices in Lincoln County, one of the cradles of the territorial Alliance. Two Republican representatives were replaced by Democratic ones in Santa Fe County. Democrats won the lone seat in the territorial house from San Juan County, a growing agricultural county in northwest New Mexico. Because of these Democratic successes, the party emerged with a two-vote majority in the house and elected William Burns from the silver county of Socorro to the speaker's post. It also narrowed the Republican margin in the council to four votes.[10]

The election results in San Miguel were particularly exciting: the People's party had won all the county's seats in the legislature and had contributed substantially to Joseph's victory. The question now arose as to the role these third party legislators would play in the Twenty-ninth Territorial Assembly scheduled to convene in Santa Fe on December 29, 1890. There were only seven Republicans and three Democrats elected to the territorial council. The two seats held by the newly elected San Miguel Populists, consequently, were important, but not decisive. In the house, on the other hand, the four Populists from the county held the balance of power; the Republican margin there was a mere eleven-to-nine. The new party's response to its potential role of power broker was of keen political interest.

In the council, Mills proved to be in harmony with the trend toward reform instituted by the young and still-to-be-coordinated third party movement in the West. On the sixth day of the session, he introduced Council Bill No. 23, "An Act to regulate transportation of freights by railroad corporations and to prevent their pooling of their earnings." The bill was sent to the committee on railroads, where it died quietly. He also introduced a memorial from the Commercial Club of Las Vegas urging protection for the Las Vegas Community Grant.[11] This effort to deal with the enclosure threat in his county, however, was premature. The territorial legislature did not take substantial steps to protect the original native grantees until the late 1890s when it incorporated the Las Vegas Grant. The final fate of the grantees, however, had to await the landmark decision of the Court of Private Land Claims in 1903, which gave the town of Las Vegas a patent for the ownership of and control over the disputed grant.[12]

Other reform endeavors met with similar results. The Republicans, led by the conservative Catron, used their numerical advantage in the council to stymie any legislation that even mildly challenged the laissez-faire philosophy prevalent in the territory. They defeated a bill calling for the confirmation of community grants, for instance. The only reform that was even partially successful was an educational bill supported by Mills. It got as far as it did only because the San Miguel Populist coordinated his efforts with a reform-minded young Republican from Silver City named Joseph A. Ancheta and with Governor Prince, who was chagrined by the fact that not one public school in Santa Fe had been opened during the previous year.[13] Mills's limited success in school reform, however, was important. It was consistent with the Populist goal of equal opportunity, educational or otherwise, and it gave the infant People's party some positive publicity to counteract its controversial association with the White Caps.

The performance of the four San Miguel Populists in the lower house, however, was a big disappointment. According to the party's founder F. A. Blake, the wily Martinez induced the four to participate in the Democratic caucuses, thus causing them not to "act as a party independent of both the old ones in the house of representatives." By their actions, they had lost a matchless opportunity, Blake claimed, to influence the course of legislation.[14]

By the year 1892, Populism was a national political movement. It showed exceptional vibrance in Colorado and exercised a noteworthy influence in Montana and Wyoming. In New Mexico, however, it expanded into only one other county Dona Ana. Even in San Miguel, the character of the party had undergone a dramatic change. Martinez deftly used his influence in 1892 to convince the Populists to fuse with the Democrats to the decided advantage of the latter. The jubilant *Albuquerque Democrat* recognized the one-sided nature of this arrangement when it boasted that eleven of the sixteen places on the joint ticket were given to Democrats.[15] More important, the displacement of Mills after his one energetic term on the council and the denial of a council seat to Blake at the People's nominating convention resulted from this fusion. Moreover, if there were any doubt as to who controlled the party, it was convincingly dispelled when Martinez was easily nominated as a fusion candidate for one of the county's two seats in the upper house. Blake undoubtedly realized that he had been displaced as a party leader when he bolted the convention, taking his closest allies with him.[16]

As far as territorial politics were concerned, the parties largely neutralized the silver issue in 1892. The domineering Catron, the Republican nominee for territorial delegate that year, gained credence with the silver mining interests of the territory by his early support of James G. Blaine for the presidency. Although Blaine was probably never a free-coinage advocate, it was widely believed in G.O.P. circles that he was much friendlier toward bimetallism than President Harrison. "Blaine and Free Coinage," consequently, became a popular slogan by June of 1892 in the movement to draft the Plumed Knight, which was headed by Colorado senators Teller and Woolcott.[17] Although Catron switched his allegiance from Blaine to Harrison at the Republican territorial convention, he had already made a favorable impression. The Catron-controlled delegates elected at the convention, therefore, were able to cast their ballots for the victorious Harrison at the Republican national convention without widespread criticism. As for territorial Democrats, the strong impression that they had made by endorsing free silver in 1890 was largely negated when their national party again nominated the outspoken gold bug Grover Cleveland.

Catron's advantage on the silver question was only a temporary one, however, as he soon learned that his biggest liability in the coming campaign was himself. Dominating Republican politics in the territory for a quarter of a century had exacted its price. Some of his party's most dedicated people resented his power, wealth, and aggressiveness. Prince, for example, once remarked that Catron was the "most arbitrary and dictatorial of men." Of course, Catron and Prince were rivals, but the governor's sentiments were not uncommon. As for Democrats and Populists, they could easily unite to stop Catron, whose association with land-grabbing and ring politics had already made him the antithesis of all they represented.[18] Although Joseph's image had been somewhat tarnished by his inability to win statehood for New Mexico, he benefited from the anti-Catron feeling and won re-election by a vote of 15,799 to 15,220. His showing was again strong in the stock-raising counties on the east side, where anti-monopoly sentiment had been strong since the 1880s; however, he was unable to carry the silver counties he had won two years earlier.[19] As for San Miguel County, the fusion ticket again triumphed, although this time it was more Democratic than Populist in orientation.

Shortly after the election of 1892, the country was overwhelmed by the worst depression to date. The whole territory was affected by the business failures, low farm prices, and high unemployment caused by the Panic of 1893. Cleveland's decision to call for the repeal of the Sherman Silver Purchase Act also adversely affected her silver mines. Local Populists, on the other hand, were unwilling to blame the depression solely on the effects of the Sherman Act. They insisted that the policies of both major parties were the cause of the panic and that innocent people were its main victims. The real sufferers, insisted the populistic San Juan Times of Farmington, were the common folk, who do not "understand the working of political machines."[20]

Throughout the West at this time, Populist organizations took independent political action in order to exploit the distress caused by the panic. New Mexico was no exception; however, the party organization in San Miguel was no longer the best vehicle in the movement's quest for power. Martinez had almost completely changed that party's original character and alienated its original leaders. Following the 1892 election, he further outraged territorial Populists when he went to Washington with a delegation of Democrats to win appointment as United States marshal. Failure to gain that position only made him more determined to make the People's party his instrument for the acquisition of political power preferment. Indeed, he not only reorganized the party, but also renamed it, calling it the Union party.[21] The Republican Las Vegas Daily Optic described Martinez's new creation as "simply the democratic party with a strong wing of the republican party attached to it"—a reference to the fact that a group of wayward Republicans called Independents had been attracted to Martinez's newest organization. As for what remained of San Miguel Populism, the Optic showed nothing but disdain:

> Its principles, objects, and aims have been allowed to fall to the ground, without even the . . . cloak of name to cover them. Bitter personal feeling dispersed this weak representative of the national populist party, in this county, like a fog before the noonday sun.[22]

By 1894, however, New Mexico Populism was changing. It was becoming a territorialwide movement. During the late summer, its center of power shifted away from San Miguel to the territory's second most populated county Bernalillo. Bernalillo, at the time, extended all the way to the Arizona border; the transfer of Populist strength to the immense county marked a decided shift of the movement westward. Mills's departure from San Miguel in 1893 to work a mining claim at Cochiti, then part of Bernalillo County, caused the county's new preeminence.[23] Mills had some formidable rivals for party leadership in a group of Albuquerque merchants, of whom M. P. Stamm, a prominent wholesale produce merchant, and Thomas F. Keleher, a businessman in the wool and hides trade, were among the most prominent.[24] Thus, not only had the Populist movement shifted westward, but it also had taken on a more urban coloring.

San Juan County in the northwest corner of the territory was another new area of Populist strength. Because of its agricultural diversity, this county produced a strongly agrarian Populist organization more like those found in less arid regions of the country, such as the wheat-raising Midwest or the cotton-producing South. The key to this unusual variation in crop production in San Juan was irrigation. The waters of the San Juan, Animas, and La Plata rivers had the potential to irrigate one million acres, according to enthusiastic local boosters. By 1892, approximately 50,000 fruit trees were in production, and the land in the county was on the verge of yielding twenty to forty bushels of wheat per acre. The busy silver camps of western Colorado had been a fine market for its products. The decline in silver prices and its adverse effects on Colorado mining, however, soon changed this once bright picture. The San Juan Populists were ready to respond promptly to the downturn. On August 18, 1894, the county committee of the new party met at Aztec to set the dates for the party's primaries and county conventions. The new political organization was also assured of maximum publicity because Fred E. Holt, editor of the San Juan Times and an avowed Populist, was quick to promote the activities of the infant party.[25]

September was the decisive month as far as the new territorial movement was concerned. During the first week, Populists from Gallup held an "enthusiastic" organizational meeting which included a series of six lectures on the virtues of the Single Tax. In the meantime, inflamed miners from the silver county of Grant were ready to join in the organization of a new party with their brethren from the silver county of Sierra. "The Populists of Grant county are on the warpath, and the democrats of that area are disrupted," chortled the Republican Albuquerque Evening Citizen in a mid-September edition.[26] On September 12, the Bernalillo Populists held their organizational meeting in Albuquerque and selected members to a county central committee, of which Stamm was the most important member. On the same day, a territorial Populist convention began with a mass meeting addressed by Lafe Pence, one of the two Populist congressmen from Colorado. Albuquerque was selected as the place for both gatherings because the territorial fair was being held at the same time and this was supposed to ensure a good attendance. Reduced railroad fares attracted both farmers and political enthusiasts. Fred Holt, the San Juan editor, may have been as exuberant about displaying the fine apples raised in his county as he was about being a Populist delegate.[27]

When the Populists began the serious business of drafting a platform and nominating a territorial delegate on September 13, delegates from almost every county were present. Two characteristics about the gathering are worth special mention. One was its composition, which was largely Anglo. The territory's newest party was not necessarily hostile to or indifferent toward the majority Hispanos, but there were close and long-standing alliances between the native population and the two older parties, with the Republicans being particularly successful in this regard. The other characteristic was the urban makeup of most of the delegates of this essentially agrarian movement, a feature quite common to the Populist leadership structure elsewhere.

Mills had issued the call for this territorial gathering, which drew heavily upon the 1892 Omaha platform and earlier Populist declarations. The delegates demonstrated their harmony with the call by repeating many of its items in the platform they drafted. For instance, in response to the controversial federal intervention in the Pullman strike, Mills suggested that the convention condemn military interference with civil authorities in time of peace; the delegates responded affirmatively with a forceful resolution. Moving in the opposite direction from Wyoming and Montana Populists, Mills called for state or territorial rather than federal control of irrigation projects; the convention agreed. This third party gathering, in essence, adopted the 1892 Omaha platform and endorsed its preamble with one important modification. Instead of insisting upon "equal rights and equal privileges securely established for all men and women in this country," the territorial convention called for equality for "*all* living in this country." The omission of the word "women," which was surprising when one considers the remarkable record in behalf of woman suffrage in such states of the Mountain West as Wyoming and Colorado, was due to the new party's pragmatism. Populists were sensitive to the strong convictions of native New Mexicans, many of whom had traditionally subordinated women in their culture.

After the Populists had embraced most of the principles and political stands of their national party, they passed ten separate resolutions, including the ones previously discussed dealing with the Pullman strike and western irrigation. Among the ones concerned with national issues was a demand that the United States begin negotiations with the Latin American republics and other bimetallic nations for a reciprocal exchange of products. Another called for a postal savings system. A third insisted upon a national currency "safe, sound, and flexible, issued by the general government only" with the stipulation that "no money [should] be issued that is not a full legal tender for every debt." As for the local issues that they approved, the delegates' call for immediate admission of New Mexico to statehood was the most compelling. In fact, most resolutions of a local nature were clearly critical of the territorial system. For example, the delegates demanded a popular referendum for all laws passed by the territorial legislature, the direct election of those territorial officials not appointed, and the direct deposit of fees into the "public treasury" so that public monies collected in the territory could not stray elsewhere. Yet as radical as some of these proposed governmental and fiscal reforms were, the delegates stopped short of endorsing Henry George's much-discussed Single-Tax doctrine.[28]

Curiously enough, free coinage, a reform that was first advocated unequivocally by territorial Democrats in 1890, did not merit a separate resolution. At least a segment of the territorial press was quick to take notice. The Republican Las Vegas Daily Optic, one of New Mexico's leading newspapers, chided the Albuquerque Populist convention for not having "one word to say about free coinage, the most important principle the Populists of Colorado have to work on." It coupled its criticism with a warning: "Dodging the silver question, Col. T.M.B. [Mills], will not aid you among the miners and laboring classes."[29] Such advice, of course, was not needed. New Mexico Populists by 1894 were as aware of the growing importance of silver as their Republican and Democratic counterparts. Nonetheless, the omission of any special reference significantly weakens the case of those historians who dismiss Mountain Populism as simply a case of silverism. Indeed, if the platform approved by New Mexico Populists in 1894 was at all reflective of their true convictions, then the newly organized territorial party was definitely a multi-issue one.

After the party had made its position on issues a matter of public record, it was ready to nominate a candidate for territorial delegate. The fact that the balloting did not begin until midnight of September 13 may account for the small number of delegates present. Mills and Stamm were the two major contenders. On the surface, it would appear that Stamm had the advantage because of a strong and loyal home delegation behind him. Mills, however, had attracted wide and favorable attention while serving in the territorial council during the Twenty-ninth Assembly. As a result, Populists outside of Bernalillo, such as Holt from San Juan County, were able to give the transplanted San Miguel leader an eight-to-five margin of victory.[30]

When the Democrats gathered in Las Vegas for their convention on September 17, they treated free silver as the "foremost" issue of the 1894 campaign. Joseph, completing his fifth term as territorial delegate, was renominated over the opposition of idealistic Albuquerque lawyer Harvey B. Fergusson. Republicans, who met later that week in Socorro, were again able to neutralize the effectiveness of the silver issue by castigating Grover Cleveland for his role in bringing about the repeal of the Sherman Silver Purchase Act. Moreover, they exploited the disappointment over Joseph's ten-year failure to win statehood; this strategy worked to the decided advantage of Catron, who was again nominated for delegate. The Republicans emphasized the traditional tariff issue. They advocated wool protection to appeal to native New Mexicans involved in sheep-raising; lead protection, to appeal to those New Mexicans involved in mining.[31]

During the 1894 campaign, the Democrats were concerned that Mills would detract from Joseph's natural support, while the Republicans were delighted with the situation. The Republican Socorro *Chieftan* declared that the Populists were "cutting the bottom out of the Democratic party in Lincoln county." A supporter in Grant County wrote to an elated Catron that 140 Populists—116 of whom were "pronounced democrats"—were ready to vote for Mills. Another Catron supporter told the persistent Republican that the Populists in Dona Ana County were primarily from the Democratic party "4 Dem[.] to 1 Rep [.]. . . ."[32] Mills, himself, in an optimistic interview with the *Santa Fe New Mexican* toward the end of the campaign, predicted that he could carry his old home county of San Miguel, the silver-rich counties of Grant and Socorro, the cattle counties of Lincoln and Colfax, and the agricultural county of San Juan—five of these six counties Joseph had carried in 1892.[33] There was speculation that Mills intended his candidacy to aid the conservative Catron. Two years later, he was still attempting to refute a rumor that had circulated throughout the territory since 1894 that he had received $5,000 from Catron to make the race.[34] Such allegations against Populists in this region were not unheard of. They were also made in Wyoming in 1896. There is no clear-cut evidence, however, that Mills was subsidized like the middle-of-the-road Populists of Wyoming were.[35] Nevertheless, Catron, to Mills's chagrin, never contradicted this damning allegation.

Since he was not a poor man and had a good legislative record, Mills seems above the charge of bribe-taking; however, it is difficult to deny that rank opportunism permeated much of the movement at this time. Blake, for example, offered to help Catron during the 1894 campaign.[36] His surprising decision may have stemmed from his bitterness toward Martinez, who had gained control of the San Miguel People's party which Blake had founded. Because Catron was the *bête noire* of reformers in New Mexico, Blake's offer of support seems unconscionable. Of course, in the area of opportunistic manipulation, Catron had no peer. Exploiting the importance of his role in winning separate status for newly created Union County, Catron, through an emissary, brought about the unlikely fusion of the Republican and Populist parties in the county so as to deny Mills all but one Union vote.[37]

Catron, however, did not need the Populist votes of Union County to win in 1894. His 18,113 to 15,351 victory over Joseph was so decisive that Mills's 1,835-vote tally (a mere 3.77 percent of the total) had no real effect on the outcome.[38] The pet issues of both Democrats and Republicans apparently made little difference in this off-year election. For example, the strenuous efforts of some Populists, particularly of Stamm, to blame the Depression of 1893 on the two older parties had no perceivable impact. Even the allegations of land-grabbing and ring politics that were so lethal to Catron two years earlier had lost their clout. New or unexpected issues met the same fate. The charge that the G.O.P. was vulnerable to the entreaties of the American Protective Association had virtually no effect for Catron and his allies had close ties with the native New Mexicans.[39] (The fusion of the Populist and Republican parties in Union County was the handiwork of Populist leaders, all of whom were Hispanos attracted to Catron in much the same way that many native leaders were.[40]) Joseph, for his part, attributed Catron's victory to his own failure as a delegate to gain New Mexico's admission to the Union as a state.[41] Republicans, on the other hand, insisted that the party's favorable stand on the protective tariff was most crucial.

Mills must have been sorely disappointed by his own performance. Of the six counties he predicted he could win, he carried only one— "San Juan of the Populists," as some of the party's detractors called it.[42] The rural subscribers of the *San Juan Times* had evidently responded favorably to the journal's Midwestern brand of agrarian protest because Mills won the normally Democratic county. He polled 233 votes to Joseph's 225 and Catron's 165. The Populist candidate also did well in Sierra County. He placed second there and probably deprived third-place Joseph of a narrow victory. His showing in Grant, on the other hand, was not as impressive. It did, however, affect the final outcome: Joseph's triumph over Catron there was closer than expected. Mills also made a small but reasonable showing in two other Democratic counties he thought he would carry. In Lincoln, his performance did not deprive Joseph of victory, but in Colfax, it did. In his old home county of San Miguel, though, the 105 votes he tallied were negligible. The victorious Catron carried that county as he did populous Bernalillo, along with such Spanish-speaking counties of northern New Mexico as Sante Fe, Mora, and Valencia.[43]

New Mexico Populists were also disappointed by their dismal performance in the legislative races. They failed to win even one seat in the Thirty-first Legislative Assembly; however, they did do better in a few local contests. In San Juan County, for example, every candidate fielded by the fledgling party was victorious. In Bernalillo, Populist cooperation with the Democrats resulted in the county's only Demo-

cratic success, the election of a probate judge. Negative results, however, were far more common. In San Miguel, the birthplace of Populism, a re-created People's party lost badly to Felix Martinez's Union
party, which no longer made any pretense of being a Populist organization. As a matter of fact, before the campaign, Martinez was planning to attend the Democratic territorial convention in Las Cruces
with a delegation of his handpicked subordinates.[44]

Following the 1894 election, silver sentiment in the territory grew
rapidly; indeed, its impact was such that it eclipsed all other political
concerns by the mid-1890s. In fact, there were times when free coinage was the only issue politicians would forthrightly address. The
newly elected Thirty-first Legislative Assembly provides an excellent
example of this silver fixation. Seats in the lower house were almost
evenly divided, and during a struggle for control, embittered Republicans bolted the session. Despite the chaos caused by this bitter
schism, the rump Democratic-controlled session found time to pass a
strong and unequivocal joint memorial calling for free coinage.[45]

Even in San Juan County, where the most agrarian kind of Populism
existed, silver began to submerge all other issues. The *San Juan Times*,
for instance, began to spend less time attacking the inequality of wealth
in the United States and more time publicizing the virtues of bimetallism. Even though editor Fred Holt, in the spring of 1895, continued to
promote the San Juan Fruit Growers Association whose goal was to
allow farmers rather than commission men to determine prices, he was
devoting an increasing amount of space to free silver. By the fall of
1896, the mania for bimetallism had reached such a point that nervous
Republicans, vulnerable because of Catron's cautious stand on the
issue, called it the "silver craze" or "free silver craze," terms that were
rapidly becoming common in the territory.[46] As a member of the
Republican central committee of San Juan County put it in a letter to
Catron: farmers in San Juan County were "thoroughly imbued with the
silver craze, and to a fanatical extent."[47]

New Mexico Populists were among the chief beneficiaries of the
silver craze, despite the omission of a special resolution in their 1894
platform. The newness of their movement was certainly one advantage: the young party had no historical burdens to carry, such as the
demonitization of silver in 1873 or the repeal of the Sherman Silver
Purchase Act in 1893. Both older parties recognized the strategic
position of the People's party in 1896, which was evident by the
increasing frequency of this political question: would the Populists

again make a separate bid for power as they did in 1894 or would they fuse with one of the two major parties as their national organization had done with the Democrats in July? On the eve of the Populist territorial convention, the influential *Santa Fe New Mexican* considered the possibilities of another unilateral bid by the Populists. Acknowledging that the vote for Mills during the previous campaign was small, the Democratic journal hastened to remind its readers of how evenly divided the Republican and Democratic count was in 1894. It solemnly predicted that during the coming campaign the People's party could very well hold the "balance of power in no less than nine counties, or just half the whole number." The *New Mexican* also refused to discount confidential Populist boasts that they could double their vote in 1896.[48] The Republican *Daily Citizen* of Albuquerque, on the other hand, was more concerned about fusion. It particularly feared the kind of fusion arrangement that would involve Democrats and Populists and did all in its power to discourage it.

Fusion, of course, was the more likely of the two alternatives. It had already occurred on the national scene with the Populist endorsement of Bryan's candidacy and on the state level with a series of cooperative arrangements that were being forged in those areas of the country where Populism was still strong. It was almost a foregone conclusion that it would occur in New Mexico. There could be one important difference: fusion in the territory could very well involve Republicans and Populists. Mills's aggressive support of Prince for the office of territorial delegate made this option most feasible. Advocacy of the Prince candidacy was not an unreasonable stand for the Populist. Ex-Governor Prince was one of the foremost silver Republicans in the West; many compared him to Colorado's great silver champion Henry Moore Teller.[49] Mills, a mining speculator as well as a political activist, was no doubt attracted to Prince because of the ex-governor's exceptional prominence on the currency question. But, unfortunately, Prince was conservative on practically every other political issue. Consequently, Stamm, who was chairman of both the Populist territorial committee and the party's national committeeman, bitterly opposed Prince's selection, preferring instead the nomination of Democrat Harvey B. Fergusson.

When the Populists convened in Las Vegas for their territorial convention in late September, the debate was no longer whether the party should fuse or not, but with whom. Prince supporters were there, lobbying among the delegates and telling them that their candidate already had the support of "six or seven republican delegations" that would comprise the membership of the Republican territorial convention scheduled to gather in Las Vegas three days later. Fergusson supporters were present, too; they were conspicuous as well as numerous. As a result it took three ballots before the seventy-seven delegates—a much larger number than in 1894—chose Prince over Fergusson. Stamm responded to this defeat by bolting the convention and taking his supporters with him. One important cause of his precipitous action was a convention resolution which freed the conservative Prince from the obligation of supporting all the planks of the Populist platform.[50]

Prince's nomination as the fusion candidate seemed almost like the complete triumph of silverism in New Mexico; however, Prince's Republican supporters had not fully reckoned with the power of "Tom" Catron. The incumbent delegate defeated his silver rival at the party convention in Las Vegas. It would now be a three-way race; Catron would face both Prince and the Democratic standard-bearer, Harvey Fergusson, who was chosen a few days later. It would be an entirely different kind of campaign for Catron this time. Silver was not a neutral issue as before. More important, the Republican delegate had become identified with a controversial silver substitute that he had used to stave off a free coinage resolution at his party's territorial convention. According to the Catron-devised substitute, there would be an unlimited coinage of all silver produced in this country and a prohibitive tariff on imported foreign bullion. In addition, all currency under ten dollars would be abolished except for silver.[51] Catron's plan, in effect, treated silver like any other commodity in need of protection instead of regarding coinage of the white metal as a panacea for practically all the nation's ills. Such a lukewarm position on silver was unacceptable to most New Mexicans. Indeed, when Prince failed to disavow Catron's substitute by breaking with his party, the Populists replaced him as their candidate with Fergusson.[52]

When the campaigning began, Fergusson had an overwhelmingly important advantage: his stand on free coinage was unequivocal. He also was a very progressive politician which appealed to Populists of the Stamm variety. With the most important issues on his side and with his characteristically spirited style of campaigning, Fergusson exuded almost complete confidence. Consequently, it was no great surprise to the electorate when he reversed Catron's healthy margin of victory in 1894 by easily defeating the embattled incumbent by a vote of 18,948 to 17,017. His totals in such normally Democratic counties as Lincoln, Colfax, Grant, and Sierra were almost staggering in their decisiveness.[53] Equally impressive was his vote in San Juan, where a fusion ticket made up mostly of Populists captured all the county's seats in the territorial legislature. Catron, as usual, did his best in those parts of northern New Mexico where the Hispano vote was large. Nonetheless, he was edged out by Fergusson in both Santa Fe and Taos counties because of the aggressive prosilver editorials of the *Santa Fe New Mexican*. As far as local races were concerned, Populists were successful only when they fused—with one exception. The People's party fielded separate candidates for county office in San Juan and won every office but two.[54]

By 1898, the Populist movement in New Mexico was all but dead. The last gasp of the People's party, symbolically enough, was not in one of the silver-producing counties near the Arizona border nor in one of the cattle-grazing counties to the east, but in the agriculturally diversified county of San Juan. In 1898, the voters of San Juan defeated every Populists candidate for county office. It took a fusion ticket of determined Republicans and Democrats, however, to vanquish this last local representative of the national People's party.[55] Even so, reform was in trouble elsewhere in the territory. Although he continued to show strength in those counties where antimonopoly and silver were important issues, Fergusson lost the delegate's race in 1898 after serving only one term.[56] His defeat may have been the result of the Republicans winning most of the credit for a wool protection measure that he successfully sponsored.[57] It looked as though the traditional territorial issues of growth and development had resumed their former importance in New Mexico.

Dealing effectively with traditional territorial issues was not a hallmark of Populist politics in New Mexico. Indeed, the Populist performance on the territorial level was not impressive—Mills's unsuccessful effort to become territorial delegate is convincing proof of this assertion. It was on the county level where the Populists really excelled. Periods of conspicuous success for the party organizations of San Miguel and San Juan counties have already been chronicled. A county-by-county analysis further documents the fact that New Mexico Populism was primarily a local movement. The two graphs included here demonstrate this contention as well as provide additional insights. The first, entitled Populist Vote for Delegate, 1894, shows how the Populist vote was concentrated in certain counties and how widely

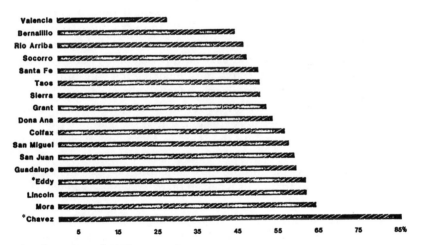

Populist Vote for Delegate, 1894

*Just for 1890 and 1892.

Democratic Vote for Delegate, 1888–92 (Average)

Statistical sources for both graphs: *The World Almanac, 1891*, 300; *The World Almanac and Encyclopedia, 1895*, 413; and *The World Almanac and Encyclopedia, 1899*, 455.

dispersed that vote was. The second graph, Democratic Vote for Delegate, 1888–92 (Average), not only shows Democratic strength in the territory, but when coupled with the first it also reveals that Populists and Democrats could run strong campaigns in the same counties.

The concentration of Populist votes in three parts of the territory is the most striking aspect of the first graph. Mills, the Populist standard-bearer, enjoyed his greatest support in the stock-grazing eastern plains, agricultural San Juan, and the silver-mining southwest. Of the six New Mexico counties where he polled more than 5 percent of the votes, three of them—Lincoln, Eddy, and Colfax—were on the territory's east side. Had Felix Martinez not manipulated the fortunes of the San Miguel's People's party in such a destructive way, the Populist showing in that eastern county might well have been the most impressive in the territory. As it turned out, San Juan County had the distinction of giving the Populist candidate his largest vote percentage. In fact, San Juan along with the two silver-mining counties of Grant and Sierra were the other three counties in New Mexico to provide Mills with his best percentages. The graph also reveals the scattered nature of the Populist vote, a likely result of inadequate organization. Populists made their best showing in the four corners of the sprawling territory: Lincoln and Eddy in the southeast, Colfax in the northeast, San Juan in the northwest, and Grant and Sierra in the southwest. The pattern would have been perfect if the Catron organization had not been so effective in influencing the vote in Union, a county created out of Colfax in time for the 1894 election. The conclusion should not be drawn, however, that Populist strength was practically nil in the territory's center. These six counties were immense, extending miles into the interior. More important, a graph such as this, which shows only percentages, can be deceptive. Although the party's vote in populous Bernalillo was less than 5 percent, the 210 votes that Mills received there were only 23 fewer than he received in San Juan.

Comparing the first and the second graphs, one can see a relationship between the Populist and Democratic vote. Of the six counties where Antonio Joseph averaged more than 55 percent of the vote for the delegate elections of 1888, 1890, and 1892, four of them (Lincoln, Eddy, San Juan, and Colfax) were among Mills's top six. In the remaining two (Grant and Sierra), Joseph won more than half the vote. Of the four counties he lost to the Republicans, Mills failed to garner 5 percent of the total vote in each. In two Republican counties Valencia and Rio Arriba in the Spanish-speaking north, Mills polled less than half a percentage point. As a matter of fact, these two counties along with Guadalupe were Mills's poorest ones.

Shown in the first graph is the local nature of New Mexico Populism, which may have been an unavoidable development for a third party in a place such as New Mexico. (Washington's control of territorial government did not create a flourishing environment for anti-establishment views.) The two graphs taken together show that Populists and Democrats were very largely drawing from the same vote. It seems apparent that Mills garnered many of his protest ballots from discontented Democrats. Democrats, however, could be a hindrance as well as a help. They could, and often did, siphon off the territory's potential Populist protest vote.

Nine

Populism in Idaho, Utah, Nevada, and Arizona
An Overview

Despite the geographical diversity found in the states stretched along the Front Range, the basic reforms advanced in each by Populists were unmistakably similar. Although silver assumed its preeminent role, especially with the advent of the presidential campaign of 1896, according to this study, antimonopolism was the most prominent of the commonly supported issues. Other issues were not ignored; the movement was unquestionably a multi-issue one before the Battle of the Standards. A brief assessment of Idaho, Utah, Nevada, and Arizona, the four commonwealths sandwiched between the Pacific Coastal and Front Range states, is important to see if the multiplicity of issues supported along the Front Range was characteristic of Populist organizations in the other states of the Mountain West. It should further clarify our understanding of western Populism as a distinct movement separate from its southern and midwestern counterparts.[1]

Idaho is a good place to start because the movement there was very much like the one in Montana. Not only do these two states share a marked geographical similarity, but they also have the same types of industry. Northern and central Idaho has mountains to match those of western Montana. Extraordinary mineral deposits exist; the lead-silver district centered in Shoshone County is the largest in the United States. The value of lead, zinc, and silver taken from the Coeur d'Alene Mountains has exceeded two billion dollars. There are also agricultural regions to compete with Montana's Gallatin and Bitterroot valleys. The cultivated lands along the Snake provide a prime example. An extensive network of canals had been built to utilize the waters of the great river as it wound its way across southern Idaho. Because of the aridity, farmers there could not have survived without this irrigation. With it they successfully raise potatoes, corn, barley, and wheat.[2]

Although mine employees became the most militant Populists, there was a strong agrarian element in Idaho (probably stronger than the one in Montana). Both the Grange and the Farmers' Alliance were active in the Gem state; by 1890, discontented elements of the Farmers' Alliance were actively involved in political protest. Rate reform was a big issue for the "have not" farmers of Idaho who were charged high freight rates by the railroads. Irrigation farmers, like their fellow farmers in Colorado, resented the high corporate-owned water companies' rates and were alarmed because eastern capitalists controlled the larger ditches.[3]

Absentee ownership was also a source of discontent in Idaho's mining region, a situation not unlike that found in Montana and Colorado. By 1892, the state's silver miners were responsible for an annual yield of eight million dollars, but the owners, who enjoyed the most benefits, lived in such "mining" capitals as London, New York, San Francisco, and Portland. Tension between absentee owners and employees erupted in 1892 when the Coeur d'Alene Miners' Union called a major strike in mineral-rich Shoshone County.[4] In 1893, the Western Federation of Miners, a union that transcended the boundaries of specific mining districts, was formed because of this strike. The state's People's party, which attracted farmers as well as mine employees, also arose out of this strike. The varied career of Ed Boyce, one of the founders of the Western Federation of Miners, is one example of the close relationship between Populist politics and mine unionism in Idaho. During the 1892 election, Boyce was elected to the state legislature as a Populist, even though he spent a portion of that year in jail because of strike activities.[5]

In 1892, Idaho Populists demonstrated the enthusiasm of any new organization's members. At two meetings in Boise, they made the party's customary endorsement of the Omaha planks and then went on to address some of the state's more contentious issues. They demanded repeal of Idaho's lien law, called for the arbitration of labor disputes (no doubt in response to delegates from the Knights of Labor), condemned the importation of cheap foreign labor such as that provided by the Chinese, and criticized the widespread monopolization of water rights. They also stressed the immensely popular free-coinage issue. As was common in the four Front Range states, however, Democrats and Republicans also gave silver a hearty endorsement.[6] The best Populist issue of 1892 was provided by Republican Governor Norman Willey when he declared martial law and sent six companies of the Idaho National Guard to join federal troops in breaking the strike called by the Coeur d'Alene Miners' Union.[7] This action, which had been condemned by Populists from the start, remained a burning issue throughout the campaign.[8]

Democrats wanted to fuse with Populists in 1892, but the confident People's party was unwilling to cooperate. Democrats, nevertheless, refrained from nominating presidential electors pledged to Cleveland, and agreed to support Populist ones instead. As a result, the Weaver-Field ticket carried the state. It was a success to match those achieved by Populists running for other national offices. For example, Henry Heitfield was victorious in winning a seat in the United States Senate; James Gunn and Thomas Glenn were elected to the national House of Representatives.[9] As in other states, the Populists' failure to fuse allowed the Republicans to win most of the state races. The Republican state ticket was elected and the party maintained control of both houses of the state legislature by comfortable margins, just as they had done in Montana in 1892.[10]

With the legislature firmly in Republican hands, Populist legislators met with the expected frustrations. Regulation of water rates had to await the creation of water districts in 1895. These districts, which were organized along the lines of school districts, did in time manage to win widespread approval.[11] On some issues, Populist lawmakers found many willing to cooperate. They were able to help pass a measure forbidding yellow-dog contracts. Of course, in their advocacy of free silver, there was no lack of support. They presented the electorate with an attractive voting record, although they lacked the strength to pass their own bills.[12]

The Idaho party enjoyed a relatively long and successful life. Because of the importance of silver, a Populist-Democratic fusion ticket won more than 78 percent of the vote cast in 1896. The Republican party was the expected loser, even though Senator Frederick T. Dubois broke with the parent party and bolted the Republican national convention with Teller after McKinley's nomination.[13] As the decade of the 1890s waned, Idaho Populists tended to identify more and more with militant unionism. In the bitter 1899 strike against the immense mining concern Bunker Hill and Sullivan, local Populist officials in the troubled Coeur d'Alene country were accused of outright complicity. When martial law was declared, hundreds of miners were herded into controversial "bullpens," while certain Populist officials, including a sheriff and two county commissioners, were incarcerated in jail cells.[14]

Populism in Utah to the south did not have the violent history of the Idaho movement, because even though the Utah party was probably the most labor-oriented one in the West, the state's political conservatism also made the party one of the smallest. Its modest size and urban complexion were not caused by any dearth of agricultural capabilities in the Beehive state—Mormon pioneering in irrigation was both a familiar and important western development. At the same time, the powerful Mormon influence did tend to discourage agrarian protest. Its theocratic framework in rural Utah society inclined farmers toward cooperation rather than competition. Such a social and economic setting also stifled the growth of the Farmers' Alliance, the Grange, and other farm organizations. Moreover, favorable agricultural conditions impeded significant reform efforts. The fact that Utah farmers produced primarily for a reliable local market made them less dependent than many other western states on the often disastrous fluctuations of an outside market.[15]

With few recruits from the countryside, Utah Populists sought support from urban areas such as Salt Lake City and Ogden, where the state's young and relatively limited industry was found. Starting later than elsewhere in the Mountain West, the People's party in Utah was not formally organized until 1893. In the fall of that year, a territorial party was organized in Salt Lake City. (Utah was not admitted to statehood until January 4, 1896.) From the beginning, a majority of its members were from laboring organizations. As expected, the omnipresent Knights of Labor was one of them. In 1889, there were twenty locals of the union in Salt Lake City alone, and although the Panic of 1893 brought about the demise of many unions, labor contined to be the foundation for the new party.[16]

The first efforts on the part of Utah Populists to seek power were feeble ones, causing one historian to characterize the movement as "listless and tame."[17] In 1895, for instance, the Populists nominated Henry W. Lawrence for governor and James Hogan for Congress. Lawrence, a strong advocate of the eight-hour day, was a Mormon excommunicate. His campaign highlighted an early friction between Mormonism and the new party.[18] Hogan, a national organizer for the American Railway Union, was a friend of Eugene V. Debs—no asset in a conservative state like Utah.[19] The poor showing of both candidates indicated that the voice of Populism in the new state would never be strong.

The spectacular growth of the silver crusade in the mid-1890s helped the new party. Utah was responsible for 13 percent of the nation's silver product, but the two major parties' identification with free coinage again tended to neutralize that issue.[20] The Battle of the Standards changed this, of course. Utah Populists then willingly fused with Democrats to become a part of Bryan's massive state victory. Four Populists were elected to the state legislature, and the party's candidates for attorney and surveyor of Uintah County were victorious.[21]

The small Populist bloc in the legislature worked primarily for labor laws and for direct legislation. An employee safety bill and one to build a miners' hospital were defeated as were efforts to institute the initiative and referendum. One Populist legislator, B. A. Harbor, successfully pushed through a mechanics' lien law and a measure to create a state board of public works. Perhaps the most intriguing aspect of Utah Populism was its marked emphasis on municipal reform. Populists gave wholehearted support to a bill providing for direct legislation in municipal government. It was passed but, unfortunately, without the necessary enabling legislation.[22]

In 1897, Lawrence ran for mayor of Salt Lake City. Again his party's stress on municipal reform characterized Utah's nonagrarian brand of Populism. The Populist candidate, a staunch antimonopolist, joined other party members in decrying the treatment of unemployed vagrants by city police. Salt Lake City Populists also showed that Single-Tax ideas, already noted in such Front Range states as Montana, were popular with the party. The Populists proposed a tax increase on vacant property being held in the city for speculation. Lawrence lost the election, polling less than 9 percent of the vote, but Populists were able to win the mayor's office in Ogden in cooperation with the Democrats.[23]

In 1898, the Populists made their last major try for office in Utah. Warren Foster, a former Alliance editor from Kansas, was nominated for Congress at a convention in which the party endorsed a stinging attack against monopolies introduced by the relentless Lawrence.[24] The delegates rejected fusion with the more conservative Democrats of the state. In the subsequent campaign, Populists downgraded the issue of free silver and stressed such issues as municipal reform, direct legislation, and the Single Tax. Indeed, it would have been difficult to characterize the Utah party as a silver one in 1898.

By 1900, the Populist movement in Utah was in fatal decline. Foster, who had continued his journalistic career by editing one of the state's three Populist newspapers, deserted the party for socialism. Although Lawrence and a few stalwart supporters remained loyal, Utah Populism lost what little effectiveness it had had.[25] Its eventual demise left an almost imperceptible historical impact. In its orientation, the Utah People's party was probably the most fascinating one in the Mountain West; its urban-labor focus gave it an almost utopian quality because it was at such variance with its particular time and place.

Nevada was the most silver-oriented of the states and territories of the Mountain West. The state's economy had been alarmingly sluggish since the decline of the fabled Comstock Lode. The sagging silver prices of the 1890s only added to its woes.[26] Not surprisingly, free coinage became an irresistible issue for this state, appropriately nicknamed the Silver state. Concern for the metal's status led to the organization of Nevada's first silver clubs in Winnemucca and Eureka in April of 1892. Their formation warned the two major parties that strict adherence to free coinage would be mandatory if they expected to win in the coming election. Both parties were in an impossible position, however; neither President Harrison nor Cleveland could inspire confidence among bimetallists.[27] The Nevada voters did not tolerate the usual efforts to equivocate on silver, which were acceptable in 1892 in the other states and territories of the region.

The shrewder leaders of both parties sensed this mood and organized an independent Silver party which was soon dominated by such prominent Republicans as the able Francis G. Newlands, William M. Stewart, one of the more strident voices for silver in the United States Senate, and Charles C. "Black" Wallace, the Central Pacific's chief Nevada lobbyist. The new party nominated electors pledged to Weaver and Field because these two candidates were not ambivalent on silver. Due almost entirely to the coinage issue, Nevada voters gave the state's three electoral votes to Weaver and Field.

They also overwhelmingly elected Newlands to the House of Representatives and chose enough legislators sympathetic to silver to ensure Stewart another term.[28]

In 1892, the new party's identification with national Populism was merely a political convenience. There was a certain irony about the arrangement, though. The Central Pacific, through its support of the Silver party, gave indirect support to a political movement that was openly hostile toward railroads. Wallace, the railroad's lobbyist, however, was evidently influential: During the next legislative session, many of the successful Silver candidates voted to abolish a state board of assessors and equalization that had boldly raised property taxes on the railroad.[29]

Subsequent events diversified the program of the Silver party and moved it to the left. Its members, for instance, developed a strong sympathy for the confused units of Coxey's Washington-bound army, and transported one these units across the state in twenty-three cattle cars provided by the Central Pacific.[30] Although pragmatic railroad owners wisely gave aid to the Coxeyites, old criticisms against the railroad were renewed shortly thereafter when federal troops were dispatched to Nevada to end the Pullman Strike. During all these turbulent events, the silver issue was able to harmonize with those spawned by the Panic of 1893. Parades in Reno in support of the Coxeyites featured silver banners. The state's prosilver press supported the American Railway Union (A.R.U.) during the Pullman Strike. One of the more prominent defense attorneys for the A.R.U. was Thomas Wren, cofounder of the pioneering Eureka silver club.[31]

By the midterm election of 1894, the Silver party was ready to offer a complete slate of candidates. Its platform more closely resembled that of national Populism in terms of issues. The Silver party advocated free coinage, of course, but it also supported other third party reforms, such as the direct election of United States senators and the compulsory arbitration of labor disputes. It even endorsed government ownership of the railroads, notwithstanding the continued influence of the Central Pacific in party affairs.

At the state convention, some Silverites made an effort to affiliate their party with the national People's party. When this effort failed, the disaffected delegates organized Nevada's first Populist party. To justify this potentially harmful split, the party's founders alleged that the railroads controlled the Silver party. The new party's platform, however, was not significantly different from that of the Silver party, although it added such controversial planks as the repeal of the National Banking Act, prohibition of any more Chinese or Japanese immigrants, and the demand that unemployed workers be used on reclamation projects. The Populists also fielded candidates for the 1894 race. They nominated James Doughty, an exrailroad worker, for Congress and "Farmer" George E. Pickham from Washoe County for governor.[32]

Nevada voters left no doubt in 1894 that they preferred the Silver party to the hastily organized People's party. The Silver organization's better known candidates won by convincing margins in the contests they entered. Republicans placed second, while frustrated Democrats and Populists struggled for third. The silver-dominated legislature that convened the following year, however, showed little sentiment for reform. They passed a law that required disclosure of campaign expenditures and a resolution that called for woman suffrage to show that Nevada had the potential of being as receptive to this issue as Idaho and Utah were.[33] Unfortunately, women had to wait until 1914 before they were fully enfranchised because of the strong forces of conservatism that operated in Nevada despite the campaign oratory that enlivened the state's arid landscape in 1894.[34]

The 1896 election followed the usual pattern. Originally Democrats, Silverites, and Populists were to fuse. After a heated debate at their September convention, the leaders of the People's party withdrew from the arrangement; they again nominated Doughty for Congress. Populist support for the eloquent Bryan in the Silver state, however, was overwhelming; his combined fusion and Populist vote accounted for more than 80 percent of the total. The Silver-Democrats (as the fusionists were called) also won every office they sought by overwhelming majorities.[35] The long-range results of this election were significant. Complicated party realignments and issues such as silver nudged this remarkably conservative state dominated by railroad and mining interests to the left. The Democrats with their strong Bryan legacy began a decade of dominance in alliance with the state's silver forces, while the once-powerful Republicans drifted into a ten-year decline. Populists, following the national trend, faded into history as the century closed despite the strong vote the ardent silverite Thomas Wren received as the Populist candidate for Congress in 1898.[36]

In Arizona, the last of the Far Western states this study surveyed, Populism faced the usual problems associated with territorial government: presidential elections were not held in the territories; major offices were appointive; delegates to Congress were nonvoting; and laws enacted by local legislatures were subject to congressional approval. Consequently, Populism in Arizona followed the same pattern as in New Mexico—it was slow to emerge, its successes were limited, and its strength was confined to certain local areas (the northern part of the state in Arizona's case). In some ways, nonetheless, the environment for third party activity was more favorable in Arizona. The percentage of Anglos in the territory was higher, for instance, which made the electorate more responsive to eastern reforms. Moreover, neither major party had as strong an alliance with the more traditional Hispanos as the New Mexico Republicans had.

The constitution drawn up in Phoenix in 1891 by delegates eager to gain Arizona's admission reflected this more liberal-minded electorate. Predating the serious growth of Populism by at least two years, this constitution established silver as legal tender in payment of state debts and urged state aid to hasten the development of railroads and other corporations. Anticipating the Populists of Colorado and New Mexico (and possibly Idaho), the convention's delegates also demanded state control over Arizona's rivers and canals.[37] Since admission to statehood was denied until 1912, this constitution ended up in a cluttered graveyard with other such hopeful documents from this part of the Southwest.

Populism in the Grand Canyon state had another advantage. Unlike the People's party in New Mexico, Arizona Populists had a prominent political leader, William O. "Buckey" O'Neill, who was the Populist candidate for delegate in 1894 and 1896. O'Neill was originally a Republican, like New Mexico's Theodore B. Mills. Several years before his death while serving as a Rough Rider in the Spanish-American War, O'Neill was elected assessor of Yavapai County. Because the Atlantic and Pacific Railway had allegedly refused to pay its fair share of the county's property taxes, O'Neill, who as sheriff once caught three train robbers for the railroad, assessed the Atlantic and Pacific $800,000. In his opinion, this figure represented an honest valuation; it amounted to about $1.25 an acre. Naturally, the railroad disagreed. It vigorously protested and took the case all the way to the Supreme Court.[38]

O'Neill became known as the "people's champion," but he was far too controversial for his own party. Republican leaders refused to nominate him for territorial delegate in 1894, but the Populists, who began organizing during the divisive gubernatorial term of Cleveland-appointee Louis C. Hughes, enthusiastically chose O'Neill as their candidate.[39] More liberal Democrats aliented by the conservative Hughes joined the Populists to give O'Neill a respectable tally, although he placed third in the voting. Conservative Republicans, however, were the chief beneficiaries. Their candidate Nathan O. Murphy took advantage of the liberal split to win election as a delegate to Congress.[40] Populists, however, remained enthusiastic about O'Neill. His rhetoric resembled that of Ignatius Donnelly, and his opposition toward business monopoly almost matched that of Davis Waite.[41] Bucking the tide toward fusionism in 1896, O'Neill ran again for the office of territorial delegate to Congress as a Populist. This time he increased his percentage of the vote to a respectable 28 percent.[42]

In many ways, the controversy over the Atlantic and Pacific gave Arizona Populism its impetus—another example of antimonopolism's potency as an issue. This southwestern railroad, of course, cannot be compared with the aggressive Northern Pacific as far as its impact on the territory was concerned. After all, the Atlantic and Pacific failed to utilize its immense federal land grant or to become a major transcontinental. Nevertheless, Arizonans, for a variety of reasons ranging from fear of corporate power to concerns about railroad taxation, regarded the Atlantic and Pacific as a formidable force.

Silver also played a role in this mineral-rich commonwealth during its brief Populist Era. In Arizona's case, however, silver seemed to benefit the Democrats almost exclusively. The chief beneficiary in the 1896 delegate race, as a matter of fact, was the Democratic candidate Marcus A. Smith, who gained the most from his party's strong free-silver stand. (Arizona residents were unable to vote for Bryan in the presidential race.) In the end, silver and the other reforms of the era did not push Arizona politics to the left as they had in Nevada. Rather, the trend was a conservative one, especially after the decline of Populist strength in 1898. Just as New Mexico had moved toward traditional Republicanism, Arizona, following a similar pattern, drifted into a decade of conservative Democratic dominance.[43]

Although this survey of Populism in Idaho, Utah, Nevada, and Arizona does not compare in terms of scope and degree to the Front Range study, it does suggest certain regional trends. Although silver was important, it was only one of several issues, especially before

1896. Above free coinage, such issues as antimonopolism, working-men's conditions, women's rights, direct legislation, and Chinese ex-clusion were important in these states, just as they were along the Front Range. Consequently, this reassessment has revealed an un-mistakable diversity of issues throughout the entire eight-state region of the Mountain West.

Ten

Mountain Populism

A Reassessment

I t is difficult to argue that in a region as diverse as the Mountain West, Populism was cohesive because of one factor. Historians, using silver as that factor, have traditionally drawn such a conclusion, however, for the West. They argued that Populism from the western edge of the Great Plains to the Sierra Nevadas was simply a silver movement. Moreover, they believed that the movement had no serious purpose beyond the obsessive determination of regional Populists to bring about free coinage. This conviction regarding silver's preeminence was so strong that until recently, historians have made no effort to test its validity. In fact, historians have largely interpreted Populism as a national movement from the standpoint of the wheat-raising Midwest and the cotton-producing South to the exclusion of the Mountain West. They regarded the movement in both of these areas as multi-issue in nature, despite the great importance of wheat to the Midwest and cotton to the South. In contrast, they looked upon devotion to Populist issues other than free coinage in the silver-producing West as superficial.

Of course, silver's importance to the western economy cannot be denied. In fact, the price of the white metal was so important that silver as a political issue was largely neutralized until the emotional Battle of the Standards was waged in the election of 1896. Democrats and Republicans tended to be most vocal in their support of free coinage regardless of the views of their national party. Only the preeminence of the Silver Question in 1896 changed this situation. McKinley's stand in behalf of gold placed regional Republicans in an almost impossible position. Prior to the Bryan-McKinley election, however, members of the two major parties were often more zealous about silver than either the People's party or any of its organizational predecessors. In 1888, for instance, Republicans in the Centennial state came out for free coinage two years before the organization of the Independent party, the forerunner of Colorado Populism. In Montana, while the Independent Labor party advanced silver in its 1890 platform as a means of ensuring full employment, the Democrats and Republicans took straightforward stands in behalf of the unrestricted coinage of silver. In Wyoming, while the fledgling People's party refrained from any direct reference to silver in 1892, Democrats advocated free coinage. Even Republicans remained bimetallist despite the lukewarm attitude toward silver of the state's two Republican senators, Warren and Carey. In the Territory of New Mexico, the contrast was even greater. One prominent territorial journal criticized the Populist party for failing to include a separate resolution in behalf of free coinage in its 1894 platform. Democrats, on the other hand, had endorsed free silver as early as 1890, while the G.O.P., dominated by the conservative Catron, equivocated on the issue. One suspects that a more detailed study of the Populist movement in the other four states of the Mountain West might reveal a similar tardiness on the part of Populists toward the endorsement of silver.

Populists in the Mountain West shared with Democrats and Republicans a concern over a number of issues. Members of both major parties were highly sensitive about silver, just as they would have been about cotton if the South were their home or about wheat if it were the Midwest. This emphasis on silver, however, did not preclude an interest in other issues. Republicans, for example, took a strong stand on the protective tariff because it was important to many of their constituents. During the early 1890s, wool protection meant more to sheep grazers in New Mexico and eastern Montana than did free coinage. Lead protection was also important in the mining states of the Mountain West. Even Wyoming, poor in precious metals, cared because it hoped its true potential in mineral wealth would one day be realized. The Democrats, who favored low tariffs, also had persuasive issues. They championed the cause of small producers in agriculture and blue-collar workers in industry and thrived on stands critical

of the relationship between Republicans and the major mining industries. Many western Democrats displayed, at least publicly, a distrust
of regional entrepreneurs. They often hurled accusations of monopoly against them. In fact, Democrats from three of the states emphasized in this study (Montana, Wyoming, and New Mexico) tended to
siphon off the protest vote that regional Populists had worked hard to
attract. Only the extraordinary power of the People's party prevented
such a development from happening in Colorado, at least during the
early 1890s.

Just as both major parties in the Mountain West dealt forthrightly
with a variety of issues, so did the Populists. Indeed, their stands on
public questions often required great courage because the issues they
dealt with were more controversial than such traditional ones as the
tariff. A study of Populist conventions in this region reveals party
platforms devoted to a myriad of political, social, and economic questions of both local and national importance. Their stands on national
issues were accurately reflected in the 1892 Omaha platform. The
common practice of Populist conventions in this region was to adopt
the Omaha platform as a statement of party principle and then to deal
with local issues through separate resolutions. A similar procedure
was often employed at the Democratic and Republican state conventions. The sincerity of the delegates of the two major parties has rarely
been questioned—not so with western Populists. Historians have
frequently regarded their enthusiastic endorsement of the Omaha
platform as a mere ritual to prove that their political cause was something more than silver.

Perhaps the best way to prove that western Populists were sincere
too is to examine the challenging local problems they were willing to
confront. Such an approach would be particularly helpful because
dealing with a local challenge often meant implementing one of the
reform planks of the Omaha platform. Platform items dealing with
alleged monopolies, such as the railroads, for instance, are illustrative
of Populist concern about issues other than silver. The vast acreage of
land granted to the transcontinental railroads by the federal government always had the potential for controversy in a developing region
such as the West. The Populists in Omaha had demanded that those
land grants not used by the railroad be returned to the public domain.
Railroads, however, represented only one kind of monopoly in this
region. Land and cattle monopolies threatened many of the West's
small farmers and stock grazers. Large irrigation companies were con-

sidered monopolistic. Mining corporations, both local and absentee-owned, were often placed in the same category. Democrats and Republicans often hesitated to challenge these local monopolies which they considered essential to the growth of the Mountain West. Populists, on the other hand, became conspicuous by their willingness to denounce them.

Certainly, the best known of the local monopolies were the railroads. The most radical plank in the Omaha platform called for the nationalization of the country's common carriers. Western Populists not only endorsed this contentious demand, but fought against these important transportation corporations whenever the power of these corporations seemed abusive or threatening. Undoubtedly, the most controversial railroad along the Front Range was the Northern Pacific in Montana. This railroad's insistence on its title to all mineral rights on its federal land grant not known at the time of its 1864 charter made it the most feared monopoly in the Treasure State until the Supreme Court ruled against the company in the Barden case. While the two older parties in Montana were distressed by the extravagant claims of the Northern Pacific, the Populists took the most aggressive stand. At their 1892 convention, they demanded that the powerful transcontinental's land grant be forfeited because the Northern Pacific had failed to complete its construction within the time specified by its charter.

Railroads were also controversial in Colorado, particularly among the dryland farmers on the eastern plains. High freight rates, among other disputed practices, fostered antimonopoly feelings among those who cultivated the so-called rain belt. The common carriers of the West, whether they caused alarm or provided reasssurance, were almost invariably among the most potent of the region's enterprises; indeed, they were often the only representatives of unbridled laissez-faire capitalism in the more remote West. Thus, the rate-fixing policies of the Union Pacific in Wyoming or the Santa Fe in New Mexico would always have a great impact on the economies of both states. Rate reform was a big issue among pioneer farmers in Idaho. The initial stimulus for the Populist movement in Arizona was the reluctance of the Atlantic and Pacific to pay its fair share of property taxes assessed in the territory. The Central Pacific attracted such controversy by its misuse of political power that the railroad felt it was expedient to haul one of Coxey's armies across the state in order to placate its working-class critics. Indeed, a major objective of the

Farmers' Alliance, which was prominent in many parts of the Mountain West, was to deal with the abuses of these transportation giants. Although the Populists drew many of their members from the Alliance, they shared with the Republicans and Democrats a strange ambivalence toward the railroads because of the essential role railroads played in the growth of the Mountain West.

Mining was another industry that exercised monopolistic power. Since they were the major employers in many parts of the West, mine owners controlled the economic lives of scores of people. The impersonality that resulted from the all-too-common practice in the industry of absentee ownership compounded the problems caused by their power. Absentee corporate owners were influential in all the states and territories of the Mountain West; to one extent or another, all the states of this region had colonial economies. Their development was dependent upon eastern and European capital or California capital in the case of Nevada. Outside capital was especially important to the region's great mining commonwealths. For example, one historian has characterized mineral-rich Colorado during the late nineteenth century as "little more than a pocket borough of the corporate oligarchy," because of the clout of these outside entrepreneurs.[1]

The formidable economic strength of mine owners compelled many employees to organize. Considerable success in unionization was achieved, especially in such mining states as Colorado, Montana, and Idaho. Union members in Colorado, for example, were able to earn $3.00 a day. Those in Montana did even better, earning up to $3.50. These unions counterbalanced the power of the mining capitalists at a time when workers could expect little sympathetic governmental intervention.

One of the major unions in the Mountain West at this time was the Knights of Labor. This union, which was instrumental in the development of Populism throughout the country, played a prominent role in the West. It was one of the chief bargaining agents for surface workers in mining. It provided an active voice for many of the region's teamsters and railroad workers. Some of the union's leaders became conspicuous in the area's local Populist organizations. F. A. Blake founded the first People's party in New Mexico, to which at least two of the Herrera brothers belonged. Henry Breitenstein and Shakespeare E. Sealy, two steadfast antimonopolists, were key organizers of the Populist movement in Wyoming. Peter Breen, District Master Workman for the Montana Knights, not only sought the gubernatorial nomination of the People's party in 1892, but also went on to become one of the cofounders of the militant Western Federation of Miners, another union supportive of Populist policies. The toughness of the urban-mining branch of Colorado Populism surely owed much to the aggressiveness of Davis H. Waite, who was a member of the Knights before he became the state's only Populist governor.[2]

Unionization not only checked the power of monopolistic mining corporations, but it also prepared the way for the implementation of those prolabor resolutions found in the Omaha document. In Montana, where urban Populists were dominant, the eight-hour day became the most important local issue. Utah's miniscule People's party had strong proponents of the eight-hour day too—the most prominent was the 1895 Populist gubernatorial candidate Henry W. Lawrence. Mine safety also had support. It was a familiar plank in nearly every party platform adopted in Montana. Reforms of this kind gained new backers as a result of the Panic of 1893. As early as January 1893, Colorado's Populist governor Waite had dealt with many of the labor issues highlighted by the panic when he recommended in his inaugural address that the state legislature enact an employer liability law, a stringent child-labor measure, and a restriction on the use of Pinkertons—issues that were most important in Montana too. During the 1894 election Populists along the Front Range also rejected fusion with the Democrats in Colorado, Wyoming, and Montana and made a separate bid for power in New Mexico because they wanted to dramatize their disenchantment with the country's traditional political support of laissez-faire capitalism.

The approach of agricultural Populists in coping with monopoly relied more on governmental intervention than on laws to protect workers against unjust corporate personnel policies. The response to the region's railroads has already been cited; government ownership of the common carriers or forfeiture of their land grants were the two major strategies advanced. In the area of water—that most valuable commodity in the arid parts of the Mountain West—Populist farmers urged a similar governmental role. They advocated public ownership of irrigation facilities in one form or another in response to water abuse. In Colorado and New Mexico, irrigation farmers regarded state ownership and management of water companies as the best solution. Colorado farmers were convinced that the water companies in their state were promising more water than the companies could deliver and were charging royalties above the standard rates. This was a familiar charge among Idaho's irrigation farmers too. In northeastern Colorado, farmers were especially hostile toward the English Company, a large monopolistic water company that also bore the stigma of being foreign-owned. Although state or territorial ownership received its share of support in Colorado and New Mexico as well as in Idaho and Arizona, it was rejected in Wyoming and Montana where Populists felt a marked distrust for their state governments. Wyoming Populists in 1892, for example, opposed Senator Warren's bill to transfer irrigation responsibilities to the states; they preferred federal supervision instead. Although provisions of the proposed Warren bill were later incorporated into the Carey Act, rural Populists in Wyoming remained skeptical. Populists in Montana were also suspicious of state control. The party's 1892 platform called upon the federal government to build and maintain reservoirs for the irrigation of arid lands.

Another source of concern for some rural Populists was the threat posed by alleged cattle monopolies. Many small stock growers in this region feared the power of the cattle companies and the state cattle associations through which the companies sought their political goals. While the state associations were eclipsed in such states as Colorado and Montana by the dominant mining enterprises, the one in Wyoming was so powerful that the state earned the nickname of the "cattlemen's commonwealth." In fact, the invasion of Johnson County by gunmen hired by the Wyoming Stock Growers Association launched the People's party in Wyoming. The Wyoming Populist platform in 1892 exploited this unpopular invasion to the fullest: the longest and most effective planks were those that excoriated the Wyoming Stock Growers Association and the state Board of Live Stock Commissioners which it controlled. So-called cattle monopolies, however, were not confined to Wyoming. Members of the Farmers' Alliance in New Mexico charged the big cattle companies of Lincoln and Colfax counties with seeking to control the scarce water resources of eastern New Mexico so that the companies could monopolize the public domain. The encroachment on the Las Vegas Community Grant in San Miguel County by determined and often wealthy Anglo cattlemen threatened the descendants of native grantees to such an extent that the first territorial People's party was organized there in 1888.

Alleged land monopolies also threatened small settlers in this region. The accumulation of land in the hands of a few was a particularly serious problem in the Territory of New Mexico where immense tracts of land, such as the one adjacent to Las Vegas, were granted to individuals or groups first by Spanish and then by Mexican governors. During the state's long territorial period, opportunistic Anglo speculators acquired many of these grants. Clever lawyers had gained possession of some by taking land as a fee when they defended the ownership rights of the original grantees or their descendants. The best known of these grants was the Maxwell one. By the 1870s, it had come under the control of the Maxwell Land Grant and Railroad Company, a Dutch firm that laid claim to approximately two million acres of land straddling the New Mexico-Colorado border. It was another conspicuous example of foreign ownership, the bane of western Populists. It was also the target of intense opposition on the part of those grazers, farmers, and miners whose land or mineral claims were jeopardized by the Maxwell's. Groups such as the Colfax County Farmers' Alliance mustered support in a struggle that deteriorated into the bitter Colfax County War. In the end, the Maxwell Company prevailed, but only after years of resistance.

There was also organized opposition to another kind of land grab, the effort to enact the Warren arid land bill into law. Voters in Wyoming regarded the Warren bill as an effort to monopolize land as well as water. Some considered state control of the arid lands proposed for irrigation to be just as alarming as state control of the canals and reservoirs. During the 1892 election, fusionist Populists and Democrats described the Warren bill as the "great Land steal"; the charge no doubt added to the woes of Wyoming Republicans who were already discredited by their party's identification with the Johnson County War.

The new party was also committed to Direct Democracy. While the party's focus in this regard did not match its solicitude toward blue-collar workers in mining and industry nor its more universal anti-monopoly stance, it was nonetheless one of the hallmarks of Populism in the Mountain West. The party's members in this region enthusiastically supported the Omaha plank which called for the direct election of United States senators. They were also advocates of the initiative and referendum. Utah Populists even agitated for direct legislation on the municipal level. Success in bringing about Direct Democracy, however, usually had to await the passage of time. For instance, the initiative and referendum did not become part of state law in Montana until 1906. Attainment of the Australian secret ballot was another story. The Montana territorial legislature provided for its passage as early as 1889, largely because of the efforts of Will Kennedy, who came the Populists' first gubernatorial candidate in 1892.

Regional Populists, moreover, played a notable part in the crusade for woman suffrage. It was in this forum that the Mountain West provided its most significant national leadership. Wyoming, of course, had the distinction of being the first state to grant women the franchise. Colorado was second; women received the vote during the Populist administration of Governor Waite. Waite, along with most party members, gave enthusiastic support to this reform, although he later bemoaned the alleged opposition of women toward his political career.[3] Utah and Idaho were also in the vanguard of female suffrage. Utah gave women the right to vote, but not to hold office, two months after Wyoming granted them the franchise, while Idaho adopted a woman suffrage law in 1896.[4] Montana was not as advanced in the campaign for women's rights, but the immense popularity of Ella Knowles, the Populist candidate for state attorney general in 1892, indicates a broad acceptance of women in politics. Nevada and Arizona were also slow in acknowledging the aspirations of women, although it would be unfair to characterize the voters of these two states as being indifferent toward the suffrage issue.[5] Only in New Mexico did Populists balk on the question of women's rights. Their attitude, however, was not unusual. All political leaders in the territory were cautious because of the traditional attitude of most Hispanos toward women in public life.

The evidence conclusively proves that Populists throughout the country were political crusaders whose concerns were not confined to free silver. Since Progressives later incorporated most of their reforms into the American political process, there has been the well-known and controversial tendency to idealize the role of these third-party advocates. This exaltation has led to the now familiar and thoroughgoing revision of the movement by a school of Populist historians who tend to be quite negative in their assessment. Prominent critics of Populism such as Richard Hofstadter and Oscar Handlin, for example, have seen such traits as nativism and anti-Semitism in the movement in those parts of the country where the People's party was strong.

Nativism was certainly present in the Mountain West. Its most notorious form was the widespread persecution of the Chinese. It was also evident in the activities of the anti-Catholic American Protective Association. Blue-collar Populists, unfortunately, engaged in discrimination and violence against Chinese immigrants in much the same way that other working people did. Anti-Chinese sentiments had no political boundaries in this region. In Nevada, for instance, an 1880 statewide referendum on Chinese immigration revealed overwhelming opposition to these Oriental people; the admission of more Chinese was rejected by a vote of 17,259 to 183.[6] As for the American Protective Association, this organization found its most congenial western home in the Republican rather than in the Populist or Democratic parties. Along the Front Range, in fact, Populists were often the targets of the A.P.A. (Examples of this for Colorado and Montana have already been cited.) Evidence of such Populist persecution in Wyoming and New Mexico is not clear-cut, although Republicans are clearly implicated in the activities of the American Protective Association in Wyoming.[7]

There is less evidence, however, to support the allegations of anti-Semitism by Populists in the Front Range states. Montana Populists in 1892 did use the term "Shylock" along with money shark, when it came to naming those responsible for the low incomes in the region. Anti-Semitic material was found in the writings and speeches of such Populist leaders as Governor Waite or Mary Elizabeth Lease, the midwestern orator who was such a popular campaign speaker in the West.[8] Nonetheless, little was found in this study to substantiate the charge that Populists were more anti-Semitic than Republicans or Democrats. The same can be said regarding the familiar revisionist charge of Populist anti-intellectualism in these states.[9]

A source of surprise in this reassessment of the movement was the variety of party doctrine and organizational activity in the Mountain West. In Montana, Colorado, and Utah, for instance, there was an unmistakable urban quality about Populism; it took the form of a pronounced antimonopolism coupled with a strong determination to improve the working conditions of mine employees and other blue-collar workers. One difference did prevail. In Colorado, the movement's agrarian members were more aggressive and prominent than those in Montana and Utah. Indeed, the Independent party, Populism's precursor in that state, was also called the Farmers' Alliance party. The agricultural and mining sectors were in better balance in Idaho than in Montana and Utah despite the publicity generated by the violent strikes of the Western Federation of Miners in the Shoshone County area. Nevada, on the other hand, had comparatively little in the way of agriculture; indeed, the party there was the most prosilver of the entire region. In Wyoming, the Populists lacked a mineral and agricultural base to create a People's party that was like those found in these more diversified states. The party there was largely comprised of small stock grazers with a few crop farmers and railroad workers and even fewer mine employees.

In New Mexico and Arizona, Populism was plagued by two handicaps. For one thing, territorial status did not give the party in either place much political latitude. To cite one example, the important territorial officials were federally appointed. Moreover, the movement's lack of success in either territory to elect a congressional delegate or a majority of territorial legislators confined the really important party accomplishments to the local level. In New Mexico, for instance, Populist candidates waxed stronger in such far-flung counties as San Miguel and San Juan than they did in other parts of the territory. In Arizona, the party's most impressive performances were confined to local areas such as those in the north where "Buckey" O'Neill played a prominent political role.

The Populist movement in the Mountain West, then, was almost as varied in the diversity of its support as it was in the complexity of the stands it took. In some respects the dissimilarity among the movement's backers was more marked in the high country of the West than it was in the Midwest and South. In the latter two sections, most Populists came from an agrarian background because these were two of the most important agricultural regions in the nation. In the Mountain West, on the other hand, agricultural land was limited; consequently, farmers had to share the movement with miners, railroad workers, and stock grazers. This heterogeneity would obviously affect the region's issues. In fact, the multiplicity of issues confronted by members of the new party in this eight-state area becomes increasingly obvious the more one delves into the history of the western movement. As has been seen, anti-monopolism was probably the most conspicuous question advanced and debated, but workingmen's issues such as the eight-hour day and those of Direct Democracy and women's rights were also important.

Dedication to the cause was another Populist trait. Among the different kinds of working people attracted to Populism's clarion call for fundamental change, many were intensely committed individuals who had become profoundly alienated. Historian Carlos A. Schwantes, as noted in the first chapter, used the expression "ideology of disinheritance" to characterize the mindset of the more zealous of the western Populists. And one senses in perusing the political broadsides and editorial pronouncements printed during this time of turmoil a real disillusionment with the system on the part of often incensed third party adherents. According to these struggling dissenters, the God-given rights to succeed and prosper in the undeveloped West had been denied by the western representatives of monopolistic corporate America. Only a program of major reform would change this depressing and decidedly unfair situation.

Yet despite the diversity of the movement, its multifaceted nature, and the dedication of its adherents, one has to admit that an exceptionally strong commitment to free coinage developed by the mid-1890s. Silver, of course, was one of the West's leading commodities; it has already been likened in this study to wheat in the Midwest and cotton in the South. This inordinate focus on silver in the Mountain West, so conspicuous by the last decade of the century, however, does not weaken the case for Mountain Populism as a mainstream movement. The People's party in the wheat-raising Midwest and cotton-producing South also shifted from a multi-issue orientation to a virtual obsession with silver. This transition, remarkable because it was so thoroughgoing, started as early as 1892, according to John D. Hicks. While Hicks saw free coinage as the only viable party issue in the Mountain West, he had to concede that its appeal had become nationwide by the campaign of 1892. "Throughout the country converts had flocked to the Populist standard for no other reason than the new party promised to do for silver what neither of the older parties dared attempt."[10]

Lawrence Goodwyn also recognized the mushrooming national appeal of silver coinage. He saw it as having a pernicious influence on the other party planks hammered out in Omaha in 1892. In his opinion, its effect on the movement's purpose and structure was obvious by 1894.

> Not only in the mining states of the plateau region, but in a number of places through the old cotton belt and the newer Western granary third party organizational difficulties had led to what Alliancemen regarded as ideological 'trimming' of the Omaha Platform.[11]

By 1896, the transformation was complete. Silver fusionists were dominant when third party delegates gathered in Saint Louis for their national nominating convention. As Robert F. Durden shows in his 1965 study *The Climax of Populism*, however, the leading silverites were from the wheatlands of the Midwest and the cotton country of the South. Spearheading fusion with the Democrats were midwestern leaders such as James B. Weaver of Iowa and Senator William Allen of Nebraska and southern leaders such as James G. Field of Virginia and Senator Marion Butler of North Carolina. The role that these men played was crucial. In essence, they were the most instrumental in persuading party members to support silver's new champion the charismatic Bryan.[12]

Many articles and monographs abound with evidence to document this transition to silver in the wheat and cotton belts of agricultural America. Not only was this drastic shift of emphasis a major area of concentration in older studies, such as those authored by Hicks and Durden, but it was also carefully traced in a number of newer ones, such as those cited in chapter one. (See also the bibliographic essay.) A major development of mainstream Populism, consequently, was the transition from a multiplicity of issues to a preoccupation with silver as the movement's last gasp.

Populism in the Mountain West was part of this familiar metamorphosis. Indeed, the focus of this monograph is to document the variety of issues advanced in this region before silver's preeminence (a significant number of which involved antimonopolism in one form or another). The study's results showed that the substance of the movement in the West as well as its evolution were fundamentally the same as in the other two strongholds of Populism. Of course, the western movement had greater occupational diversity—it was the least agrarian of the three regions—but in most basic considerations its similarities to the movements in the Midwest and South were striking.

Notes

CHAPTER 1   MOUNTAIN POPULISM: A MAINSTREAM
MOVEMENT?

1 John D. Hicks, *The Populist Revolt: A History of the Farmers' Alliance and the People's Party* (Minneapolis: The University of Minnesota Press, 1931), 228.

2 Thomas A. Clinch, *Urban Populism and Free Silver in Montana: A Narrative of Ideology in Political Action* (Missoula: University of Montana Press, 1970), 58.

3 O. Gene Clanton, *Kansas Populism: Ideas and Men* (Lawrence: The University Press of Kansas, 1969), 127.

4 Hicks, *The Populist Revolt*, 262.

5 Ibid., 263; Robert W. Larson, "Populism in the Mountain West: A Mainstream Movement," *The Western Historical Quarterly*, XIII (April, 1982), 144; Russell R. Elliott, *History of Nevada* (Lincoln: University of Nebraska Press, 1973), 185–87.

6 Clinch believes, as a matter of fact, that there are strong indications that fusion would have resulted in "heavy majorities" for cooperating Democrats and Populists. Clinch, *Urban Populism and Free Silver in Montana*, 65.

7 The population of San Miguel surpassed its closest rival Bernalillo by more than three thousand at this time. U.S., Congress, House, *Compendium of the Eleventh Census: 1890, Part 1. Population*, 52nd Cong., 1st Sess., 1890, House Doc. 340, 280–82.

8 Robert W. Larson, *New Mexico Populism: A Study of Radical Protest in a Western Territory* (Boulder: Colorado Associated University Press, 1974), xiv.

9 Hicks, *The Populist Revolt*, 268. Italics are Hicks's.

10 Richard Hofstadter, *The Age of Reform: From Bryan to F.D.R.* (New York: Alfred A. Knopf, 1955), 50.

11 David B. Griffiths, "Populism in Wyoming," *Annals of Wyoming*, XL (April, 1968), 63–65.

12 John K. Yoshida, "The Wyoming Election of 1892" (Master's thesis, University of Wyoming, 1956) and Thomas Krueger, "Populism in Wyoming" (Master's thesis, University of Wyoming, 1960).

13 See note 2 for full citation.

14 Stephen J. Leonard, "Denver's Foreign Born Immigrants, 1859–1900" (Ph.D. dissertation, Claremont Graduate School and University Center, 1971), 201.

15 James Edward Wright, *The Politics of Populism: Dissent in Colorado* (New Haven: Yale University Press, 1974).

16 See note 8 for full citation.

17 Lawrence Goodwyn, *Democratic Promise: The Populist Movement in America* (New York: Oxford University Press, 1976), 319.

18 Ibid., xx. Italics are Goodwyn's.

19 Ibid., 201–210. According to one Populist historian, Goodwyn took those Populists who were strongly attracted to silver and who dominated the movement on the northern prairies and excommunicated them as "pseuo-Populists"; they were very simply party members "who did not fit his schema." James Turner, "Understanding the Populists," *Journal of American History*, LXVII (September, 1980), 357.

20 This same discussion of Goodwyn's book, almost verbatim, is included in Larson, "Populism in the Mountain West," 146–47.

21 Stanley B. Parsons, Karen Toombs Parsons, Walter Killilae, and Beverly Boyers, "The Role of Cooperatives in the Development of the Movement Culture of Populism," *Journal of American History*, LXIX (March, 1983), 866. McMath's review appeared in the June 1977 issue of the *American Historical Review* and Cannon's appeared in the August, 1977 issue of the *Journal of Southern History*. The authors of this article also list in their documentation of this study two major texts that present Goodwyn's views as the standard interpretation of the Populist movement. They are *The American People* co-authored in 1980 by David Burner, Eugene D. Genovese, and Forrest McDonald and *The American People: A History* co-authored a year later by Arthur S. Link, Stanley Coben, Robert V. Remini, Douglas Greenberg and Robert C. McMath, Jr.

22 Parsons and others, "The Role of Cooperatives in the Development of the Movement Culture of Populism," 867–84.

23 Turner, "Understanding the Populists," 357–58. For Turner's analysis and statistical evidence, see pp. 359–73. Not all students of Populism, however, have accepted Turner's conclusion. Donna A. Barnes on pp. 30–31 of her *Farmers in Rebellion: The Rise and Fall of the Southern Alliance and People's Party in Texas* (Austin: University of Texas Press, 1984) questioned Turner's use of statistical data. In categorizing Texas counties as Populist or Democratic, for example, Turner placed seven counties in the Democratic column that reported a Populist gubernatorial vote of at least 40 percent in 1894, hardly a percentage that could qualify them as "Democratic strongholds." She also questioned Turner's assertion that the scarcity of railroads produced the geographical isolation where Populism dominated by showing that there was a similar number of rail lines in those Populist and Democratic counties where protest was strong.

24 Clanton's most recent published findings are presented in " 'Hayseed Socialism' on the Hill: Congressional Populism, 1891–1895," *The Western Historical Quarterly*, XV (April, 1984), 139–62. Bicha's perceptions regarding Populist behavior in Congress are included in his *Western Populism: Studies in an Ambivalent Conservatism* (Lawrence, Kansas: Coronado Press, 1976).

25 Carlos A. Schwantes, "Protest in a Promised Land: Unemployment, Disinheritance, and the Origin of Labor Militancy in the Pacific Northwest, 1885–1886," *The Western Historical Quarterly*, XII (October, 1982), 373–75.

26 Bruce Palmer, *"Man over Money": The Southern Populist Critique of American Capitalism* (Chapel Hill: University of North Carolina Press, 1980), 114.

27 As quoted in Peter H. Argersinger, *Populism and Politics: William Alfred Peffer and the People's Party* (Lexington: University of Kentucky Press, 1974), 302. For information about Peffer's leadership in railroad regulation, see pp. 6–7, 25, 27.

28 As quoted in Larson, *Populism in New Mexico*, 3.

CHAPTER 2   COLORADO: THE ORIGINS OF PROTEST

1 Rodman Wilson Paul, *Mining Frontiers of the Far West, 1848–1880* (New York: Holt, Rinehart and Winston, 1863), 314.

2 Robert G. Athearn, *The Coloradans* (Albuquerque: University of New Mexico Press, 1976), 17.

3 Wright, *The Politics of Populism*, 12.

4 Paul, *Mining Frontiers of the Far West*, 124.

5 Leon W. Fuller, "Colorado's Revolt Against Capitalism," *Mississippi Valley Historical Review*, XXI (December, 1934), 346.

6 Ibid.; Wright, *The Politics of Populism*, 96–97.

7 Fuller, "Colorado's Revolt Against Capitalism," 347.

8 Paul, *Mining Frontiers of the Far West*, 124.

9 Wright, *The Politics of Populism*, 13.

10 Fuller, "Colorado's Revolt Against Capitalism," 348.

11 The Baring family has been exceptionally prominent in the financial affairs of Britain's once sprawling Empire. An example of its continuing significance is the fact that the family firm was put in charge of the liquidation of the country's assets in the United States during World War II. A good history of the firm's first century is Ralph W. Hidy, *The House of Baring in American Trade and Finance: English Merchant Bankers at Work, 1763–1861* (Cambridge: Harvard University Press, 1949).

12 Fuller, "Colorado's Revolt Against Capitalism," 348.

13 Wright, *The Politics of Populism*, 19–20.

14 Ibid., 18, 23.

15 The first assembly of the Knights established in the state involved the coal miners of Erie, who received their charter in August of 1878. Percy

Stanley Fritz, *Colorado, The Centennial State* (New York: Prentice-Hall, Inc., 1941), 368. For a good unpublished history of this labor organization in Colorado, see Gregory Alexander Bence, "The Knights of Labor in Colorado" (Master's thesis, University of Northern Colorado, 1974).

16 A discussion of Buchanan's influence on Knight activity in neighboring New Mexico is found in Robert W. Larson, "The White Caps of New Mexico: A Study of Ethnic Militancy in the Southwest," *Pacific Historical Review,* XLIV (May, 1975), 181–82.

17 Wright, *The Politics of Populism,* 112–13.

18 John D. W. Guice, *The Rocky Mountain Bench: The Territorial Courts of Colorado, Montana, and Wyoming, 1861–1890* (New Haven: Yale University Press, 1972), 128–30.

19 Wright, *The Politics of Populism,* 30.

20 August 12, 1882, issue as cited in Gene M. Gressley, *Bankers and Cattlemen* (New York: Alfred A. Knopf, 1966), 41.

21 Wright, *The Politics of Populism,* 34.

22 Ibid., 38. Not all of the state's cattlemen agreed with the Association as far as the national cattle trail was concerned. Those whose lands would be crossed quite naturally objected to it. See Ora Brooks Peake, *The Colorado Range Cattle Industry* (Glendale, Calif.: The Arthur H. Clark Company, 1937), 31–33

23 Larson, "Populism in the Mountain West," 151. No doubt to curry public favor, the controversial "English Company" contributed $15,000 in 1889 to meet one of the conditions of the state legislature for the establishment of a State Normal School at Greeley in the irrigated South Platte River Valley. It also contributed part of the forty-acre site required by law before the new school could become a reality. Albert F. Carter and Elizabeth Hays Kendel, *Forty Years of Colorado State Teachers College Formerly the State Normal School of Colorado, 1890–1930* (Colorado Teachers College Education Series, No. 11. Greeley, Colorado: The Tribune-Republican Publishing Company, 1930). For a copy of S. B. 104 creating the State Normal School, see *Laws Passed by the General Assembly of the State of Colorado Relating to the University of Northern Colorado, 1889–1983.* Collected by Robert Markham and Betty Mooso (UNC Archives Studies, Vol. III. Greeley, Colorado: University Archives, James A. Michener Library, 1983).

24 Wright, *The Politics of Populism,* 39.

25 Ibid., 35.

CHAPTER 3   COLORADO POPULISM

1 Wright, *The Politics of Populism,* 59–60.

2 Ibid., 80–81.

3 Interestingly enough, there were only 611 Chinese in the entire state in 1880. Ibid., 26–27. See also Athearn, *The Coloradans,* 178–79.

4 The Democratic national platform of 1880 provided the strongest expression of anti-Chinese sentiment: "No more Chinese immigration, except for travel, education, and foreign commerce, and that even carefully guarded." The Republicans that year were not quite as forceful, but they did pledge "to limit and restrict" Chinese immigration, and after the Chinese exclusion act had been passed in 1882, they promised in their 1884 national platform to sustain that law and improve it, if necessary. Kirk H. Porter and Donald Bruce Johnson, *National Party Platforms, 1840–1968* (4th ed.; Urbana: University of Illinois Press, 1972), 57, 62, 73.

5 Wright, *The Politics of Populism*, 27.

6 Ibid., 68.

7 Ibid., 42. For an illuminating discussion of the prominent role that the Grange played in the establishment of the state agricultural college in Fort Collins, see James E. Hansen II, *Democracy's College in the Centennial State: A History of Colorado State University* (Fort Collins, Colorado: Colorado State University, 1977), 24–25.

8 Lynn Marie Olson, "The Essence of Colorado Populism: An Analysis of the Populists and the Issues of 1892" (Master's thesis, University of Northern Colorado, 1971), 52–56.

9 Wright, *The Politics of Populism*, 42.

10 Ibid., 43–44. The growth rate of the Colorado Alliance was threefold in one year, there being only 5,000 members in 1890. Harold J. Kountze, Jr., "Davis H. Waite and the People's Party in Colorado" (Master's thesis, Yale University, 1944), 2.

11 For a thorough discussion of the issues and personalities involved in the struggle between the "Gang" and "Gang Smashers," see John Foster Powers, "'Blaine and Free Coinage': Factionalism and Silver in the Republican Pre-Convention Campaign of 1892 in Colorado" (Master's thesis, Colorado State College, 1968), 27–51.

12 Wright, *The Politics of Populism*, 117.

13 Many leaders of the new party thought this was inevitable. Benton, for instance, told hometown readers some weeks later that such government ownership was "clearly beneficial," and the only thing that had kept it from coming about sooner was popular "intertia." *Greeley Tribune*, September 22, 1892.

14 Wright, *The Politics of Populism*, 118. Also informative as far as this first third-party convention is concerned is Leonard Peter Fox, "Origins and Early Development of Populism in Colorado" (Ph.D. dissertation, University of Wisconsin, 1916), especially chapter four.

15 Wright, *The Politics of Populism*, 118.

16 Ibid., 119. For an analytical account of the intense partisanship that preceded the Republican state convention, see R. G. Dill, *The Political Campaigns of Colorado: With Complete Tabulated Statements of the Official Vote* (Denver: The Arapahoe Publishing Company, 1895), 135–48.

17 Wright, *The Politics of Populism*, 120.

18 Routt was a good choice. Both the "Gang" and the "Gang Smashers" had tried to court him because he stood for some of the same reforms they claimed to support, including the protection of state school lands, a most popular position. Powers, " 'Blaine and Free Coinage,' " 43–44. See also Robert Charles Voight, "The Life of John Long Routt" (Master's thesis, Colorado State College of Education, 1947), 75–78.

19 Wright, *The Politics of Populism*, 121–22. J. D. Burr in his congressional race lagged only slightly behind John G. Coy. He won 6.19 percent of the total vote, polling 5,207 votes out of 84,115 cast. There were, however, more votes cast in the congressional contest. *The World Almanac, 1891* (New York: The Press Publishing Co., 1891), 278. For a county-by-county breakdown of the state races for that year, see Colorado, *House Journal of the General Assembly of the State of Colorado*, Eighth Session (Colorado Springs: The Gazette Printing Company, State Printers, 1892), 23–26. All published state records in this chapter are found in the Colorado State Archives, Denver.

20 Wright, *The Politics of Populism*, 124–25.

21 Wright provides a more detailed analysis of the issues that divided miners and farmers at this time. Ibid., 130–31.

22 Ibid., 128; Carl Abbott, *Colorado: A History of the Centennial State* (Boulder: Colorado Associated University Press, 1976), 127–28. Abbott sees labor as well as agrarian discontent as a factor in the organization of the new party.

23 Karel D. Bicha, *Western Populism: Studies in an Ambivalent Conservatism* (Lawrence, Kansas: Coronado Press, 1976), 67, 74.

24 Chief justice of the three-man state supreme court was Joseph C. Helm. Colorado, *Reports of Cases Determined in the Supreme Court of the State of Colorado*, Edited by William E. Beck, XVI (New York: Banks and Brothers, Law Publishers, 1892), introduction. Helm would later become the chief stumbling block in the way of third-party control of Colorado. He was nominated as a Republican candidate for governor in 1892 and lost to the Populist candidate by only 5,436 votes out of 93,756 cast in a three-way race. It appears that the main charge against the court was the retention of a clerk who had allegedly appropriated funds for his own use. *Rocky Mountain News*, September 10, 1891, Western History Department, Denver Public Library.

25 Wright, *The Politics of Populism*, 128–29.

26 Ibid., 134.

27 Ibid., 135–36.

28 Curiously Judge Gresham had had no previous association with the third-party movement. Yet because of his correct stands on silver, rail regulation, and labor issues, he appeared as an attractive choice to many Populists. Consequently, there was prevalent pre-convention talk that Gresham would be offered and would accept the party's nomination. The rumor that he had been converted to free silver by reading Ignatius Donnelly's *Caesar's Column*

no doubt strengthened the judge's appeal. According to Hicks, Gresham's "acceptance could then be used as evidence that respectable people were becoming Populists—even men of high standing in the old parties." The conversion of such a man to Populism must have appealed to the more conservative and cautious members of the new party. Gresham's abrupt withdrawal from consideration before the end of the convention terminated this presidential boom, much to the relief of some Populists. The entire episode suggests a pragmatism in the thinking of many of the new party's proponents. For a more complete account of this unusual development, see Hicks, *The Populist Revolt*, 233–34.

29 For the complete platform see Porter and Johnson, *National Party Platforms*, 91–93, and for the resolutions, many of which were designed to attract the labor vote, see Hicks, *The Populist Revolt*, 443–44.

30 July 29, 1892, as quoted in Wright, *The Politics of Populism*, 140. The vote in the Waite-Thompson contest was a convincing one, but not overwhelmingly so. Waite won by a count of 174½ to 144½. John Robert Morris, "Davis Hanson Waite: The Ideology of a Western Populist" (Ph.D. dissertation, University of Colorado, 1965), 47.

31 Abbott, *Colorado*, 128.

32 Waite's percentage of the vote was 47.19. His chief opponent, Helm, the Republican candidate, won 41.39 percent of the vote (see note 24). Although most Democrats joined the fusion movement to get Waite elected, Democratic loyalists, known as White Wing Democrats, nominated Joseph Maupin, who carried only one county and secured a mere 9.54 percent of the total vote. Wright, *The Politics of Populism*, 153. In some respects, the stern-looking Helm was a perfect foil for Waite's outspoken antimonopoly views. The *Montezuma Journal* characterized Helm as a "corporation hireling" whose conservative views as a Colorado Supreme Court justice clearly marked him as an implacable foe of the working class. See Jane Werner, "The Press and the Populists," *The Colorado Magazine* XLVII (Winter, 1970), 50.

33 These three counties were important ones; they were among the ten which polled the largest number of votes in 1892. 2,241 votes were cast in Laramie, 2,716 in Weld, and 3,623 in Boulder. Colorado, *Senate Journal of the General Assembly of the State of Colorado*, Ninth Session (Denver: The Smith-Brooks Printing Company, State Printers, 1893), 34–35.

34 Wright, *The Poitics of Populism*, 153.

35 Clanton, *Kansas Populism*, 177.

36 Hicks, *The Populist Revolt*, 301. For a more sharply focused discussion on the importance of silver as an issue in 1892 see Larson "Populism in the Mountain West," 152–53.

37 David Lawrence Lonsdale, "The Movement for an Eight-Hour Law in Colorado, 1893–1913" (Ph.D. dissertation, University of Colorado, 1963), 32–33.

38 Wright, *The Politics of Populism*, 163–65. Of particular interest is Table

12 on p. 64, in which the vote and disagreement scores of the parties in the legislature on sixteen key questions are tabulated.

39 Waite had said in his inaugural address that there was "nothing of greater importance to the people of Colorado than the railroad question" and none for which there was greater public sentiment for action. Colorado, *Message of Gov. John L. Routt and Inaugural Address of Gov. Davis H. Waite to the Ninth General Assembly, State of Colorado, 1893*, Ninth Session (Denver: The Smith-Brooks Printing Co., State Printers, 1893), 35–36, in Office of the Governor, Inaugural Addresses, 1876–1925, Colorado State Archives, Denver.

40 Waite, although he embraced many of the social prejudices of his day, including ambivalent attitudes toward Catholics and Jews, was apparently most sincere in his gubernatorial advocacy of woman suffrage. Undated type-written memo entitled "Religion and Morals in Politics, Mrs. Ellen Foster's idea that the question of Morals has no place in Politics." Governors of Colorado, Special Series: Waite's Letters and Speeches, 1892–1896, Colorado State Archives, Denver. Hereafter cited as Waite's Letters and Speeches. Waite later questioned his support for woman suffrage when a majority of Colorado women allegedly voted against his bid for reelection. For an analysis of his shifting attitudes toward the female vote see John R. Morris, "The Women and Governor Waite," *The Colorado Magazine* XLIV (Winter, 1967), 11–19.

41 Wright, *The Politics of Populism*, 166–67.

42 Ibid., 174. Waite also feared land monopolies. In his inaugural address he had recommended that the State Land Board be stripped of its power to convey state lands to private parties. Moreover, he raised serious questions regarding alien-owned lands as well as lands that were part of old Mexican grants located in the southern part of the state. His sentiments were deeply felt: "Perhaps the most general evil that afflicts mankind is the land monopoly. So criminally wasteful has been the land policy of the United States that an area of public lands nearly equal to all of the New England States and New York and Pennsylvania combined, has been given to railway corporations." Colorado, *Message of Gov. John L. Routt and Inaugural Address of Gov. Davis H. Waite . . .* , 44–45.

43 Wright, *The Politics of Populism*, 174, 176–77. The governor's disappointment must have been acute. Only eleven laws were passed; Waite had outlined thirty-three problem areas for the special session to consider. Moreover, some of the laws that were enacted did not address the state's current problems in a meaningful way. Changes in the foreclosure and attachment laws, for instance, applied only to future contracts.

44 Ibid., 170. Many of Waite's supporters honestly believed that the governor's remarks were distorted by the eastern press. One correspondent wrote Waite that his speech was "so distorted that I do not recognize or harmonize the quotations in the eastern papers with the utterance as I read it at the time." J. C. Sibley to Waite, September 27, 1893. Waite's Letters and Speeches.

45 Waite wrote the President of Mexico that it was not impossible for silver-producing states to avail themselves of the Constitutional clause which empowers them to make gold and silver coins "a tender in payment of debt." Waite to Porfirio Diaz, September 19, 1893, Waite's Letters and Speeches. Ironically, the governor later wrote the dictatorial Diaz of a global conspiracy by the money power "against liberty all over the world." March 9, 1894. Also in Waite's Letters and Speeches.

46 Wright, *The Politics of Populism*, 161–62; Carl Ubbelohde, Maxine Benson, and Duane A. Smith, *A Colorado History* (3rd ed.; Boulder, Colorado: Pruett Publishing Co., 1972), 220–21. The two board members were D. J. Martin and Jackson Orr. Orr was strongly identified with the third-party movement, being both an Independent and a Populist.

47 Waite's official position was to prevent violence. He instructed the commander of the state militia on March 17, 1894, to "repair at once" to Cripple Creek and use "all possible means to prevent bloodshed." Waite to Adjutant General T. J. Tarsney, Waite's Letters and Speeches.

48 The issue, however, was not an eight-hour workday in the mines, but a question of fair compensation for extra time worked. Lonsdale, "The Movement for an Eight-Hour Law in Colorado," 46.

49 *Denver Republican*, September 14, 1894, as quoted in Wright, *The Politics of Populism*, 188–89.

50 Ibid., 191–93, 199–20. Another group affected by the attacks of the A.P.A. was the Spanish-speaking one in southern Colorado. But it was not as politicized as the immigrant groups in the mining counties, especially the Irish, and, therefore, not as important to the outcome of the election. Waite was, unfortunately, guilty of sharing many of the bigoted attitudes of Gilded Age Americans. A prolific writer, the governor has left to posterity some rather damning anti-Catholic and anti-Semitic remarks. See Morris, "Davis Hanson Waite," 234–36, 241–43.

51 McIntire's record on this issue is unimpressive. Not one Catholic was allowed to hold public office after McIntire was elected. Morris, "Davis Hanson Waite," 238.

52 McIntire's percentage was 51.66. The third candidate in the race was Democrat Charles Thomas, who polled only 8,337 votes for a mere 4.61 percent of the ballots tallied. *The Tribune Almanac for 1896* (New York: New York Tribune Association, 1896), 228–29.

53 For a careful quantitative analysis of the 1894 returns, see Wright, *The Politics of Populism*, 175–204. The ten counties regarded as Alliance strongholds in 1891 were Weld, Larimer, Huerfano, Las Animas, Conejos, Costilla, Otero, Saguache, Rio Grande, and Montrose. Of the ten only Saguache, Montrose, and Rio Grande remained with Waite in 1894. For a county-by-county breakdown of the gubernatorial vote see *The Tribune Almanac for 1896*, 228–29.

54 A vivid account of Teller's dramatic break with the Republican party at the national nominating convention in Chicago is provided by H. Wayne Morgan, *From Hayes to McKinley: National Party Politics, 1877–1896* (Syracuse: Syracuse University Press, 1969), 500–501.

55 Wright, *The Politics of Populism*, 207–16.

56 Ibid., 216.

CHAPTER 4   WYOMING POPULISM

1 Krueger, "Populism in Wyoming," 10–11.

2 Ibid., 14; Griffiths, "Populism in Wyoming," 60. See also Larson, "Populism in the Mountain West," 153–54, for a discussion of how Wyoming's particular environment influenced the growth of Populism in that state.

3 As quoted in Krueger, "Populism in Wyoming," 59.

4 As quoted in T. A. Larson, *History of Wyoming* (2nd ed.; Lincoln: University of Nebraska Press, 1978), 161.

5 Krueger, "Populism in Wyoming," 51–52.

6 U.S. Department of the Interior, Census Office, *Compendium of the Eleventh Census: 1890*, Part III (Washington: Government Printing Office, 1897), 432–33.

7 Larson, *History of Wyoming*, 153–55, 168–71, 273.

8 Ibid., 273; Griffiths, "Populism in Wyoming," 60–61.

9 Larson, *History of Wyoming*, 273–74.

10 Ibid., 274–75. Of course, the classic work on the Johnson County War is the colorful but highly slanted account by Cheyenne journalist, Asa Shinn Mercer, first published in 1894. The edition used in the study by this writer is A. S. Mercer, *The Banditti of the Plains or the Cattlemen's Invasion of Wyoming in 1892 (The Crowning Infamy of the Ages)*, Foreword by William H. Kittrell (Norman: University of Oklahoma Press, 1975).

11 Barber himself used the term insurrection in his April 12, 1892, telegram to the President. See Mercer, *The Banditti of the Plains*, 74–75. For a brief but objective account of the confrontations at the KC and TA ranches, see Larson, *History of Wyoming*, 276–78. Still valuable for its discussion of the causes and events of the Johnson County War is Ernest Staples Osgood's *The Day of the Cattlemen* (Minneapolis: The University of Minnesota Press, 1929), 236–55. But the best single source on the famous range war probably is Helen Huntington Smith, *The War on Powder River* (New York: McGraw-Hill, 1966).

12 Mercer, *The Banditti of the Plains*, 76; Lewis L. Gould, *Wyoming: A Political History, 1868–1896* (New Haven: Yale University Press, 1968), 142.

13 Larson, *History of Wyoming*, 283.

14 A clouded picture which remains with us today emerged soon after the invasion. J. Elmer Brock, a longtime Johnson County resident who knew many of the participants, claimed that the invasion of Johnson County was really a

goodwill mission. The invaders planned to hold a mass meeting in Buffalo to acquire the cooperation of small stockmen. They also intended to post the names of confirmed rustlers, giving them twenty-four hours to leave on pain of death. Mari Sandoz, on the other hand, in her book *The Cattlemen*, insists that the invaders carried a list of seventy names marked for death. Ibid., 275–76.

15 Gould, *Wyoming: A Political History*, 141–42.

16 Krueger, "Populism in Wyoming," 11, 13.

17 The Laramie platform is reprinted in Krueger, "Populism in Wyoming," Appendix A, 72–73; the Saint Louis one in Hicks, *The Populist Revolt*, Appendix A, 427–28. Griffiths notices two differences in the platforms. The Laramine one goes beyond the original by advocating the direct issuance of currency by the government and the exemption of all incomes under a thousand dollars in any income tax. Griffiths, "Populism in Wyoming," 58.

18 Krueger, "Populism in Wyoming," 19.

19 Ibid., 18–19.

20 Hicks, *The Populist Revolt*, 444. The reference to Wyoming as a territory is a curious one; Wyoming was granted statehood on July 10, 1890. See also Larson, "Populism in the Mountain West," 154.

21 The term Cheyenne Ring had been used by Democratic newspapers since the late eighties to discredit their Republican rivals. After the Johnson County War, however, the effectiveness of this so-called ring had increased to such an extent that even Republican leaders had to acknowledge its existence. Gould, *Wyoming: A Political History*, 171–72.

22 Krueger, "Populism in Wyoming," 22.

23 *Daily Boomerang* (Laramie), June 30, 1892. Newspapers utilized in this chapter are from the Wyoming State Archives and Historical Department in Cheyenne.

24 Krueger, "Populism in Wyoming," 25, 26. For useful biographical information about Tidball, see pp. 8–10 in Krueger's thesis.

25 *Daily Boomerang* (Laramie), September 23, 1892.

26 Griffiths, "Populism in Wyoming," 63. For a more detailed account, see Yoshida, "The Wyoming Election of 1892," 53–54.

27 One Laramie Populist, E. E. Wheeler, insisted that he would not leave the party because this would make "150 poor, honest ranchmen and their families" vulnerable to the "most diabolical conspiracy that ever degraded a civilized people." His remark was aimed at the Republicans, but the party's close ties with the cattlemen's association undoubtedly implicated that organization. Krueger, "Populism in Wyoming," 29.

28 *Daily Boomerang* (Laramie), September 23, 1892.

29 Ibid., June 30 and September 23, 1890.

30 Griffiths, "Populism in Wyoming," 64.

31 Republican gubernatorial candidate Ivinson admitted that the "great Land Steal," an obvious reference to Warren's arid land bill, hurt his party

badly in 1892 along with the Johnson County War and the close Republican connection with that invasion. Gould, however, presents convincing evidence that Warren sincerely believed that his bill would solve the problems of irrigation in the arid West. Nevertheless, because the senator was such a large landowner and stock grazer, his opponents could not resist characterizing him as a monopolistic land grabber. See Gould, *Wyoming: A Political History*, 130–33, 171–72.

32 Anne Carolyn Hansen, "The Congressional Career of Francis E. Warren from 1890 to 1902," *Annals of Wyoming*, XX (January, 1948), 18–19.

33 Griffiths, "Populism in Wyoming," 64–65.

34 *The Tribune Almanac for 1893* (New York: New York Tribune Association, 1893), 307. The election votes broken down by counties for both presidential electors and candidates for state office were officially canvassed on December 31, 1892, and carried in the *Sheridan Post* on January 12, 1893.

35 Historians of Wyoming Populism simply cannot agree on the main reason for the defeat of the Weaver-Field slate. Yoshida in his "The Wyoming Election of 1892" insists that many Democrats violated their fusion pledge and voted for Harrison. He receives some support for this assertion from T. Alfred Larson. Krueger, on the other hand, argues that many Republicans crossed over to vote for Osborne but refused to support Weaver. He uses the vote in Johnson County to buttress his position. In 1890 the Republicans carried Johnson County handily, but in 1892 there was a dramatic reversal. Weaver carried the county, but by a much smaller majority than the Democrats, who won their largest majority in Johnson County. Thus, Republicans in the north were able to draw a distinction between the state and national organizations of their party. Griffiths, "Populism in Wyoming," 65, 66; Larson, *History of Wyoming*, 287; Krueger, "Populism in Wyoming," 32–34.

36 Following the decline of Populism as a political force in Wyoming, Tidball became a socialist, even editing a socialist newspaper in Sheridan. Krueger, "Populism in Wyoming," 9.

37 Griffiths, "Populism in Wyoming," 65, 66.

38 *Sheridan Post*, February 23, 1893.

39 Griffiths, "Populism in Wyoming," 66.

40 Larson, *History of Wyoming*, 289.

41 Yoshida, "The Wyoming Election of 1892," 127.

42 Krueger, "Populism in Wyoming," 37.

43 Larson, *History of Wyoming*, 295–96.

44 Krueger, "Populism in Wyoming," 40–41.

45 *Cheyenne Daily Leader*, August 12, 1894.

46 Krueger, "Populism in Wyoming," 43, 47. The estimate ranges from eleven to thirteen percent.

47 Fred A. Shannon, *American Farmers' Movements* (Princeton, New Jersey: D. Van Nostrand, Inc., 1957), 72.

48 Krueger, "Populism in Wyoming," 48.

49 Ibid., 56–57.

50 Larson, *History of Wyoming*, 293. According to Gould, Brown's "ego was greater than his common sense." He was not only lured into a much more extensive campaign with the railroad passes, but was provided with fake letters of support and outright donations from Republicans. Gould, *Wyoming: a Political History*, 253.

51 The count was 10,655 for Bryan and 10,072 for McKinley, giving the silver-thumping Democrat a narrow 583-vote margin. *The World Almanac and Encyclopedia, 1899* (New York: The Press Publishing Co., 1899), 476. Warren boasted that Wyoming Republicans had "scored the greatest success in the United States" in keeping Bryan's majority so small. Bryan carried Colorado by a margin of six to one and Montana by a margin of four to one. But both of these states had important silver resources. Larson, *History of Wyoming*, 294–95.

52 The potential Populist vote was there to make a difference. In 1894 the controversial Tidball running for governor polled 2,176 votes out of 19,290 cast, a tally that could have significantly tilted either of the two major races in 1896. *The World Almanac and Encyclopedia, 1895* (New York: The Press Publishing Co., 1895), 435.

53 Larson, *History of Wyoming*, 294.

54 Krueger, "Populism in Wyoming," 63. The other two from Sheridan were J. F. Brown and George Brundage, while Melvin Nichols, a silver Republican convert from Crook, was the fourth elected to the House.

55 Griffiths provides a brief account of Populist activity for the elections of 1898, 1900, 1902, 1904, 1906, 1908, 1914, and 1916. Griffiths, "Populism in Wyoming," 70–71.

56 Larson, *History of Wyoming*, 284–85. Intimidation of voters, particularly by employers hostile to Populism, and factional disputes within the party are other reasons given by Larson.

CHAPTER 5   MONTANA: THE ORIGINS OF PROTEST

1 The typical Populist was an urban trade unionist or middle-class intellectual from such strongholds of party activity as Butte, Anaconda, Great Falls, and Helena. Clinch, *Urban Populism and Free Silver in Montana*, 170.

2 K. Ross Toole, *Montana: An Uncommon Land* (Norman: University of Oklahoma Press, 1959), 67–70. Typical of many mining rushes, when a major strike occurred on the Alder Gulch in May of 1863 there was an influx of miners from Bannack to stake out their claims. Within a year Virginia City had a population of 10,000, and nearby Nevada City was Montana's second-largest community. William L. Lang and Rex C. Myers, *Montana: Our Land and People* (Boulder, Colorado: Pruett Publishing Company, 1979), 34.

3 Clinch, *Urban Populism and Free Silver in Montana*, 1–3. In 1892 the

value of silver production was $22,500,000 as compared to gold, which was slightly below $3,000,000. Although the state's first recorded silver find occurred at Argenta near Bannack in 1864, the really big years for silver mining occurred in the mid-seventies. Michael P. Malone and Richard B. Roeder, *Montana: A History of Two Centuries* (Seattle: University of Washington Press, 1976), 141–44.

4 Toole, *Montana: An Uncommon Land* 163–64. Copper king Marcus Daly originally interested George Hearst and James Ben Ali Haggin in his scheme to mine copper at Butte by taking the two San Franciscans down a 500-foot shaft to show them the richness of the copper deposits owned by their Anaconda Gold and Silver Mining Company. The result was the formation of the Anaconda Copper Mining Company, the creation of the town of Anaconda twenty-six miles away where the great copper smelter was built, and the transformation of the state's mining economy in a revolutionary way. William E. Farr and K. Ross Toole, *Montana: Images of the Past* (Boulder, Colorado: Pruett Publishing Company, 1978), 34–35.

5 Clinch, *Urban Populism and Free Silver in Montana*, 2.

6 Ibid., 5. For a fascinating insight into the heterogeneous nature of mining-camp populations, see *Copper Camp: Stories of the World's Greatest Mining Town, Butte, Montana*, Compiled by workers of the Writers' Program of the Work Projects Administration in the State of Montana (New York: Hastings House, Publishers, 1951).

7 The original name of the organizaton was the Butte Workingmen's Union, but by 1885 so many miners belonged that it changed its name to the Butte Miners' Union. Lang and Myers, *Montana: Our Land and People*, 157. See also Clinch, *Urban Populism and Free Silver in Montana*, 6 and Malone and Roeder, *Montana: A History of Two Centuries*, 156.

8 Clinch, *Urban Populism and Free Silver in Montana*, 6.

9 Members of the Butte Miners' Union, as a matter of fact, encouraged non-miners to join the trade-oriented Knights rather than join their union. Lang and Myers, *Montana: Our Land and People*, 157.

10 There were thirty-three separate unions representing skilled and unskilled workers in Butte around the turn of the century, according to the city's business directory. For a list of them see ibid., 159.

11 Union members in Montana were interested in a wide range of workingmen's issues. The Knights of Labor, for instance, demanded at their annual convention in Butte that no child under fifteen be employed in any industrial establishment. *Butte Mining Journal*, January 24, 1892. All Montana newspapers utilized in this study are from the Montana Historical Society Library in Helena.

12 Miners in Colorado averaged only three dollars a day, even though a greater percentage of Colorado's work force was unionized in 1892 than in any other state. See chapter two, p. 21, and chapter three, p. 32.

13 The federal reclamation projects that came later did not help much either. Under the Carey Act of 1894 only three irrigation projects were completed and under the Newlands Act of 1902 only four. Clinch, *Urban Populism and Free Silver in Montana,* 14–15.

14 Frank Grant, "Rocky Mountain Husbandman: Embattled Voice of the Montana Farmer," *Montana, the Magazine of Western History,* XXIV (April, 1974), 36.

15 Toole, *Montana: An Uncommon Land,* 142.

16 Clinch, *Urban Populism and Free Silver in Montana,* 13–14. The fact that Montana's state cattle association did not enjoy the coveted position that the state's mining enterprises did should not lead to the conclusion that the cattlemen of the state were lacking in prominence or influence. Russell B. Harrison, son of Senator Benjamin Harrison, was secretary of the Montana Stockgrowers Association before his father became president. Gressley, *Bankers and Cattlemen,* 82.

17 Lang and Myers, *Montana: Our Land and People,* 86.

19 Toole, *Montana: An Uncommon Land,* 91–94.

19 Ibid., 228–42; Clinch, *Urban Populism and Free Silver in Montana,* 15. As an indication of how important wheat farming became during the twentieth century, there were 44 million bushels of wheat raised in 1924 and almost 94 million in 1950. These farmers suffered much, however, because of the severe droughts that started with World War I and continued through the Great Depression.

20 Clinch, *Urban Populism and Free Silver in Montana,* 21–22.

21 Benjamin Horace Hibbard, *A History of the Public Land Policies* (New York: The Macmillan Company, 1924), 264.

22 Clinch, *Urban Populism and Free Silver in Montana,* 24.

23 As quoted in Grant, "Rocky Mountain Husbandman," 41–42.

24 Clinch, *Urban Populism and Free Silver in Montana,* 27–28.

25 Ibid., 16.

26 The official name of the original Grange was the National Grange of the Patrons of Husbandry.

27 M. L. Wilson made that assertion in an article on Montana agriculture written about the time of World War I. It is a debatable interpretation. See Grant, "Rocky Mountain Husbandman," 38–39.

28 Clinch, *Urban Populism and Free Silver in Montana,* 16–17; Larson, "Populism in the Mountain West," 156.

29 Clinch, *Urban Populism and Free Silver in Montana,* 16–17, 49. One must assume from Ravens's appearance before the state gathering that the new state Alliance was affiliated with the Northern Alliance.

30 Grant, "Rocky Mountain Husbandman," 39, 41–42.

31 *Rocky Mountain Husbandman* (White Sulphur Springs), August 21, 1890.

CHAPTER 6   MONTANA POPULISM

1 Clinch, *Urban Populism and Free Silver in Montana,* 7, 11, 45.

2. Ibid., 46.

3 Ibid., 45.

4 Montana, *Laws, Resolutions, and Memorials of the Territory of Montana, Passed at the Sixteenth Regular Session of the Legislative Assembly,* Sixteenth Session (Helena: The Journal Publishing Co., 1889), 135–45.

5 *Semi-Weekly Inter Mountain* (Butte), June 19, 1892.

6 Clinch, *Urban Populism and Free Silver in Montana,* 45.

7 Ibid., 45–46.

8 *Rocky Mountain Husbandman* (White Sulphur Springs), August 21, 1890.

9 Clinch, *Urban Populism and Free Silver in Montana,* 47.

10 In addition to electing Breen as their leader, the Knights also passed resolutions in favor of free silver and against child labor and Chinese employment that were later approved by the delegates who met in Anaconda as part of the new third-party movement. *Butte Mining Journal,* January 24, 1892.

11 Clinch, *Urban Populism and Free Silver in Montana,* 47.

12 January 24, 1892.

13 January 24, 1892.

14 As quoted in the *Butte Mining Journal,* January 17, 1892.

15 *Semi-Weekly Inter Mountain* (Butte), January 20, 1892.

16 Clinch, *Urban Populism and Free Silver in Montana,* 48.

17 This resolution along with the organizational plan for the new party appeared in the January 24, 1892, issue of the *Journal.*

18 As quoted in the *Butte Mining Journal,* January 24, 1892.

19 *Butte Mining Journal,* January 24, 1892. These resolutions or principles are also listed and discussed in Clinch, *Urban Populism and Free Silver in Montana,* 48–49.

20 Clinch, *Urban Populism and Free Silver in Montana,* 48–50.

21 *Semi-Weekly Inter Mountain* (Butte), June 19, 1892.

22 Ibid.

23 Ibid.

24 Clinch, *Urban Populism and Free Silver in Montana,* 9–11.

25 *Butte Mining Journal,* January 24, 1892. The Butte Miners Union perhaps symbolized labor's intransigent attitude toward the Chinese as much as any workingman's organization. The union issued a directive that any member found "patronizing Chinese, directly or indirectly, on or after the 15th day of January, 1892, will be fined a sum of $5.00." *Butte Mining Journal,* January 17, 1892. The *Helena Herald* believed that once a law were passed prohibiting Chinese immigration, the new party would have no more reason to exist. The *Butte Mining Journal* disagreed: "We supposed its object was for the general betterment of the working class, and not simply an anti-Chinese organization." *Butte Mining Journal,* January 31, 1892.

26 Larson, *History of Wyoming*, 141–44. It cannot be established, however, that the union gave official direction to the use of violence.

27 *Semi-Weekly Inter Mountain* (Butte), June 19, 1892.

28 Ibid. According to the *Inter Mountain*, one party worker, James Donovan, was "so disgusted with the methods of [the] men who ran the convention yesterday" that he was going to return to one of the old parties. Of course, one must keep in mind that the *Semi-Weekly Inter Mountain* was a Republican paper.

29 Clinch, *Urban Populism and Free Silver in Montana*, 51–52.

30 Ella Knowles's Republican opponent was Henri Haskell, who won the race. She later married Haskell and went by the name of Ella Knowles Haskell throughout the remainder of her political career.

31 Clinch, *Urban Populism and Free Silver in Montana*, 54, 55–56, 58. According to a report in the *Butte Bystander* on September 17, 1892, the national committee of the People's party had decided that Weaver, because of his good reception in Montana, would probably return to Butte to campaign in late October. But there was an avalanche of criticism and ridicule for the Populist candidate in the Republican and Democratic press of the state.

32 Clinch, *Urban Populism and Free Silver in Montana*, 59–61.

33 Pemberton was highly regarded. His endorsement by the Democrats was lauded by the *Butte Bystander* as an act of "good judgment," which would make the judge a "good sure winner." *Butte Bystander*, September 17, 1892.

34 Clinch, *Urban Populism and Free Coinage in Montana*, 62–63.

35 *The Tribune Almanac for 1893*, 288.

36 Ibid.; Clinch, *Urban Populism and Free Silver in Montana*, 64.

37 Clinch, *Urban Populism and Free Silver in Montana*, 64, 65–66.

38 Montana, *Laws, Resolutions, and Memorials of the State of Montana Passed at the Third Regular Session of the Legislative Assembly*, Third Session (Butte City: Inter Mountain Publishing Co., 1893), 66–67.

39 Clinch, *Urban Populism and Free Silver in Montana*, 67.

40 Ibid., 31–35.

41 Ibid., 85–87, 101, 102.

42 The platform of the Industrial Legion was almost identical with the Populists' Omaha one. It made such demands as a national currency "safe, sound, and flexible," free coinage, a subtreasury, government ownership of railroads, and a return to the people of land not in actual use. *Montana Populist*, June 1, 1893.

43 The *Butte Bystander*, originally published by the influential Silver Bow Trades and Labor Assembly, became the official voice of the Western Federation of Miners. It was also aggressively Populist.

44 Clinch, *Urban Populism and Free Silver in Montana*, 106–110. The most bloody engagement fought by Hogan's army occurred at Billings on April 25 when men deputized by Federal Marshal William McDermott clashed with Hogan's Coxeyites. One Billings resident was killed, and a number of men on

both sides were wounded. The *Butte Bystander* probably spoke for many of the state's working people when it lamented the violent encounter but placed the responsibility for it "squarely on the shoulders of federal authorities." *Butte Bystander*, April 28, 1894. The sentiments of the state militia were also suspect. About a year before Hogan's army was stopped, the *Montana Populist* insisted that the plutocracy could depend upon the militia to shoot strikers. *Montana Populist*, June 1, 1893.

45 Clinch, *Urban Populism and Free Silver in Montana*, 91–93, 119–20. Malone and Roeder believe that after 1893 the majority of Populists came from the mining areas, "especially from hard-pressed silver towns" of the state. Malone and Roeder, *Montana: A History of Two Centuries*, 162.

46 Populist intransigence on the subject of fusionism caused considerable frustration among Democrats. The obviously Republican *Helena Independent* took glee from the Democrats' predicament. "The populist organs in this state have become so cocky over two or three little victories at the spring election that they announce that democrats will be invited to vote their ticket next fall, but there will be no offers of fusion. This leaves those weak-kneed democrats who have been eager to form a co-partnership [with] populists in an interesting predicament." As quoted in *Butte Bystander*, May 12, 1894.

47 Because of Smith's newness to the party, there was a spirited contest between Smith and one of the more established Populists, Joseph Oker. Oker spoke thirty-five minutes to convince the delegates of his worth, ten minutes longer than Smith did. *Montana Silverite*, June 29, 1894. One reason for Smith's popularity was his defense, along with George Haldorn, of William Hogan and his Coxeyites at their federal trial in Helena. Clinch, *Urban Populism and Free Silver in Montana*, 110.

48 A much more militant candidate than Smith was George W. Reeves. the Populist candidate for associate justice. Prior to his nomination Reeves gave a speech most critical of the two older parties entitled the "Evils of Class Legislation." *Montana Populist*, March 3, 1894. During the campaign he declined to attend an important meeting with this terse telegram message: "Am defending men of A.R.U. charged with blowing up engine. Can't be with you." *Butte Bystander*, August 18, 1894.

49 Hartman's legal connections with the Northern Pacific probably hurt him, but not enough. They were not, however, forgotten. The *Havre Herald* reminded railroad employees that Hartman was a "paid attorney" for the Northern Pacific. "Will the railroad men of Montana vote for him in preference to Bob Smith, the workingmen's friend?" As quoted in the *Butte Bystander*, August 18, 1894.

50 Clinch, *Urban Populism and Free Silver in Montana*, 117–19. The A.P.A. was even more active in Colorado in 1894 (see chapter three), and again the Republican party was the most congenial of the political parties toward this nativist organization. Many Democrats and Populists were bitter against both

the American Protective Association and the G.O.P. because of their association with each other. Populist Will Kennedy was most antagonistic toward the
two; he crusaded for the abolition of the A.P.A. in the pages of his Boulder
Age. The *Bystander* tried to dismiss the nativist organization with bravado,
but it was not always convincing: "The Apaists naturally belong to the republican party, but against the united populists every one [sic] they don't
stand a ghost of a show." *Butte Bystander*, March 9, 1895. Many Republicans,
of course, were embarrassed and outraged by A.P.A. support. For a thorough
study of this organization, see Donald L. Kinzer, *An Episode in Anti-Catholicism: The American Protective Association* (Seattle: University of Washington Press, 1964).

51 Clinch, *Urban Populism and Free Silver in Montana*, 119.

52 Another long-standing concern of the Populists was the creation of a
separate silver party if they did not do something decisive about the coinage
issue. More than two years before fusion talk really became serious, Absalom
F. Bray warned party members that they must "cover the financial question
fully and in a manner not to be misunderstood" by Montana voters. "If we do
not do this a silver party will be formed which will—if it does not win—
defeat the populist party." *Butte Bystander*, January 13, 1894.

53 Clinch, *Urban Populism and Free Silver in Montana*, 138.

54 Ibid., 138–43. After the silver Republicans had failed to nominate a
presidential elector, they agreed to support the three fusionist electors chosen
by the Populists and Democrats: Martin Maginnis, Henry Frank, and Daniel
Brown.

55 *The World Almanac and Encyclopedia, 1899*, 452. The two Republican
counties were eastern ones: Custer and Dawson.

56 Clinch, *Urban Populism and Free Silver in Montana*, 153.

57 Ibid., 154–55.

58 Ibid., 155–57.

59 *The World Almanac and Encyclopedia, 1899*, 452. Campbell received
Hartman's support, which was vital because the fusionists (Silver Republicans
and Populists) nominated Thomas C. Marshall. Campbell's two opponents
together polled more votes than he. The final tally was Campbell, 23,351;
Marshall, 14,823; and Hogan, 11,607.

60 Clinch, *Urban Populism and Free Silver in Montana*, 159.

61 Ibid., 160–65.

62 Edwards had to defeat three candidates in that confusing election. He
bested his nearest opponent, Republican Samuel G. Murray, by 4,923 votes.
The World Almanac and Encyclopedia, 1901 (New York: The Press Publishing Co., 1901), 462. Caldwell Edwards was one of the few agrarian candidates
to win high office at this time. One of the leaders of the old Gallatin County
Farmers' Alliance, himself a Single Taxer in 1890, Edwards had a long-standing reputation for incorruptibility. When he was nominated for Congress by

the newly organized Populist party in 1892, he claimed he could resist the "corrupting influences which permeated Washington political life," having done so in the territorial legislature, where he was never approached by the "emissaries" of the railroads and other monopolistic enterprises. *Semi-Weekly Inter Mountain*, June 19, 1892.

63 Clinch, *Urban Populism and Free Silver in Montana*, 166–67.

64 Ibid., 168.

CHAPTER 7   NEW MEXICO: THE ORIGINS OF PROTEST

1 Lynn I. Perrigo, *The American Southwest: Its Peoples and Culture* (New York: Holt, Rinehart and Winston, 1971), 50.

2 Robert W. Larson, *New Mexico's Quest for Statehood* (Albuquerque: The University of New Mexico Press, 1968), 65, 71.

3 Warren A. Beck, *New Mexico: A History of Four Centuries* (Norman: University of Oklahoma Press, 1962), 258, 263.

4 Ibid., 255–56.

5 Ibid., 243–45.

6 Moreover, most of New Mexico's territorial delegates spent an inordinate amount of time lobbying for statehood right up to the time of admission. Larson, "Populism in the Mountain West," 159.

7 Prince to J. J. Trujillo, January 2, 1892, as quoted in Larson, *New Mexico Populism*, 4.

8 Larson, *New Mexico Populism*, 51.

9 Beck, *New Mexico*, 258, 260, 262.

10 Ibid., 245–46.

11 Larson, *New Mexico Populism*, 51. For a more detailed account of gold and silver production in the territory at this time, see Herbert Theodore Hoover, "Populism and the Territories" (Master's thesis, New Mexico State University, 1961), 54–57.

12 Larson, "The White Caps of New Mexico," 173–74.

13 Victor Westphall, *The Public Domain in New Mexico, 1854–1891* (Albuquerque: University of New Mexico Press, 1965), 78–79.

14 Frank D. Reeve, *History of New Mexico* (2 vols., New York: Lewis Historical Publishing Company, Inc., 1961), II, 210–11.

15 Larson, *New Mexico Populism*, 7.

16 Ibid., 11.

17 Ibid., 22–23. Probably the most detailed account of the complicated history of the Maxwell Grant is Jim Berry Pearson's *The Maxwell Land Grant* (Norman: University of Oklahoma Press, 1961).

18 Larson, *New Mexico Populism*, 23–24, 26; Beck, *New Mexico*, 170. A second opponent of the Maxwell Company was another Methodist minister, Oscar P. McMains, who carried on his war against the company for more than

twenty years. For a thorough account of McMain's crusade, see Morris F. Taylor, *O. P. McMains and the Maxwell Land Grant Conflict* (Tucson: University of Arizona Press, 1979).

19 For a lengthy discussion of this remarkable letter written by Governor Ross to John O'Grady on March 26, 1887, see Larson, *New Mexico's Quest for Statehood*, 141–43. The death of Tolby was attributed to the Santa Fe Ring as much as it was to the closely allied Maxwell Company.

20 Larson, *New Mexico's Quest for Statehood*, 143. For a detailed account of Catron's extensive business activities, see Victor Westphall, *Thomas Benton Catron and His Era* (Tucson: University of Arizona Press, 1973).

21 Owens has suggested three classifications for the territorial party system: one-party, two-party, and no-party. In a no-party system, such as New Mexico's, major parties worked together in a coalition where considerable harmony was achieved despite the routine noises of partisanship. See Kenneth N. Owens, "Patterns and Structure in Western Territorial Politics," *The Western Historical Quarterly*, I (October, 1970), 377, 386–92.

22 Leo Grebler, Joan W. Moore, and Ralph C. Guzman, *The Mexican-American People: The Nation's Second Largest Minority* (New York: The Free Press, 1970), 50. For one of the most thoroughgoing discussions of the land-grant question, see the chapter on the Santa Fe Ring in Howard Roberts Lamar, *The Far Southwest, 1846–1912: A Territorial History* (New Haven: Yale University Press, 1966), 136–170.

23 Andrew Bancroft Schlesinger, "Las Gorras Blancas, 1888–1891," *Journal of Mexican American History*, I (Spring, 1971), 93–94.

24 Larson, *New Mexico Populism*, 43. For a history of the New Mexico Knights, see Robert W. Larson, "The Knights of Labor and Native Protest in New Mexico" in Robert Kern (ed.), *Labor in New Mexico: Unions, Strikes, and Social History since 1881* (Albuquerque: University of New Mexico, 1983), 31–52.

25 John K. Martin, Frank C. Ogden, and J. B. Allen to Powderly, August 8, 1890, as quoted in Walter John Donlon, "Le Baron Bradford Prince, Chief Justice and Governor of New Mexico Territory, 1879–1893" (Ph.D. dissertation, University of New Mexico, 1967), 233.

26 Larson, "The White Caps of New Mexico," 175. After spening time in the gambling halls of Wyoming, Herrera and his brother homesteaded for a number of years in Brown's Park, Colorado, See Grace McClure, *The Bassett Women* (Athens, Ohio: Swallow Press/Ohio University Press, 1985), 10. McClure is currently working on a biography of Herrera.

27 Family tradition is the source of this incident which involved Herrera and his neighbor, the owner of the Black Tree Trunk Ranch near San Geronimo. The account was related to this writer in an interview with Mrs. Ruth Brito, Herrera's great grandniece, and her son and daughter-in-law, Mr. and Mrs. Al Brito of Denver, February 27, 1972.

28 Larson, "The White Caps of New Mexico," 175–76.

29 The governor made his request to the Secretary of the Interior, John W. Noble, on August 12, 1890, even urging that official to use his influence with the War Department to acquire the troops from Santa Fe and Fort Union for that purpose. In the end the government refused to intervene unless civil authority in New Mexico was challenged in such a way that it would shatter the public peace. Larson, *New Mexico Populism*, 39.

30 Herrera had originally joined the Knights in one of the two states, his commission as district organizer being a renewal, according to an August 8 letter from three San Miguel Knights to Powderly (see note 25). Robert J. Rosenbaum, *Mexican Resistance in the Southwest: "The Sacred Right of Self-Preservation"* (Austin: University of Texas Press, 1981), 121, 209–10.

31 Rosenbaum feels that Herrera did not have to teach or provide effective "techniques of protest." Direct and forceful action was natural to those native New Mexicans involved in both fence-cutting and labor agitation. See ibid., 122–23.

32 Larson, "The White Caps of New Mexico," 179.

33 Larson, *New Mexico Populism*, 42–44.

CHAPTER 8   NEW MEXICO POPULISM

1 Larson, *New Mexico Populism*, 42.

2 Biographical sketches for both Mills and Martinez are included in ibid., 44–46.

3 Ibid., 81; Larson, "The White Caps of New Mexico," 183.

4 Larson, *New Mexico Populism*, 46.

5 October 4, 1890. Issues of the *Sun* are located in a collection of newspapers that belonged to Mills, which are currently located at New Mexico Highlands University in Las Vegas.

6 Larson, *New Mexico Populism*, 53.

7 Hoover, "Populism and the Territories," 48.

8 Larson, *New Mexico Populism*, 54–55.

9 *The World Almanac, 1891*, 300.

10 Larson, *New Mexico Populism*, 58.

11 Ibid., 59.

12 Larson, "The White Caps of New Mexico," 184.

13 Larson, *New Mexico Populism*, 60–61.

14 Ibid., 66–67.

15 October 15, 1892. Issues of the *Democrat* are located in the State Records Center and Archives in Santa Fe.

16 Larson, *New Mexico Populism*, 76.

17 Powers, "'Blaine and Free Coinage,'" 190. The catchy slogan appeared on the badges worn by Colorado delegates at the Republican national convention in Minneapolis.

18 Larson, *New Mexico Populism*, 74.

19 *The World Almanac and Encyclopedia, 1895*, 413.

20 August 31, 1894. Issues of the *Times* are located on microfilm at the *Daily Times* (Farmington).

21 Larson, *New Mexico Populism*, 81, 85–86.

22 More extensive comments are found in the September 18, 1894, edition of the *Optic* and are quoted in ibid., 86.

23 Larson, *New Mexico Populism*, 87.

24 Information on the occupations of both Stamm and Keleher was found in the *Southern Pacific Coast Directory, 1888–9* (San Francisco, no date), 444, 447.

25 Larson, *New Mexico Populism*, 56–57, 88.

26 As quoted in ibid., 89.

27 Larson, *New Mexico Populism*, 90.

28 Ibid., 90–91, 92–93.

29 September 15, 1894, issue as quoted in ibid., 94.

30 Larson, *New Mexico Populism*, 93.

31 Ibid., 97.

32 Quotations are taken from the October 26, 1894, issue of the *Chieftain* and from letters found in the extensive Thomas B. Catron Papers, Special Collections Division, University of New Mexico Library, Albuquerque. See ibid., 113–14.

33 The interview was carried in the November 2, 1894, issue of the *Las Vegas Daily Optic*. See Larson, *New Mexico Populism*, 113.

34 Mills denied this charge in an October 13, 1896, letter to Prince, the contents of which are discussed in detail in Larson, *New Mexico Populism*, 169–71.

35 For a discussion of Populist subsidization in Wyoming, see chapter four, p. 59.

36 "I think some effective work can be done to aid you in this county," Blake wrote Catron on September 24, 1894, referring to populous San Miguel County. See Larson, *New Mexico Populism*, 114.

37 Lewis C. Fort, an East Las Vegas attorney and former member of the territorial council, was the Catron lieutenant responsible for this remarkable development. Reasons for Fort's successes are analyzed in Larson, *New Mexico Populism*, 115.

38 *The World Almanac and Encyclopedia, 1895*, 413.

39 As was the case with so many states and territories in the Mountain West at this time, New Mexico was vulnerable to the propaganda of the A.P.A. and like organizations, even though it was the least likely place for success because of the large Spanish-speaking Roman Catholic majority. For more information about the New Mexico effort see Larson, *New Mexico Populism*, 109–10, 150–51.

40 Ibid., 115. Emiterio Gallegos, Mateo Lujan, Saturnio Pinard, and Francisco Gallegos were the Populist leaders involved in this fusion arrangement.

41 Given the importance of mining and sheep-raising in New Mexico, the attack on President Cleveland's gold-bug views and his free wool policy also cost the Democrats in the 1894 election. Larson, "Populism in the Mountain West," 161.

42 The term, meant to be derogatory, was taken from a San Miguel Spanish language newspaper published by Felix Martinez, *La Voz de Pueblo.*

43 *The World Almanac and Encyclopedia, 1895,* 413.

44 Larson, *New Mexico Populism,* 96, 117.

45 Ibid., 119; Larson, *New Mexico's Quest for Statehood,* 199–200.

46 Larson, *New Mexico Populism,* 120, 143.

47 J. D. Kello to Catron, October 18, 1896, as quoted in ibid., 143.

48 September 23, 1896 as quoted in Larson, *New Mexico Populism,* 128.

49 Prince worked to advance silver through such regional and national organizations as the Trans-Mississippi Congress and the proposed Trans-Montane League. He wrote a book on free coinage *The Money Problem, or Bi-Metallism vs. a Single Gold Standard,* which also brought him much prominence. Larson, *New Mexico Populism,* 121–23; Larson, *New Mexico's Quest for Statehood,* 184, 190.

50 Larson, *New Mexico Populism,* 131–33, 135.

51 For the details of the Catron substitute, see Larson, *New Mexico's Quest for Statehood,* 186–87.

52 Prince's removal as the Populist candidate for delegate was made under the most controversial and embarrassing of circumstances. Prince claimed he was replaced before he received the notification offering him the nomination, an offer he intended to refuse. Larson, *New Mexico Populism,* 138–40.

53 *The World Almanac and Encyclopedia, 1899,* 455.

54 Larson, *New Mexico Populism,* 154–55. One of the fusion candidates elected to the council to represent both San Juan and Rio Arriba counties was Antonio Joseph, who was later elected council president.

55 Ibid., 163, 164.

56 Fergusson's margin of defeat was greater than his margin of victory in 1896. He lost to Pedro Perea, a Catron lieutenant, by a vote of 18,722 to 16,659. See *The World Almanac and Encyclopedia, 1899,* 455, for a county by county breakdown.

57 Larson, *New Mexico Populism,* 160–61. The Republicans were evidently more persuasive in convincing New Mexico voters that the wealthy sheep-owner Solomon Luna was more effective in achieving the duty on wool than Fergusson.

CHAPTER 9   POPULISM IN IDAHO, UTAH, NEVADA, AND ARIZONA: AN OVERVIEW

1 For a brief, preliminary assessment of these four states, see Larson, "Populism in the Mountain West," 162–64.

2 F. Ross Peterson, Idaho: *A Bicentennial History* (New York: W. W. Norton and Company, Inc., 1976), 10, 104, 123. Ultimately, the development of the Snake River Valley would make it one of the great reclamation projects of the twentieth century.

3 David Burke Griffiths, "Populism in the Far West, 1890–1900" (Ph.D. dissertation, University of Washington, 1967), 296–97, 299; C. J. Brosnan, *History of the State of Idaho* (New York: Charles Scribner's Sons, 1918), 186–87. For a more lengthy study of the origins of Populist protest and their political manifestations, see William Joseph Gabourg, "Dissension in the Rockies: A History of Idaho Populism" (Ph.D. dissertation, University of Idaho, 1966).

4 Griffiths, "Populism in the Far West," 297.

5 Peterson, *Idaho: A Bicentennial History*, 110. For a study of Boyce's unusual career which took him throughout much of the mining West, see John Fahey, "Ed Boyce and the Western Federation of Miners," *Idaho Yesterdays*, XXV (Fall, 1981), 18–30.

6 Griffiths, "Populism in the Far West," 298–99.

7 Peterson, *Idaho: A Bicentennial History*, 109.

8 Recognizing from the beginning the political value of this issue, the Populists at their organizational meeting in May unequivocally condemned state and federal intervention in the strike. See Griffiths, "Populism in the Far West," 298.

9 Peterson, *Idaho: A Bicentennial History*, 110.

10 The Republican majority in the eighteen-seat senate was four, and in the thirty-six-seat house, it was sixteen. *The World Almanac and Encyclopedia, 1895*, 394.

11 Brosnan, *History of the State of Idaho*, 186–87.

12 Griffiths, "Populism in the Far West," 304.

13 Byron Defenbach, *Idaho: The Place and Its People*, I (Chicago: The American Historical Society, Inc., 1933), 453, 454.

14 Peterson, *Idaho: A Bicentennial History*, 111.

15 David B. Griffiths, "Far Western Populism: The Case of Utah, 1893–1900," *Utah Historical Quarterly*, XXXVII (Fall, 1969), 397.

16 Griffiths, "Populism in the Far West," 348, 356.

17 Charles S. Peterson, *Utah: A Bicentennial History* (New York: W. W. Norton and Company, Inc., 1977), 170.

18 One historian claims that Lawrence was an "impossible candidate," about whom Mormons had many unpleasant memories. Wayne Stout, *History of Utah* (Salt Lake City: privately printed, 1968), 29.

19 Griffiths, "Far Western Populism: The Case of Utah," 398.

20 In 1890 Utah produced eight million ounces of silver or thirteen percent of the national product. Griffiths, "Populism in the Far West," 348.

21 Griffiths, "Far Western Populism: The Case of Utah," 402.

22 Ibid., 402–03.

23 Ibid., 403, 404. Of 12,690 votes cast in the Salt Lake City race, Lawrence won only 1,087. Griffiths, "Populism in the Far West," 370.

24 The planks of the 1898 platform are listed in Stout, *History of Utah*, 55.

25 Griffiths, "Far Western Populism: The Case of Utah," 404–06.

26 Mary Ellen Glass, *Silver and Politics in Nevada, 1892–1902* (Reno: University of Nevada Press, 1969), 27–30.

27 Russell R. Elliott, *History of Nevada* (Lincoln: University of Nebraska Press, 1973), 184.

28 Russell R. Elliott, *Servant of Power: A Political Biography of Senator William M. Stewart* (Reno: University of Nevada Press, 1983), 154–58. Stewart appeared with Weaver during Weaver's campaign visit to Nevada in 1892 where the two men shared a four-horse coach drawn through the streets of Virginia City on August 7. One Nevada newspaper predicted that Stewart would be Secretary of State if Weaver were elected.

29 The elimination of the state board saved the Central Pacific about $2,640 per mile. This figure was the difference between the lower assessments by county boards and those of the state board. Ibid., 187–88.

30 Glass, *Silver and Politics in Nevada*, 80–81.

31 Elliott, *History of Nevada*, 189–91.

32 Ibid., 191–92; Glass, *Silver and Politics in Nevada*, 86.

33 Elliott, *History of Nevada*, 194–95. Idaho adopted woman suffrage by popular vote in 1896. Utah gave women the right to vote but not to hold office in 1870, two months after Wyoming led the nation, giving women the right to hold office and vote. T. A. Larson, "Dolls, Vassals, and Drudges—Pioneer Women in the West," *The Western Historical Quarterly*, III (January, 1972), 11–12, 14. Utah Populists were almost as conspicuous as Colorado ones in their support of women's rights, advocating suffrage at their first party gathering.

34 Perhaps pragmatism would be a better term than conservatism in describing the attitude of many of the state's political leaders toward woman suffrage. Opportunistic Senator Stewart, for example, backed woman suffrage as early as 1874 when he voted for an amendment to a bill which supported that issue. Yet the Senator's own personal record on the employment of women made him vulnerable to criticism. Indeed in a letter Stewart wrote in 1892 he had to deny that he was hostile to woman suffrage. See Elliott, *Servant of Power*, 135–36.

35 Elliott, *History of Nevada*, 196–98.

36 Wren polled 3,111 votes of 8,907 cast, a respectable margin considering that he was facing the popular Newlands, whose silver credentials were as impressive as his own. *The World Almanac and Encyclopedia, 1899*, 454.

37 Jay J. Wagoner, *Arizona Territory, 1863–1912: A Political History* (Tucson: The University of Arizona Press, 1970), 288–89.

38 Ibid., 341–43; Lamar, *The Far Southwest*, 481.

39 Wagoner, *Arizona Territory*, 434.

40 Ibid., 309; Lamar, *The Far Southwest*, 480–81.

41 O'Neill was particularly bitter about the record of both major parties as far as the Homestead and Pullman strikes were concerned. He believed that federal intervention in the Pullman Strike was not only unfair but anti-labor. "Wealth might have its trusts, its combines and pools," O'Neill said, "but labor, when it dared to raise its hand against being reduced to the level of industrial slavery, at once became an outlaw." For other quotations and insights, see Ralph Keithly, *Buckey O'Neill . . . He Stayed with 'Em While He Lasted* (Caldwell, Idaho: The Caxton Printers, Ltd., 1949), 181–84.

42 O'Neill, whose tally was 3,895, trailed his second-place Republican opponent by only 195 votes. *The World Almanac and Encyclopedia, 1899,* 430.

43 Lamar, *the Far Southwest*, 481–82. By the time of Arizona's admission, the conservative trend had been significantly reversed. In fact, the territory's constitutional convention in 1910 was a pro-labor body. The *Arizona Republican* reflected the lingering anti-Populist feelings of conservatives in the territory when it called the document drafted by that convention "The Populistic-Socialistic Constitution." Wagoner, *Arizona Territory*, 464.

CHAPTER 10   MOUNTAIN POPULISM: A REASSESSMENT

1. Fuller, "Colorado's Revolt Against Capitalism," 347. For full citation see chapter two, note 5.

2 Marjorie Horbein, "Davis Waite, Silver, and Populism," *Essays and Monographs in Colorado History* (1983, No. 1), 76.

3 Waite had a change of heart after the 1894 election. Because many of the women enfranchised by his party voted against him in 1894, he had serious reservations about continued Populist support for woman suffrage. A bitter speech he made on the subject in Minnesota prompted Ignatius Donnelly to write him, claiming that the effect of Waite's remarks was to end "woman's suffrage in the People's party." Wright has pointed out, however, that Waite lost the same counties in 1894 that he lost in 1892 before women had the franchise. See Wright, *The Politics of Populism*, 198–99. For additional information on Waite and the woman vote, see chapter three, note 40.

4 For a thorough discussion of the suffrage movement throughout the West, see Larson, "Dolls, Vassals, and Drudges—Pioneer Women in the West," 5–16. See chapter nine, note 33, for full citation regarding suffrage in Utah and Idaho.

5 Although women were not enfranchised in Nevada until 1914, there were early efforts made by supporters in the state legislature to get them the vote. Powerful Senator Stewart was one of these strong backers, at least publicly. Despite some questions regarding the senator's sincerity (see chapter nine, note 34), Susan B. Anthony was convinced enough to write him a letter in 1900 thanking him for his support. Elliott, *Servant of Power*, 135–36. In

Arizona two territorial governors called for suffrage legislation during the nineties. Action was not taken, however, until 1903 when the legislature passed a suffrage bill. But the vote in the council was predicated on the understanding that the governor would veto the bill (which he did). Arizona's last effort as a territory to give women the franchise occurred at the constitutional convention of 1910 where delegates refused to submit a suffrage measure to the electorate as a popular referendum. Wagoner, *Arizona Territory*, 298, 311, 319, 406, 472.

6 Elliott, *Servant of Power*, 94.

7 The major target for the A.P.A. in the Cowboy state were 4,000 Catholics in southeastern Wyoming, many of whom were railroad workers. These people were particularly resented because many of them kept their jobs with the railroad during the Panic of 1893. Sullen A.P.A. members had infiltrated the Republican party in the rail center of Cheyenne, where they helped elect a Republican mayor even before the panic could further poison relations there between religious and ethnic groups. See Gould, *Wyoming: A Political History*, 206–07.

8 Hofstadter has pretty well publicized Lease's anti-Semitism. In her book *The Problem of Civilization Solved*, Lease called Grover Cleveland "the agent of Jewish bankers and British gold." Hofstadter, *The Age of Reform*, 79. Waite was not as public about his prejudices. In private correspondence, however, he referred to Jews as "shylocks" on some occasions. His most anti-Semitic reference, though, was to "jew extortioners"; he claimed the government wanted to turn the little people of the country over to their "tender mercies." See Morris, "Davis Hanson Waite," 241–42.

9 In my study of New Mexico Populism, I found the evidences of anti-intellectualism to be no stronger for Populists than for Republicans or Democrats. Populists from Grant County did support the concept of rotation in office because they believed that no special qualifications for office holding were needed. Far more damaging was the outrage expressed by a Republican candidate for school superintendent who blamed his defeat on the "villainous" charge that, if he were elected, he would require his teachers to read and write. See Larson, *New Mexico Populism*, 106–08.

10 Hicks, *The Populist Revolt*, 301.

11 Goodwyn, *Democratic Promise*, 388.

12 Robert F. Durden, *The Climax of Populism: The Election of 1896* (University of Kentucky Press, 1965), 23–44.

Bibliographical Essay

For many years, I have been puzzled by the scanty attention given the Populist movement in the Mountain West. My disappointment has been especially keen because the standard general histories of Populism have been thorough in dealing with the movement in the Midwest and South. Especially effective in this regard was John Hicks's *The Populist Revolt: A History of the Farmers' Alliance and People's Party* (Minneapolis: The University of Minnesota Press, 1931). Hicks's coverage of the wheat-raising Midwest and the cotton-producing South was excellent. For over fifty years, no student could make a serious study of the third party movement without consulting this seminal work. Hicks's justification for his brief treatment of western Populism was that free coinage was the only issue that really mattered to supporters of the People's party. He was backed in this one-issue interpretation by Richard Hofstadter in *The Age of Reform: From Bryan to F.D.R.* (New York: Alfred A. Knopf, 1955). Even the most recent general history of the movement Lawrence Goodwyn's *Democratic Promise: The Populist Movement in America* (New York: Oxford University Press, 1976) did not deviate from this emphasis on silver.

Beginning in the late 1960s, several books and articles were published about the Populist movement in certain individual states and territories of the Mountain West. Each presented the idea that Populism in this region was not a one-issue movement but a multi-issue one. Particularly effective in conveying this insight was James Edward Wright's *The Politics of Populism: Dissent in Colorado* (New Haven: Yale University Press, 1974). Wright greatly strengthened his multi-faceted conclusions about Colorado Populism by a systematic quantification of the data he uncovered. The late Thomas A. Clinch in his *Urban Populism and Free Silver in Montana: A Narrative of Ideology* in *Political Action* (Missoula: University of Montana Press, 1970) also brought other issues to light. Another historian who produced the same effect was David B. Griffiths. In his "Populism in Wyoming," *Annals of Wyoming*, XL (April, 1968), 57–71, he showed that the outrage over the invasion of Johnson County was more important to the growth of Wyoming Populism than free silver. Griffiths primarily depended upon his dissertation, "Populism in the Far West, 1890–1900" (Ph.D. dissertation, University of Washington, 1967), for some of his insights although he also drew upon two master's theses: Thomas Krueger's "Populism in Wyoming" (Master's thesis, University of Wyoming, 1956) and John K. Yoshida's "The Wyoming Election of 1892" (Master's thesis, University of Wyoming, 1960). Most important in determining the scope and direction of this study, however, was my own research for my monograph *New Mexico Populism: A Study of Radical Protest in a Western Territory* (Boulder: Colorado Associated University Press, 1974). As a result of delving into sources for this study and the preparation of a later one "Populism in the Mountain West: A Mainstream Movement," *The Western Historical Quarterly*, XII (April, 1982), 143, I became convinced of the multi-faced nature of the western movement.

During the 1970s I decided to pull these studies together and supplement their findings with research in the libraries and archives of four western states: Colorado, Wyoming, Montana, and New Mexico. These Front Range states have most of the characteristics of Populism for states in this area and make excellent subjects for type studies. I also decided to complement these findings by making a brief survey of the other four states of the Mountain West: Idaho, Utah, Nevada, and Arizona. I needed more thorough research and documentation, though, to demonstrate that this movement was like its midwestern and southern counterparts as far as its varied commitments were concerned. Below are other sources consulted in order to make this regional synthesis and analysis more complete:

MANUSCRIPTS AND NEWSPAPERS

During the preparation of my New Mexico study, I discovered that newspapers were more informative primary sources for a Populist study than were manuscript collections or government documents. While this dependence on news journals was frustrating in writing the history of such a controversial movement, it was actually an asset in determining which Populist issues were important for the overall regional picture. Newspaper accounts stressed party positions as well as emphasized the significance of campaigns and election returns. Consequently, I found the printing of party platforms or statements in these periodicals immensely useful in understanding a new third party movement such as Populism. The newspaper reports on the proceedings and debates at state party conventions also helped me to measure the enthusiasm or controversy generated by the issues promoted. Moreover, I found that in those states where the People's party was strongest, news coverage of all kinds was better.

I did not have to make an extensive perusal of Colorado newspapers because Wright had used so many in his study; nevertheless, the issues of the *Rocky Mountain News* (Denver) and the *Greeley Tribune* proved most helpful. Particularly beneficial was the manuscript collection of one of the region's most famous Populists, Governor Davis H. Waite. I found his correspondence at the Colorado State Archives in a collection known as Governors of Colorado, Special Series: Waite's Letters and Speeches, 1892–1896, to be most valuable in understanding the motives and sentiments of this Colorado leader.

Newspapers helpful in recording and interpreting the Wyoming movement were the *Daily Boomerang* (Laramine), the *Sheridan Post*, and the *Cheyenne Daily Leader* which I found in the Wyoming State Archives and Historical Department in Cheyenne. These journals, published during the early 1890s, supplemented those newspapers that I utilized in the studies of Griffiths, Kreuger, and Yoshida.

I also discovered that several Montana newspapers were helpful. One Republican journal the *Semi-Weekly Inter Mountain* (Butte) gave a comprehensive account of the party's 1892 nominating convention; more sympathetic to the convention's proceedings, however, was the *Butte Mining Journal*. Other newspapers supportive of Montana Populism were the *Butte Bystander* (issues of which were available from 1892 to 1895) and the *Montana Populist* and *Montana Silverite*. I found the relevant issues of the *Rocky Mountain Husbandman* valuable from the agrarian viewpoint. These journals, which were also essential to Clinch's study, are in the Montana Historical Society library in Helena.

As previously mentioned, I relied heavily on newspapers for my New Mexico study. These same sources again proved helpful. The collection of trade journals and small territorial newspapers collected by Theodore B. Mills, Populist candidate for territorial delegate in 1894, is one of the best of its kind. Known as the T. B. Mills Collection, it is in the New Mexico Highlands University Library. Other good repositories for newspapers as well as manuscript collections are the State Records Center and Archives, Museum of New Mexico, and the State Library (all in Santa Fe) and the University of New Mexico Library in Albuquerque (location for Populist opponent Thomas B. Catron's papers). I found the *San Juan Times* helpful because of its strong support for territorial Populism. (Microfilmed copies of which are found in the editorial offices of the *Daily Times* in Farmington.)

OFFICIAL RECORDS

Public records used in this study were helpful in a number of ways. For instance, they enabled me to document election returns. In Colorado, two publications *House Journal of the General Assembly of the State of Colorado*, Eighth Session (Colorado Springs: The Gazette Printing Company, State Printers, 1892) and *Senate Journal of the General Assembly of the State of Colorado*, Ninth Session (Denver: The Smith-Brooks Printing Company, State Printers, 1893) provided needed election results. Certainly, public records were useful for other purposes. *Reports of Cases Determined in the Supreme Court of the State of Colorado*, edited by William E. Beck, XVI (New York: Banks and Brothers, Law Publishers, 1892) helped to identify a controversial state judge who later tried to unseat Waite as governor, and *Message of John L. Routt and Inaugural Address of Gov. Davis H. Waite to the Ninth General Assembly, State of Colorado, 1893*, Ninth Session (Denver: The Smith-Brooks Printing Company, State Printers, 1893) duplicated Waite's entire inaugural message. Because of the major role played by small stock grazers in Wyoming's Populist movement, I found the state's occupational breakdown given in the Department of the Interior publication *Compendium of the Eleventh Census 1890*, Part III (Washington, D.C.: Government Printing Office, 1897) useful. It gave me statistical data to support evidence of the clout these people had in the 1892 election. I used the Montana official records to document legislative activities. The act calling for the Australian secret ballot introduced by Will Kennedy, who later became a Populist gubernatorial candidate, was printed in *Laws, Resolutions, and Memorials of the Territory of Montana, Passed at the Sixteenth Regular Session of the Legislative Assembly*, Sixteenth Session (Helena: The Journal Publishing Co., 1889). An eight-hour day law for stationary engineers was published in *Laws, Resolutions, and Memorials of the State of Montana, Passed at the Third Regular Session of the Legislative Assembly*, Third Session (Butte City: Inter Mountain Publishing Co., 1893). I also employed information from a number of government documents used in my New Mexico study but added to the current study *Compendium of the Eleventh Census: 1890, Part 1. Population*, 52nd Cong., 1st Sess., 1890, House Doc. 450 to document the 1890 population edge enjoyed by San Miguel County over Bernalillo County.

ALMANACS

I found almanacs especially useful for election returns. I consulted these to get tallies for races ranging from presidential contests to elections for control of the state or territorial legislature. *The Tribune Almanac for 1893* (New York: New York Tribune Association, 1893) was valuable in this regard as was *The Tribune Almanac for 1896* (New York: New York Tribune Association, 1896). Also important in providing returns were *The World Almanac, 1891* (New York: The Press Publishing Co., 1891); *The World Almanac and Encyclopedia, 1895* (New York: The Press Publishing Co., 1895); *The World Almanac and Encyclopedia, 1899* (New York: The Press Publishing Co., 1899); and *The World Almanac and Encyclopedia, 1901* (New York: The Press Publishing Co., 1901). I utilized returns from the 1891, 1895, and 1899 editions of the *World Almanac* for the county-by-county breakdown of election returns in the Territory of New Mexico to show that the Populist candidate for territorial delegate in 1894 drew most of his strength from those counties carried by the incumbent Democratic delegate in 1888, 1890, and 1892.

BOOKS AND ARTICLES

Besides those previously mentioned, I used a number of secondary sources to reconstruct Populism in the Mountain West. Some dealt with the growth of the movement; others provided background information relevant to its advent. Important in this regard was Howard Roberts Lamar, *The Far Southwest, 1846–1912: A Territorial History* (New Haven: Yale University Press, 1966), which was a history of New Mexico, Colorado, Utah, and Arizona during the territorial period.

Lamar's chapters on New Mexico and Arizona were particularly useful. Lynn I. Perrigo's *The American Southwest: Its People and Culture* (New York: Holt, Rinehart and Winston, 1971) was another fine regional history. Background information of a more national scope was found in H. Wayne Morgan's *From Hayes to McKinley: National Party Politics, 1877–1896* (Syracuse: Syracuse University Press, 1969). Vital for the politics of the period because of its reproduction of party platforms was Kirk H. Porter's and Donald Bruce Johnson's *National Party Platforms, 1840–1968* (4th ed.; Urbana: University of Illinois Press, 1972).

Of those histories of national Populism already mentioned, I found those by Hicks and Goodwyn particularly valuable. Other studies, however, were consulted for comparative purposes. Those I utilized for the Midwest included O. Gene Clanton's *Kansas Populism: Ideas and Men* (Lawrence: The University Press of Kansas, 1969) and his more recent study of the largely midwestern Populist voice in Congress " 'Hayseed Socialism' on the Hill: Congressional Populism, 1891–1895," *The Western Historical Quarterly*, XV (April, 1984), 139–62; Peter H. Argersinger's *Populism and Politics: William Alfred Peffer and the People's Party* (Lexington: University of Kentucky Press, 1974); and Stanley B. Parson's *The Populist Context: Rural versus Urban Power in a Great Plains Frontier* (Westport, Conn.: Greenwood Press, 1973). For the South, I found Bruce Palmer's *"Man over Money": The Southern Populist Critique of American Capitalism* (Chapel Hill: University of North Carolina Press, 1980); Sheldon Hackney's *Populism to Progressivism in Alabama* (Princeton, N.J.: Princeton University Press, 1969); and Donna A. Barnes's *Farmers in Rebellion: The Rise and Fall of the Southern Farmers' Alliance and the People's Party in Texas* (Austin: University of Texas Press, 1984) useful. Important because it dealt with cooperation among midwestern and southern leaders at the Populist Saint Louis convention in 1896 was Robert F. Durden's *The Climax of Populism: The Election of 1896* (University of Kentucky Press, 1965). Provocative because of its analysis of the climate of protest in the Pacific Northwest (an area outside the familiar Populist strongholds) was Carlos A. Schwantes's "Protest in a Promised Land: Unemployment, Disinheritance, and the Origin of Labor Militancy in the Pacific Northwest, 1885–1886," *The Western Historical Quarterly*, XII (October, 1892), 373–90.

Two recent articles deserved a special category because they suggested important new interpretations for the Populist movement. They were the study by Stanley B. Parsons, Karen Toombs Parsons, Walter Killilae, and Beverly Boyers, "The Role of Cooperatives in the Development of the Movement Culture of Populism," *Journal of American History*, LXIX (March, 1983), 866–85, which effectively challenged one of Goodwyn's major interpretations and James Turner's "Understanding the Populists," *Journal of American History*, LXVII (September, 1980), 354–73 which argued that geographical isolation was an important factor in the decision by many farmers to choose Populism as their vehicle for protest.

Books and articles dealing with regional industries were also useful because economic decline was a major cause of protest in the West. Relevant to agricultural problems in the area was Fred A. Shannon's *American Farmers' Movements* (Princeton, New Jersey: D. Van Nostrand, Inc., 1957). Frederick Jackson Turner also dealt with troubled farmers from this period in "The Problem of the West," *The Atlantic Monthly: A Magazine of Literature, Science, Art, and Politics*, LXXVII (September, 1896), 290–300. I found John D. W. Guice's *The Rocky Mountain Bench: The Territorial Courts of Colorado, Montana, and Wyoming* (New Haven: Yale University Press, 1972) germane to agriculture during the territorial period. Guice's description of Colorado's advanced irrigation system, known as the "Colorado System," was especially helpful. As far as land policy was concerned, I found that Benjamin Horace Hibbard's *A History of Public Land Policies* (New York: the Macmillan Company, 1924) was still the seminal work in this area. I also consulted several excellent studies on stock grazing in this region. Ernest Staples Osgood's *The Day of the Cattlemen* (Minneapolis: The University of Minnesota Press, 1929) remained the standard. Gene M. Gressley's *Bankers and Cattlemen* (New York: Alfred A. Knopf, 1966) provided a commercial and financial dimension not found in most histories of this industry. Ora B. Peake's *The Colorado Range Cattle Industry* (Glendale, Calif.: The Arthur H. Clark Company, 1937) was illuminating for stock grazing in Colorado. Mining, it seemed, was more thoroughly covered in most state histories of this region than the other industries. Even so, Rodman Wilson Paul's *Mining Frontiers of the Far West, 1848–1880* (New York: Holt, Rinehart and Winston, 1963) was still superb in coordinating the major gold and silver rushes in the nineteenth-century American West. Education, while not an industry, was important to agrarians in this region. Two monographs useful in understanding this association in Colorado were James E. Hansen II, *Democracy's College in the*

Centennial State: A History of Colorado State University (Fort Collins, Colorado: Colorado State University, 1977) and Albert F. Carter and Elizabeth Hays Kendel, Forty Years of Colorado State Teachers College, Formerly the State Normal School of Colorado, 1890–1930 (Colorado Teachers College Education Series, No. 11. Greeley, Colorado: The Tribune-Republican Publishing Company, 1930).

Secondary sources relevant to protest and Populism in Colorado, the first Front Range state analyzed in this study, included some excellent state histories. I used Percy Stanley Fritz's Colorado, The Centennial State (New York: Prentice-Hall, Inc., 1941); Carl Abbott's Colorado: A History of the Centennial State (Boulder: Colorado Associated University Press, 1976); Robert G. Athearn's The Coloradans (Albuquerque: University of New Mexico Press, 1976); and Carl Ubbelohde's, Maxine Benson's, and Duane Smith's A Colorado History (3rd ed.; Boulder, Colo.: Pruett Publishing Co., 1972). Worthwhile because of its analysis of Colorado Governor Waite was Karel D. Bicha's Western Populism: Studies in Ambivalent Conservatism (Lawrence, Kansas: Coronado Press, 1976). Marjorie Hornbein provided other insights in to Waite's stormy political career in "Davis Waite, Silver, and Populism," Essays and Monographs in Colorado History (1983, no. 1), 1–24 and John R. Morris's "The Women and Governor Waite," The Colorado Magazine XLIV (Winter, 1967), 11–19. Useful for insights into the overall movement are Jane Werner's "The Press and the Populists," The Colorado Magazine, XLVII (Winter, 1970), 42–61 and D. Michael McCarthy's "Colorado's Populist Leadership," The Colorado Magazine, XLVIII (Winter, 1971), 30–42. Also helpful because of the political and economic background they presented were two older sources: R. G. Dill's The Political Campaigns of Colorado: With Complete Tabulated Statements of the Official Vote (Denver: The Arapahoe Publishing Company, 1895) and Leon W. Fuller's "Colorado's Revolt Against Capitalism," Mississippi Valley Historical Review, XXI (December, 1934), 343–60.

Certainly, the most comprehensive history of the Front Range state of Wyoming is T. A. Larson's standard History of Wyoming (2nd ed.; Lincoln: University of Nebraska Press, 1978). Larson's work complemented Lewis L. Gould's excellent study, Wyoming: A Political History, 1868–1896 (New Haven: Yale University Press, 1968) in which he effectively culled the extensive Francis E. Warren Papers. Also germane to Wyoming politics was Anne Carolyn Hansen's "The Congressional Career of Francis E. Warren from 1890 to 1902," Annals of

Wyoming, XX (January, 1948), 3–49. The event that did the most to give life to Wyoming Populism, however, was the Johnson County War. Two essential accounts of that famous range war that I used were A. S. Mercer's *The Banditti of the Plains or the Cattlemen's Invasion of Wyoming in 1892 (The Crowning Infamy of the Ages)*, Foreword by William H. Kittrell (Norman: University of Oklahoma Press, 1975) and Helen Huntington Smith's *The War on the Powder River* (New York: McGraw-Hill, 1966). (The latter should be read to balance the biases of the former.)

There were some excellent histories on Montana, too. Particularly helpful in the preparation of this monograph were K. Ross Toole's *Montana: An Uncommon Land* (Norman: University of Oklahoma Press, 1959) and William L. Lang's and Rex C. Myers's *Montana: Our Land and People* (Boulder, Colo.: Pruett Publishing Company, 1979). Also I found most illuminating the study by Michael P. Malone and Richard B. Roeder, *Montana: A History of Two Centuries* (Seattle: University of Washington Press, 1976). Beneficial because of its representative photographs was William E. Farr's and K. Ross Toole's *Montana: Image of the Past* (Boulder, Colo.: Pruett Publishing Company, 1978). Two more focused studies also proved useful. Frank Grant's "*Rocky Mountain Husbandman*: Embattled Voice of the Montana Farmer," *Montana, The Magazine of Western History*, XXIV (April, 1974), 34–42 was important because it dealt with the influence of farm editor Robert N. Sutherlin, and thus, provided insights into the movement's agrarian roots. Worthwhile in another way was the book compiled by the Works Projects Administration during the early forties: *Copper Camp: Stories of the World's Greatest Mining Town, Butte, Montana* (New York: Hastings House, Publishers, 1951). This volume was significant because it dealt with the remarkable ethnic diversity found among Butte's miners, a not uncommon characteristic of western mining camps.

Hispanos, of course, comprised the largest group of non-Anglo-Saxon people in the Mountain West; they were concentrated in the Territory of New Mexico. Good for the historical background of these people was the study by Leo Gebler, John W. Moore, and Ralph C. Guzman, et al., *The Mexican-American People: The Nation's Second Largest Minority* (New York: The Free Press, 1970). Essential in understanding the resistance of Hispanos to Anglo encroachments on their land was Robert J. Rosenbaum's *Mexicano Resistance in the Southwest: "The Sacred Right of Self-Preservation"* (Austin: University of

Texas Press, 1981). Also helpful in this regard were Andrew Bancroft Schlesinger's "Las Gorras Blancas, 1888–1891," *Journal of Mexican American History*, I (Spring, 1971), 87–143, and my "The White Caps of New Mexico: A Study of Ethnic Militancy in the Southwest," *Pacific Historical Review*, XLIV (May, 1975), 171–85 and "The Knights of Labor and Native Protest in New Mexico" in Robert Kern (ed.), *Labor in New Mexico: Unions, Strikes, and Social History Since 1881* (Albuquerque: University of New Mexico Press, 1983) 31–52. Informative because it provided additional knowledge about little known White Cap resistance leader Juan Jose Herrera was Grace McClure's *The Bassett Women* (Athens, Ohio: Swallow Press/Ohio University Press, 1985). On a different but related subject, I used Victor Westphall's *Public Domain in New Mexico, 1854–1891* (Albuquerque: University of New Mexico Press, 1965) to document the competition among both groups for water and land in New Mexico. Related to this topic because of Thomas Catron's dominant role as a land-grabber is *Thomas B. Catron and His Era* (Tucson: University of Arizona Press, 1973, also by Westphall. Invaluable for the famous struggle over the Maxwell Grant were Jim Berry Pearson's *The Maxwell Land Grant* (Norman: University of Oklahoma Press, 1961) and the late Morris Taylor's *O. P. McMains and the Maxwell Land Grant Conflict* (Tucson: University of Arizona Press, 1979). On the subject of territorial government two sources proved useful: Kenneth N. Owens's "Patterns and Structure in Western Territorial Politics," *The Western Historical Quarterly*, I (October, 1970), 373–92 and my *New Mexico's Quest for Statehood* (Albuquerque: University of New Mexico Press, 1968). Two of the general histories of New Mexico that I utilized were Warren Beck's *New Mexico: A History of Four Centuries* (Norman: University of Oklahoma Press, 1962) and Frank D. Reeve's *History of New Mexico*, II (2 vols., New York: Lewis Historical Publishing Company, Inc., 1961).

I also used books and articles for the brief survey of Idaho, Utah, Nevada, and Arizona Populism. For Idaho, they included C. J. Brosnan's *History of the State of Idaho* (New York: Charles Scribner's Sons, 1918); Byron Defenbach's *Idaho: The Place and Its People*, I (Chicago: The American Historical Society, Inc., 1933); F. Ross Peterson's *Idaho: A Bicentennial History* (New York: W. W. Norton and Company, Inc., 1976); and John Fahey's "Ed Boyce and the Western Federation of Miners," *Idaho Yesterdays*, XXV (Fall, 1981), 18–30. For Utah, I utilized the study by David B. Griffiths, "Far Western Populism: The Case of Utah, 1893–1900," *Utah Historical Quarterly*, XX-

XVII (Fall, 1969), 396–407; the one by Charles S. Peterson, *Utah: A Bicentennial History* (New York: W. W. Norton and Company, Inc., 1977); and that of Wayne Stout, *History of Utah* (Salt Lake City: privately printed, 1968). Griffiths's article was immensely useful; it uncovered information about the little-known Populist movement in Utah and revealed its almost exclusive urban base. Helpful in understanding Utah's pioneering stance on woman suffrage (a reform that often received major Populist support) was T. A. Larson's "Dolls, Vassals, and Drudges—Pioneer Women in the West," *The Western Historical Quarterly*, III (January, 1972), 5–16. Nevada Populism's response to the state's all-encompassing silver issue was effectively chronicled in the study by Russell R. Elliott, *History of Nevada* (Lincoln: University of Nebraska Press, 1973) and the one by Mary Ellen Glass, *Silver and Politics in Nevada, 1892–1902* (Reno: University of Nevada Press, 1969). Especially pertinent because it dealt with Nevada's best known silverite was Russell R. Elliott's *Servant of Power: A Political Biography of Senator William M. Stewart* (Reno: University of Nevada Press, 1983). Having had the opportunity to visit Arizona's Library Archives and Public Records in Phoenix, I found information about third party activity to be more scanty in the Grand Canyon state than in any other state studied. Lamar's *The Far Southwest*, however, was helpful as was Jay J. Wagoner's *Arizona Territory, 1863–1912: A Political History* (Tucson: The University of Arizona Press, 1970) and Ralph Keithly's *Buckey O'Neill . . . He Stayed With 'Em While He Lasted* (Caldwell, Idaho: The Caxton Press, Ltd., 1949).

These books and articles were located in a number of archives and university libraries in the West, particularly along the Front Range. My own library at the University of Northern Colorado in Greeley deserves special mention in this regard. The collection of books in one public library, the Western History Department collection at the Denver Public Library also proved invaluable. More useful for this study, however, was the Newberry Library in Chicago. There I systematically used the books of the Edward E. Ayer Collection and the library's general collections.

UNPUBLISHED DISSERTATIONS AND MASTER'S THESES

In a relatively specialized field of history, dissertations and theses are often important sources of information. Aspects of western Populism fall into that category. In Colorado, for instance, the causes of Populist activity were carefully dealt with in a doctoral dissertation written in

1916. Leonard Peter Fox's "Origins and Early Development of Populism in Colorado" (Ph.D. dissertation, University of Pennsylvania, 1916) was indeed a pioneering work. Useful in dealing with groups sometimes susceptible to Populist appeal was Stephen J. Leonard's "Denver's Foreign Born Immigrants, 1859–1900" (Ph.D. dissertation, Claremont Graduate School and University Center, 1971). In somewhat the same category was the late Gregory Alexander Bence's "The Knights of Labor in Colorado" (Master's thesis, University of Northern Colorado, 1974). Populist governor Waite has prompted two thorough studies: Harold J. Kountze, Jr.'s "Davis H. Waite and the People's Party in Colorado" (Master's thesis, Yale University, 1944) and John Robert Morris's "Davis Hanson Waite: The Ideology of a Western Populist" (Ph.D. dissertation, University of Colorado, 1965). For an overall view of the movement in the Centennial state, Lynn Marie Olson's "The Essence of Colorado Populism: An Analysis of the Populists and the Issues of 1892" (Master's thesis, University of Northern Colorado, 1971) was worthwhile. As far as issues relevant to Populism were concerned, David Lawrence Lonsdale's "The Movement for an Eight-Hour Law in Colorado, 1893–1913" (Ph.D. dissertation, University of Colorado, 1963) and John Foster Powers's " 'Blaine and Free Coinage': Factionalism and Silver in the Republican Pre-Convention Campaign of 1892 in Colorado" (Master's thesis, Colorado State College, 1968) provided useful background. Helpful, too, because it dealt with an important political personality of the early Populist Era was Robert Charles Voight's "The Life of John Long Routt" (Master's thesis, Colorado State College of Education, 1947).

Essential for their information about Wyoming Populism were the previously mentioned unpublished studies of Griffiths, Krueger, and Yoshida. Griffiths's ground-breaking dissertation also supplied little-known information about Populism in the states of Montana, Idaho, and Utah. Helpful for the Idaho movement was William James Gabourg's "Dissension in the Rockies: A History of Idaho Populism" (Ph.D. dissertation, University of Idaho, 1966). Two unpublished studies were also useful for the New Mexico portion of the study. They were Herbert Theodore Hoover's "Populism in the Territories" (Master's thesis, New Mexico State University, 1961) and Walter John Donlon's "Le Baron Bradford Prince, Chief Justice and Governor of New Mexico Territory, 1879–1893" (Ph.D. dissertation, University of New Mexico, 1967).

Index

Absentee ownership, 151; of Colorado mining operations, 19, 21; of Colorado water companies, 23, see also English Company; in Idaho, 137; lost effectiveness as Colorado political issue, 41; of Maxwell Grant, 154; in Montana, 75; owners' collapses damaged states they invested in, 97; resistance to in Colorado, 27, 29

Adams, Alva B., 42

Age of Reform, The (Hofstadter), 7

Agriculture: development of in Montana, 77; limits on in West diversified Populism, 157; in Mountain West, 15

Alienation, as motive to join Populists, 12

Alien landownership: see Absentee ownership

Allen, William, 159

Amalgamated Copper, 101

American Protective Association (A.P.A.), 26, 41–42, 99, 155; persecution of southern Colorado Hispanos, 169 n50; Republican support of, 156

American Railway Union, 57; see also Pullman Strike

Anaconda Company, 75

Anaconda convention, 88–89; modern resolutions of, 90

Ancheta, Joseph A., 120

Anderson, Reese, 74

Angus, Red, 48

Anticapitalism, 30–31; Panic of 1893 vindicated Populists', 56–57

Anti-Catholicism: see American Protective Association (A.P.A.)

Anti-intellectualism, 156

Antimonopolism, 13; at Douglas, Wyoming convention, 53; in early Colorado Independent party, 29; essential to Wyoming Populism, 60–61; fear of Arizona railroads, 145; in Montana, 82; most prominent common Populist issue, 136, 149–50

Anti-Semitism, 89, 156

Argersinger, Peter H., 10, 13

Arid land bill, 154; monopolistic fears of, 61

Arizona: constitution (1891), 144; territorial government in, 144

Arizona Populism: Atlantic and Pacific controversy started, 145; climate far better than New Mexico's, 144; disaffected major party leaders supported, 145; leadership of, 144; similar to New Mexico's, 144

Armijo, Manuel, 109

Atchison, Topeka and Santa Fe Railway: see Santa Fe Railroad

Atlantic and Pacific Railway, 144

Australian secret ballot, 30, 39, 85, 154–55

Baily, Morton, 42

Barbed-wire fencing, 108

Barber, Amos W., 48, 49, 51

Barden et al. v. Northern Pacific Railroad Company, 96

Baring Brothers and Company, 20

Bartlett, I. S., 50

Bartlett, Mrs. I. S., 50, 56

Battle of the Standards, 43, 99, 147; see also Silver issue

Beaubien, Carlos, 109

Beecher, D. F., 95